Blque Sheep
Herd of The Unheard

By
Tiffany Thompson

Copyright © 2024 Tiffany Thompson
All rights reserved.

No part of this book may be reproduced, stored in a retrieval system, or transmitted in any form or by any means—electronic, mechanical, photocopying, recording, or otherwise—without prior written permission of the author, except in the case of brief quotations embodied in critical articles or reviews.

This is a work of nonfiction. While every effort has been made to ensure accuracy, certain names, locations, and identifying details have been changed to protect the privacy of individuals.

ISBN: 979-8-218-58353-8

Printed in the United States of America

For permissions or inquiries, please contact: Blquesheep@gmail.com

Published by Tiffany Thompson

Dedication

To the little girl who dreamed of escaping the pain

To the teenager who wanted revenge but found her strength,
To the lost young woman who searched for her way,
And to the grown woman who saw it through—this is for you.

To my siblings, who shaped pieces of my journey.
To my beautiful daughter, who became not just a part but the biggest part of my purpose in the pain, mommy loves you more than words can ever say. May you one day read this with pride, knowing that mommy fought a good fight so you wouldn't have to.
For my amazing, God sent angels of support along my journey! My forever sisters of strength and love! I appreciate, need, and love you all more than you know!

To my parents, who birthed one strong, badass black sheep amongst the herd.
To my aunties and uncles, who taught me lessons in love and resilience.
And to my dear, sweet lady—the closest thing to a mother—who I know is smiling down on me, remembering our girl talks about

seeing this day. I did it, Aunty! Another one to add to your love wall up in heaven.

Finally, to you, the reader—my herd. Here's to the wool being lifted from our eyes, to see our journeys of truth, and to break the silence together.

This is for you. This is for us.

Contents

Dedication	3
Introduction: Breaking the Silence	7
Chapter 1	9
Chapter 2	12
Chapter 3	26
Chapter 4	29
Chapter 5	33
Chapter 6	38
Chapter 7	47
Chapter 8	57
Chapter 9	73
Chapter 10	93
Chapter 11	104
Chapter 12	115
Chapter 13	124

Chapter 14 139

Chapter 15 144

Chapter 16 153

Chapter 17 163

Chapter 18 173

Chapter 19 188

Chapter 20 211

Chapter 21 225

Chapter 22 242

Chapter 23 247

Chapter 24 259

Chapter 25 264

Chapter 26 272

The Road to Healing 293

Steps Toward Self-Discovery 318

Introduction: Breaking the Silence

There comes a moment in every survivor's life when the silence becomes too loud, the pain too suffocating, and the past too unbearable to carry alone. For years, I lived in that silence, hidden beneath layers of fear, shame, and a desperate need to protect the very people who hurt me. I was trapped in a world where love was conditional, safety was an illusion, and trust was a weapon wielded by those I should have been able to rely on the most. Growing up, I learned to measure my words, to tiptoe around the truth, and to bury my hurt so deep that even I could almost forget it was there. But pain has a way of resurfacing, of clawing its way back into the light no matter how hard you try to suppress it. And when it does, it demands to be acknowledged, to be felt, and to be spoken.

This memoir is my truth, laid bare in all its raw, unfiltered emotion. It is the story of a little girl who learned to navigate a world of uncertainty, where the people who were supposed to protect her became the source of her deepest wounds. It is the story of a young woman who carried that pain into her adult life, making choices shaped by trauma and searching for love in all the wrong places. And it is the story of a survivor who, against all odds, found the courage to break the silence, to confront her past, and to reclaim her voice. In these pages, you will find no sugarcoating, no glossing over the ugly truths. You will feel the weight of every word, the sting of every betrayal, and the bittersweet triumph of each hard-won victory.

This memoir is my attempt to break that silence, to give voice to the pain that has haunted me for so long. It is a journey into the darkest corners of my past, a confrontation with the demons that have shaped my life. Writing these words is an act of defiance, a reclamation of the power that was stolen from me. As I share my story, I hope to find healing and closure. But more than that, I hope to shed light on the insidious nature of abuse to expose the hidden wounds that so many carry in silence. My story is not unique; it is the story of countless others who have endured similar pain.

To them, I say: you are not alone. Your suffering matters, and your voice deserves to be heard. This is my story. It is one of heartbreak and resilience, of loss and redemption. But most of all, it is a story of survival, a testament to the power of the human spirit to rise above even the darkest of circumstances. If you're reading this, know that you, too, have the power to break the silence.

Chapter 1

To understand my story, you need to know the backdrop against which it unfolded. We lived in a modest house, a place that should have been a sanctuary but instead became a prison. The walls of our home were witnesses to the violence and terror that defined our daily lives. The air inside was thick with tension, a palpable sense of dread that never dissipated. My mother was a master of the facade, presenting a charming and composed exterior to the outside world. But behind closed doors, her true nature emerged.

She was a volatile storm, unpredictable and merciless. Her outbursts were sudden and explosive, leaving us reeling in their wake. She thrived on control, deriving satisfaction from our fear and helplessness. My earliest memories are tainted with the confusion and fear that accompanied my mother's erratic behavior. I remember the way she would snap over the smallest things, her anger disproportionate and terrifying. A misplaced toy, a spill, a wrong answer – any minor infraction could trigger her wrath. Her punishments were swift and severe, leaving no room for mistakes or forgiveness.

She had a particular way of making me feel small and insignificant. Her words were sharp blades, cutting deep into my self-esteem. She belittled me, mocked my achievements, and undermined my confidence at every turn. I learned to stay silent, to shrink into myself in the hope of avoiding her attention. But it was never enough.

Her need for control was insatiable, and I was her favorite target. Amidst the darkness, there were fleeting moments of light. My father, though deeply flawed and often complicit, offered glimpses of kindness and understanding. He was a gentle soul, caught in the web of my mother's manipulation. I had once believed that he tried to protect us, to shield us from her worst excesses, but he was no match for her relentless cruelty.

However, it was in healing that I would find that there was not much weight to that thought, let alone proof. This is a heartbreaking revelation that I will get into later in my story. I remember the rare times he would take us out, away from the suffocating atmosphere of our home. We would go to the park, the beach, or anywhere that offered a brief respite from the chaos. In those moments, I felt a semblance of normalcy, a taste of the childhood I yearned for. But these moments were fleeting, and the return to reality was always brutal.

The silence that surrounded our suffering was deafening. We were isolated, our pain hidden behind the facade of a happy family. My mother's manipulation extended beyond our household, ensuring that no one suspected the truth. She wore her mask well, playing the role of the perfect wife and mother with chilling precision.

We learned to keep our pain hidden, to bury our trauma deep within ourselves. Speaking out was not an option; the fear of retribution was too great. We suffered in silence, our cries for help stifled by the weight of our shame and fear. The isolation was suffocating, compounding the sense of helplessness that defined our existence.

Chapter 2

Early Signs and Realization: As a child, an unsettling awareness gnawed at me – something was deeply wrong with my mother's behavior. Some days, she was an unapproachable fortress of anger. I developed a ritual of "temperature checking" her by calling her name and studying her reactions. The tapping feet, shaking legs, heavy breathing, and irritated expression were harbingers of a stormy day. Approaching her was a gamble, each step laden with the dread of potential outbursts.

The earliest signs of her abuse towards my father were etched in the venom she spat about him during phone conversations. She degraded him, spreading lies and depicting him as the opposite of the kind, genuine man I knew. Her words were weapons, wielded with the intent to wound, and she seemed to derive a twisted pleasure from knowing it hurt me. Physical abuse became a staple in our household. She hit us, including my father, if we dared to disagree. My father never retaliated, always meeting her disrespect with a dignity that seemed to inflame her further.

Countless nights, her screams and the sound of objects crashing to the floor would jolt me awake. Our cries meant nothing to her as if our suffering was mere background noise to her relentless rage. I can recall a night amongst many in which I was awakened by such a traumatic noise. A noise that sounded as if the devil himself was in my home.

I ran into my parent's bedroom, where I discovered my mother spread across their bed with my father standing over her. Her head was thrown about, cursing my father and spitting at him as if a dark force possessed her. I remember my brothers and I crying as I looked into her eyes. They seemed very black and vacant of a soul. My father stood over her with a bible, dousing her in olive oil. She shouted, "Fuck you! You can't have her! She's mine!" as if Satan was speaking through her. My father then began to shout while pressing a cross drawn in the oil, "Come out of her, Satan! I rebuke you in the name of Jesus! You must flee! She is the child of God!".

He shouted at us to leave the room, insisting that our mother would be okay. But nothing felt okay. I bolted to my room, slammed the door shut, locked it, and collapsed into a flood of tears. My body shook as I prayed—prayed with every ounce of my being that God would strip the demon from my mother, that she would somehow return to the person I desperately needed her to be. But I was too young, too innocent, to understand that what I had witnessed was just a shadow of the darkness that lived inside her. It was only the beginning—a mere glimpse into the abyss of my mother's evil.

This wasn't a one-time horror. It became a ritual, a twisted protocol we were forced to follow as children. We were trained like soldiers, told that when she became "possessed," we had to grab her arms and legs and pray with all our might. We clutched the Bible, our tiny hands trembling, and screamed for Satan to let her go. But deep down, I knew this was no possession—it was her chance to unleash the venom she harbored, the hatred she had for us. Each episode ended the same: with me trembling, tears streaming down my face, my heart pounding so hard it felt like it would burst.

To say I slept would be a lie. I didn't sleep—I waited with eyes wide open, the fear gnawing at my insides like a relentless beast. What would she do to me if I dared to close my eyes? What could she do? The terror consumed me. Night after night, I lay awake, the comfort of my headphones and endless CDs the only things keeping me from losing my mind entirely. Music became my refuge, my escape from the nightmare that never seemed to end.

She was like a black mommy dearest, a living version of the movie "Precious," a master of pretense who wore her mask of normalcy with unsettling ease. Authenticity terrified her, so she buried it deep, hiding behind a facade that never cracked. Nothing came without a price—not even the smallest sliver of affection. Love wasn't something she gave freely; it was a transaction, a bartered commodity. And she never let me forget that. She had a way of reminding me, in the most subtle and insidious ways, that everything was conditional, everything had strings attached.

She was skilled at keeping her skeletons and demons out of sight, locked away in the dark recesses of her mind. But I knew they were lurking just beneath the surface, ready to be unleashed whenever it suited her. That was my life—constantly waiting, bracing myself for the next wave of her darkness to crash over me. Her emotional immaturity was boundless as if I was more of the adult and parent than her.

Whenever I found the courage to express myself, to articulate the emotions she tried so hard to suppress in me, it would send her into a rage. My ability to regulate my feelings, to speak with clarity and confidence, was something she despised. She would never admit that my strength in this area intimidated her; it was just one of the many things she envied about me. Instead, she channeled her insecurities into venomous attacks, both physical and emotional.

She would lash out, hurling insults with a ferocity that left me reeling, calling me every name in the book. She labeled everything I did or said as "disrespectful," twisting my words and actions to fit her narrative. That word "disrespectful"—became a weapon, wielded to keep me in line, to crush any semblance of self-worth or autonomy I tried to hold onto. Along with countless Bible scriptures, she used it as a tool of control, masking her cruelty in the guise of righteous discipline.

Religious manipulation was her masterpiece, one of the many twisted talents she wielded with pride behind the façade of our family walls. It was her cruel art, and she painted with lies, wielding the holy as her brush. The irony, though, was never lost on me. A woman who rarely set foot in church with my father, my brothers, and me had somehow made herself the queen of that sanctuary whenever she graced it with her presence. Her performances were legendary, her star power unmatched. She didn't just attend; she *owned* it, stealing the stage as if God himself had stepped aside to give her the spotlight.

Friendships? Relationships? Those were foreign languages to her. The church walls, like every other space in her life, were just another place to conquer, not to connect. Fellowship was supposed to be sacred, a bond of shared faith, but to her, it was just another stage. She could fake it—God, how she could fake it—but not for long. Eventually, her mask would slip, her true self creeping out like smoke through cracks in the walls. For the fleeting encounters, though, she was a saint, leaving just enough of an impression to dazzle those who didn't stick around to see the aftermath.

And then there were her "testimonies." We called it testifying in church, but for her, I had my name: *testilying*. She'd climb up to that pulpit like she was auditioning for a role only she could imagine, competing for attention in ways that still make my stomach turn. She couldn't even let the sick have their moment—

sickness became her stage, too. Where most people prayed in quiet humility for others, she made every illness a spotlight on herself.

She turned disease into currency, asking for prayers for a new illness every month. Cancer, tumors, diseases I hadn't even heard of—she claimed them all. And I, still too young and naive to question it, accepted it as truth. Because at that time, I was only scratching the surface of her cruelty, her hunger for attention. But over time, I would learn there was no bottom to her. No limit to how far she'd go for her fix of recognition.

I'll never forget watching her take her place at the altar, tears streaming down her face, the congregation surrounding her in love and pity. They hung on her every word as she sobbed about her supposed battles with chemo, radiation, and surgeries. The pastor prayed over her, and I sat there, quiet in my disbelief, watching as she put on her greatest performance yet. She would cry, fall to the floor, and wail her gratitude to God for letting her survive another day. It was theater, plain and simple, and she was the star.

I used to think maybe she believed her lies, that somewhere deep down, she convinced herself of her stories. But no. She *knew*. And she didn't care. All that mattered was the attention, the validation, the spotlight. Even as a child, I knew something was wrong—her need for that much attention felt like a black hole, sucking everything and everyone around her dry. But I didn't yet realize how bottomless it truly was. Not then.

If there's a record book for surviving every disease known to mankind, she should've been in it. But her true accomplishment wasn't survival—it was deception. Watching her manipulate an entire room full of faithful people, twisting their love, their hope, and their prayers, made me feel like I was watching something unholy in a place meant to be sacred. It was her stage, her audience, her moment, and she knew exactly how to bring down the house.

Her relentless mission to capture every heart, every soul, was never enough. Beneath the façade, her true terror lay in being exposed—her greatest fear was someone daring to pull back the curtain and reveal her for the devil she truly was. And anyone, even in the sanctuary of the church, who so much as questioned her became a threat. Yet, her downfall was always her own doing. No one needed to challenge her; she was her own worst enemy, inevitably unraveling the web of lies and manipulation she so carefully spun.

I remember one moment so vividly, one of her many failed power plays that turned the spotlight back onto her for all the wrong reasons. We were both in the church choir, though "we" implies some choice on my part. I was painfully shy and terrified of crowds, and the thought of singing in front of people made my stomach churn. But saying no wasn't an option. It never was with her. If I dared to refuse, the punishment was relentless bullying, accusations of disobedience, and threats of eternal damnation for not doing "God's will."

On this Sunday, I was assigned a solo. Not by the choir director, though it was framed that way—this was my mother's doing. She had planted the seed, whispered the suggestion, and maneuvered me into the spotlight. At first, I tried to pass the microphone back, but one look at her eyes—those hard, menacing eyes—and I knew better. So, I took the mic and sang.

Looking back, I realize now what she was trying to do. She envied me, envied everything about me, and this was her way of humiliating me. She expected me to fail, to stumble, to embarrass myself, and to confirm whatever twisted narrative she had in her head. But something remarkable happened instead: I discovered a part of myself I didn't know existed. I sang, and it wasn't terrible. It was good. The crowd responded, clapping and cheering, and for a moment, I felt something I hadn't felt in a long time—pride.

But my mother couldn't allow that. She couldn't stand to see anyone else in the spotlight, not even her child. As the applause rang out, she was already moving, stealing her way to the microphone under the guise of being "moved by the Spirit." She snatched the moment back with calculated grace, turning it into another opportunity to play the role of the "good mother."

She began to sing, her voice powerful and commanding as she walked off the pulpit and into the congregation. She knew how to move a crowd; I'll give her that. Her gestures were dramatic; her performance was larger than life. Hands raised, tears streaming, shouts of praise filling the room—it looked like worship. But I knew better.

Even in this holy moment, there was nothing holy about her motives. She wasn't singing for God. She was using her talent—the voice she should have used to praise the Lord—to do the devil's work. And, as always, there was an agenda. This time, it was a personal attack. Her song and her theatrics were aimed at two specific people in the congregation. She increased her volume and pointed her finger at them, her voice dripping with false righteousness as she sang words meant to condemn, not uplift.

"God sees you," she sang, her eyes locked on them, her voice trembling with fake compassion. "It's okay to come home." To the untrained eye, it looked like an act of grace, a call to repentance. But I knew her too well. This wasn't an invitation; it was a challenge. A veiled threat. Her words were daggers wrapped in velvet, designed to wound while appearing holy.

The two individuals, caught in her crosshairs, stayed composed. They called her by name, asked her—pleaded with her—to back off, to remove her finger from their faces. Their restraint was remarkable, their fury visible but contained. Even as she pushed and prodded, they refused to let her drag them down, especially not in the house of the Lord.

But I saw it. I saw the rage simmering beneath their calm exterior. And for a moment, I wondered if they would break, if they would let her pull them into her chaos. They didn't, though.

They held their ground, their dignity, while she flailed and postured, her mask slipping further with every note.

It was one of those moments where her true self shone through, no assistance needed from anyone else. She exposed herself, as she always did, and I watched, a strange mixture of shame and relief swirling in my chest. Shame for being tied to her. Relief for knowing that no one, not even her, could hide forever.

My father, who was to preach the message for that morning, stood up from the pulpit and, as always, so graciously made his way down to gather her. By the time he had reached her, her mask had come off, and a fight broke out. My father, along with a few others from the congregation, had to surround her and the other two and make their way out of the church. My father is holding onto her as she is screaming insults their way and swinging at them.

I cannot begin to express the embarrassment I felt at that moment. Service ended at that moment, and I followed slowly behind. Although the congregation knew that she was my mother, I would rather be seen walking out of the church alone than to be seen with her. My heart craved to be normal, so any moment that I could at least try to separate myself from her, I would, even if I was lying to myself for the moment. After that day, I never once questioned why my mother never attended church with us as a family regularly and only showed up now and then. Her absence was a temporary moment of peace for me from the true hell that existed outside those walls.

Her religious manipulation knew no limits. It was as boundless as her capacity for cruelty. She wielded premonitions, dreams, and so-called divine messages as tools to enact her twisted agendas, draping her malice in the facade of faith. "The Lord has sent me a vision," she would declare, her voice laced with a counterfeit conviction. But her words were not prophecy; they were poison.

When my aunt passed, she unleashed one of her most vile creations—a "dream" from God himself. She paraded her story to my father and her circle of flying monkeys, those who hung on her every word and carried out her bidding without question. "God showed me she's burning in hell," she claimed with chilling certainty, describing vivid images of my aunt engulfed in flames. And as she burned, my mother said, she apologized—to her, of all people. Not for any true wrongdoing but for the "sins" of standing up for me, protecting me, holding my mother accountable, and refusing to enable her abuse.

It wasn't enough that my aunt had passed. My mother couldn't let her rest, even in death. She had to twist the knife deeper to rewrite her legacy into something grotesque and false. Her hatred for my aunt—the woman who was the closest thing I'd ever had to a real mother—oozed out of every word. This wasn't a message from God; it was a testament to her own sick, envious heart.

Long before my aunt's passing, my mother's disdain for her had already surfaced. She had once expressed outright that she wished my aunt would just die already. Not content with private malice, she spread rumors among her minions, whispering that someone had found my aunt unresponsive on her kitchen floor. The lie spread like wildfire, reaching my brother's ears and sending him into a spiral of panic so intense he had to leave work. This was her way—never doing the dirty work herself but orchestrating chaos through others, pulling strings from the shadows.

My aunt, my "sweet lady," was everything my mother was not. She was warm, safe, and unconditional love. She couldn't have children of her own, and I've often thought that maybe God saved her just for me. In a life so devoid of maternal care, she was my sanctuary. Her impact on me was profound, a gift I carry with me to this day. And my mother? She couldn't stand it. She couldn't stomach our bond or the way my aunt's love filled the void she had left in me. Her envy dripped into every interaction, every scheme, every venomous word she spat to tear down what we had.

This so-called dream was no different—a grotesque perversion of both my aunt's memory and God's name. It was her way of desecrating something beautiful, of twisting her jealousy and bitterness into a weapon. Narcissists like her have a way of exposing themselves in their lies, their cruelty so transparent to anyone who dares to truly listen. Every word she spoke to destroy someone else was a mirror, reflecting the depths of her darkness.

What made the situation even more grotesque was her audacious request following my aunt's death. She reached out to another one of my aunts, feigning sentimentality, and asked for something to keep in "precious memory" of her. But not just any keepsake would do. She specifically asked for my aunt's wedding ring. The same ring that carried a history of suspicion, manipulation, and deceit.

The significance of this ring was deeply tied to a moment I will never forget. After my Navy boot camp graduation, a proud milestone in my life, my aunt—true to her loving, supportive nature—traveled to celebrate with me and brought my parents along. After the ceremony, we spent time together, catching up and sharing in the joy of the moment. Back at their hotel, my aunt suddenly became flustered when she realized her ring was missing. It was unlike her to misplace something so valuable, so we all jumped into action, searching the room from corner to corner. But the ring was nowhere to be found.

And then, like clockwork, my mother proclaimed, "I found it, thank God!" Her voice carried a hollow relief, one that felt off even then. The room wasn't large, and we had all combed through it meticulously. The idea that she just happened to stumble upon the ring felt implausible. Yet, we let it go. On the ride back to base, though, my mother couldn't let it go. She went on and on, weaving a story about how she felt my aunt might have suspected her of trying to steal the ring and only pretended to find it after being caught.

My aunt, of course, had never accused anyone. But my mother's defensiveness spoke volumes. She was overexplaining, divulging details only a thief would know, inadvertently exposing herself. This wasn't a moment of remorse or guilt—she lacks the capacity for that. It was her compulsion to control the narrative, to paint herself as the victim, even when there was no accusation. It was a classic tell, one I had grown accustomed to seeing, though it didn't make the realization any less painful.

So, you can imagine my horror when she requested that very ring after my aunt's passing. It wasn't about cherishing a memory or holding on to something meaningful. It was about triumph. The ring, to her, wasn't a keepsake but a trophy—a dark symbol of her conquest. It was her twisted version of a prize, a way to relive the moment she believed she had outsmarted everyone.

The request was less about my aunt and more about her vile satisfaction, much like a villain in a novel asking for the spoils of a defeated adversary. It was her way of relishing her malice, of reminding herself of a moment she deemed victorious. In that ring, she saw not love or loss but proof of her ability to manipulate, deceive, and still emerge with what she wanted. It wasn't sentiment—it was gloating. A reminder of how she could twist even the purest relationships into opportunities for evil.

Chapter 3

For those fortunate enough to have never encountered someone like my mother, it's hard to grasp the extent of their manipulation. Their words can seem convincing, their personas almost magnetic. But to those of us who've lived it, who've been battered by the storms they create, the truth is painfully clear. They are their undoing, their need for attention and validation driving them to reveal far more than they intend. My mother thought she was spinning a tale to paint herself as righteous, but all I saw was the ugliness of her soul laid bare.

The contradiction that was my father still baffles me to this day. A man who stood as a devoted servant of God, a loving father figure in the public eye, and someone who preached kindness, love, and standing for what was right—yet somehow allowed, tolerated, and even enabled my mother's unrelenting cruelty. For so long, I believed the goodness in me came from him. He taught me to love others and to fight for justice, even when it was unpopular. He was the man who ensured our family's devotion to the church, even riding bikes to service when there were no other means. He was admired by all, his warm smile and open heart drawing people to him.

But the truth unraveled painfully before my eyes. The man I idolized revealed himself to be a walking contradiction. He abandoned his teachings and aligned himself with my mother, participating in her campaign of destruction against me, his daughter. The dissonance between the man people praised and the man I came to know was a reality I could barely comprehend.

Some said he must have been cursed by my mother, bewitched into submission. It wasn't hard to believe. My mother's ties to the dark arts were not hidden; voodoo and witchcraft were tools she actively wielded. I recall, as a child, stumbling across voodoo dolls in her purse, unaware of their significance. But as I grew older, the depth of her malice became clear.

One of her most chilling acts was the creation of a shrine dedicated to me. In the locked confines of her closet—a place no one else could access—she set up candles and placed my photographs among them. By those candles, she wrote curses on slips of paper, wishing for my downfall, even my death. The sight of that shrine, discovered later, was a stark and terrifying revelation of the depths of her hatred.

Locks were a common theme in my childhood home, symbols of control and deprivation. Cabinets containing food, dishes, and utensils were locked, and the refrigerator was secured with a padlock. Meals were rationed out sparingly, while snacks and other foods were stashed away in their bedroom behind another lock. The power dynamic was clear: we were to beg for even the most necessities, feeding my mother's sadistic pleasure in holding the literal and figurative keys.

At the time, the lock on her closet didn't raise suspicion. It was just another locked door in a house where they were ubiquitous. But in hindsight, that locked closet contained more than candles, pictures, and curses—it was a warning. It represented the danger I lived with daily but hadn't fully recognized. That shrine was a chilling confirmation of just how deep her hatred ran and how far she was willing to go to maintain control, even at the expense of her own family.

Chapter 4

My mother's abuse was multifaceted – physical, psychological, and emotional. She was diabolically strategic in her cruelty. At times, she'd lull me into a false sense of security with kindness, only to weaponize my confidence against me later. She twisted my words and fabricated lies, her deceit a web that only became clear to me in adulthood. She was a master manipulator, mirroring others to gain their trust and then betraying it with surgical precision.

She gaslighted me, warping my reality with outlandish claims that left me questioning my sanity. Her obsession with sexualizing everything made my skin crawl. She was obsessed with labeling me as a "whore," twisting every narrative about me to fit her vile fantasies. It wasn't enough for her to let my accomplishments stand on their own; she had to tarnish them, turn them into sordid tales that stripped away my hard-earned achievements. In her eyes, I had "fucked my way to the top," using my looks as a currency for every bit of success I obtained, no matter how big or small.

Nothing was off limits, to include my platonic male friendships, down to my own Father and brothers.

Yes! Father and brothers, too, were a part of her sick and evil narrative of me. Telling all that would listen, that I slept with them all too. It wasn't just a lie—it was a carefully crafted campaign to discredit me, to paint me as something I was not. She spread these fabricated stories like poison, recruiting others into her twisted narrative and turning them against me without a second thought, her family became her echo chamber, mimicking her venom. They verbally bullied me, ridiculed my lighter skin complexion, and called me conceited, as if my very existence was an affront to their reality.

And as they joined in her hate, I was left wondering what was worse: the mother who led the charge in my character assassination or the people who followed her so blindly, so willingly, reveling in the destruction of my spirit.

She portrayed herself as the victim, and they all bought into her act. How could anyone sit there and listen to a mother speak about her daughter with such malice and then feel compelled to join her? How could they not see how disturbing it was, this allegiance they pledged to her cruelty? For an adult child to decide to cut off their parents completely—shouldn't that raise a red flag? It's natural for a child to crave a relationship with their parents, so why did no one stop to ask what she had done to make me want to sever ties so completely?

If this were an abusive boyfriend, girlfriend, or spouse telling these tales of hatred about someone who left them, people would rally to protect the victim. They would chastise the abuser, offer compassion, and encourage the decision to walk away. Yet, when it comes to parents and their children, those lines blur. Somehow, the abuse is rationalized, the blame shifts and the child becomes the villain in a story where they are just trying to survive.

Every aspect of my life was scrutinized—my grades, my interests, my appearance—nothing was off-limits from her ridicule. My tears seemed to fuel her, not soften her. Apologies didn't exist in our house. Instead, she played the victim, twisting reality until I was gaslit into believing that, somehow, I was the problem. But in her cruelty, she would also wear the mask of a mother who "cared" when it suited her, leaving me clinging to moments of false hope. What a mind fuck it was for me and kept me in total confusion of who she was to me. Reminds me of the sour patch kid that pushes you down and then helps you up and does it for all your life.

I remember one day at school in the third grade, I received a poor grade on a journal assignment. Growing up in an environment where I was constantly torn down, I had become a relentless people-pleaser, desperate to gain approval, especially from her. I was an A and B student, always striving for those marks, foolishly believing it would make her proud enough to love me. That grade, to my wounded mind, felt like it could shatter the fragile possibility of love from her.

I thought that, for once, she'd come through for me. I imagined her as the mother I desperately wished she could be—a protector, someone who would care, someone who would save the day. But what happened next was far from the comforting fantasy I clung to. She stormed into my school the very next day, unannounced, crashing through the office like a hurricane and barging into my classroom while the teacher was mid-lesson.

She didn't care about the frightened eyes of the children or the stunned silence that filled the room. My heart sank with every step she took toward the teacher's desk. I sat there, consumed by shame, hoping, praying that no one would notice me, that the floor might swallow me whole. I wanted nothing more than to be invisible, to not be her daughter in that humiliating moment.

She didn't stop at words. When the teacher, visibly shaken, instructed her to leave and schedule a meeting, my mother lashed out, shouting, "You better be lucky you're pregnant; otherwise, I'd grab your white ass up across this desk, bitch!" I sat frozen, mortified, while the class watched in disbelief. They had only glimpsed the surface of her rage, a fraction of the chaos that was my daily life. For them, it was a terrifying spectacle. For me, it was a front-row seat to the nightmare I lived with every single day.

At that moment, I didn't just wish to be invisible—I wished to be anyone but her child. I prayed to be anything but tethered to her, but the torment was only beginning, and that day was just another chapter in the endless saga of her abuse.

Chapter 5

She moved very cowardly, like at home as well in some instances. More so in her attempts to paint and control the narrative of her and my father and how he was viewed. Now that I am aware that she was quite envious of our relationship with our father, it makes sense that she was strategic in how she wanted to paint him. She would plant the seed in his head, and my father would follow through with his discipline of us according to what she said. I know now to be orchestrated scenarios where my father would discipline us, only to swoop in and play the caring mother, casting him as the villain while she wore the mask of the loving parent.

This fed into her plot to attempt to sever our bond with our father. He was very straightforward, swift, and stern in his words and punishments, and it was damn near impossible to get him to bend. She moved like a coward, but her cowardice was calculated, especially when it came to manipulating how we saw our father. Now that I understand her deep envy of the bond we had with him, it's clear that every move was strategic, every word designed to control the narrative. She needed to be the hero in her twisted story, and she was ruthless in how she cast the roles.

She'd plant seeds of doubt, twisting situations to make him the villain. My father, strict and unwavering, would take her word at face value. She'd set the stage, creating these orchestrated moments where he'd discipline us—harshly, swiftly—while she stood in the shadows, waiting for her moment to swoop in like the "caring" mother. I see it now, the way she wore that mask, the false protector, the one who "understood" us while casting him as the unfeeling, hard-handed enforcer.

It wasn't just discipline. It was manipulation, designed to drive a wedge between us and him, to tear apart any loyalty or love we might still have had for our father. The more he punished us, the more she played the savior, feeding into the narrative she so desperately wanted us to believe that she was the loving parent and he was the villain. But my father—he wasn't just strict; he was resolute. His words were final, his punishments immovable. Once he'd decided on a course of action, there was no swaying him. And she knew that. She used his sternness like a weapon against us, all the while keeping her hands clean, her face adorned with that false smile of compassion. In her cruelty, she manipulated not only us but him too, turning him into an unwitting pawn in her game to sever the bond we had with him.

Looking back, I can see how calculated it all was—how she fed off the chaos she created, always needing to control, always needing to be seen as the better parent, even if it meant poisoning the very relationships she claimed to cherish. It's terrifying to realize just how deep her need for control went and how willing she was to use those closest to her to maintain it.

My father was nothing more than a puppet in my mother's sick game. I never understood how she could claim to hate him so deeply yet remain in the marriage and, worse, try to sever the bond between him and his children. How could a woman have it all—a loyal husband, devoted to a fault, amazing children, an incredible family—and still be filled with such a twisted desire to portray herself as the victim in her own home, painting us as monsters? She stayed, not out of love or duty, but for the sick satisfaction of controlling us under the guise of motherhood.

Her outlets for spewing venom were many, but her number one confidante was her mother and sister. Any and everything that happened in our household was broadcasted to them like a twisted, live drama. And as much as they thought they were privy to the truth, they didn't realize they were just pawns in her game, too. She lied about us to them, just like she lied to us about them. One minute, she was telling us how horrible her mother and sister were to her, how they hurt her, and how she was "done" with them for good. The next minute, she was crying to them about how awful we were. The manipulation was endless.

And it was all for control.

My father was cast as the villain, the family a bunch of ungrateful monsters, while she wore the mask of the suffering saint, carrying all the weight on her back. Her family despised him, believing her lies about him being useless, cold, and unloving. But in truth, as flawed as he was, he was the safest parent I had. He was direct, stern, and unyielding in his discipline, but he wasn't cruel, at least not until my adult years when he turned. Unlike my mother, he didn't thrive on chaos. Over time, he became my hero, the parent I turned to when the walls of her lies and manipulation became too much to bear. I became a daddy's girl, a bond she resented and sought to destroy at every turn.

She orchestrated chaos, pitting my father against her family and then turning them against me. And as much as she played the innocent victim when it came to their disgust toward me, I now know she was the architect of it all. She planted seeds of disdain, painting me as the spoiled, light-skinned child who thought she was better than everyone else, the smart, quiet one who made their insecurities flare. She turned them into her weapons, and I was their target. She discarded me like an unwanted burden, dropping me off at my grandmother's house after poisoning her mind with lies—lies my grandmother was wise enough not to fully entertain.

But even then, the damage was done. Those who lent an ear to my mother's slander, those who nodded along or fed into it, were revealing something deeper—**their true feelings about me**. And that truth cut me to my core. It wasn't just betrayal; it was a silent confession that I wasn't worth love, understanding, or even the benefit of the doubt.

To realize that people you trusted were so quick to abandon you is a bitter pill—one that burns your throat and lingers in your gut long after you've tried to swallow it. I hadn't done anything to deserve this cold absence of love, but still, I was punished, cast aside, and made to feel unworthy. How do you recover from that? How do you not hear the silence?"

Chapter 6

Going to my grandmother's house wasn't any escape—it was just another circle of hell. I never felt welcome there, and no matter what I said or did, my accomplishments were diminished. My grandmother would always find a way to one-up me with tales of my cousins' successes. She was just an older version of my mother—bitter, jealous, and cold. Favoritism towards my brothers was clear, but even they weren't spared from her twisted dynamics. She despised them too, not for who they were, but for who they belonged to.

But what hurt the most wasn't just her words or the rejection—it was the deep, dark secret that hid in that house.

One of my cousins made me their target. They were obsessed with me, always telling me how pretty I was, how special. I knew something was wrong, but I didn't have the words to describe the pit of dread in my stomach every time I had to be near them. When I voiced my discomfort, it was dismissed, as if my words held no weight, as if my fear wasn't real. And so, it escalated—beyond my worst nightmares.

I still remember the night that changed everything. A sleepover at my grandmother's house, the kind that should have been filled with laughter and childhood innocence. But that night, as I lay in bed, I felt a hand crawl up my nightgown. I woke to see their eyes on me, dark with something sinister I didn't fully understand but feared with every fiber of my being. I closed my eyes, trying to escape the reality of what was happening. I didn't fight back—I was too scared, too small, and all I could do was cry in silence, hoping it would end soon.

But it didn't end that night.

It went on for years. Each encounter became worse, the fear gripping tighter. They tried to push me further, intimidating me, wanting more than I was ever willing to give. But I fought, no matter how small or powerless I felt. I never let them take everything. I survived, just like I did in my own home with my mother. Survival was my only goal—to get through one more night, to count the hours or days until I could escape. Even though I knew deep down that being vocal about the abuse would do nothing but make things harder for me, a part of me still held onto the desperate hope that someone, anyone, cared. That maybe, just maybe, if I could hint enough, cry enough, or show enough fear, my mother would take notice and save me. I remember how I would break down, sobbing every single time she told us she was dropping me and my siblings off at that place. Any good mother, any mother who truly knows her child, would've seen my tears for what they were: a cry for help, a sign of distress. But not her.

She never questioned it. Never wondered why I was so terrified. Never challenged those who made me feel so small, so scared. It didn't matter that I was a good kid, that I did everything I was told—even if it was out of fear or out of my desperate need for her approval, her love, or at the very least, her liking me. I convinced myself that if she saw my discomfort if she could see the fear in my eyes or the trembling in my voice, maybe, just maybe, some flicker of maternal instinct would kick in. Maybe then she would protect me. Keep me away from that place. Shield me from the pain I couldn't escape.

But it never came.

I would cry to the point of begging her, pleading to go to my other grandmother's house—my father's mother. That house was my sanctuary. It was everything my mother's world wasn't: warm, welcoming, full of love. My father's side of the family made me feel safe like I belonged. There, I was never treated as an inconvenience, never made to feel small or unwanted. I loved it there. I loved them. And for that, my mother despised it. She despised anything that brought me joy. Anything or anyone that made me feel happy or loved became her target because her goal was always to tear me down, to strip away any sense of worth or happiness I could cling to.

She knew how much I cherished my father's side of the family, and that was exactly why she did the opposite of what I needed. She would chastise me for the love I had for them, for the joy I found in their presence. And I truly believe she knew something was wrong—she had to know. But she didn't care. She didn't care enough to stop it, didn't care enough to protect me from that nightmare, because caring about me never fit into her plans. Everything was about her—her wants, her desires, her selfish needs. She was always off with some other man, fulfilling her self-centered ambitions, and it was always at the expense of her children, her spouse, and her family.

But speaking up? That was pointless. No one would listen, not to me. In my world, my voice was always drowned out by the lies they chose to believe. It was always easier for them to believe the lies, no matter how obvious. Lies were safer, more entertaining—less painful than facing the truth. I held on to those painful experiences with him through my childhood, my teenage years, and right up until my last encounter with him, during my freshman year of college, when I was 18.

I was staying on campus, which felt like my refuge. The campus was about to shut down for Thanksgiving, and the thought of going home made my skin crawl. College had become my escape, my way out of that nightmare. Then my mother called. She asked me what my plans were for the holiday. I told her I was planning to spend Thanksgiving with my father's side of the family at my grandmother's house like I always did. Returning to her world was not an option. I couldn't bear the thought of stepping foot back into that godforsaken place. But just the sound of my plans—of me choosing to be anywhere but with her—lit a fire of fury inside her, as I knew it would. She launched into her usual tirade, accusing me of being stuck-up, of neglecting her side of the family, and not understanding why I didn't spend time with them.

My grandmother had no idea about the abuse that happened in that house. I kept it from her, just like I kept it from everyone else. I wore the shame of it like a cloak, too afraid, too mortified to burden anyone with the truth. My father's side of the family knew who my mother was—they had dealt with her toxicity long before I was born—but they didn't know the depths of the pain she caused me. They had no idea how deeply it cut. So, as usual, I gave in to her. I decided to spend Thanksgiving with her family. I had no car, so a friend dropped me off, and we planned for her to pick me up after the holiday.

That was the day I had my final run-in with him—the cousin who had violated me for so many years. I hadn't seen him in years. I thought that part of my life was over. I thought I had buried the pain deep enough that it would never resurface. But he had other plans.

When I arrived, my grandmother was her usual self—cold, distant, barely acknowledging me. As always, I felt like an outsider. I kept my head down and tried to survive the day, telling myself it was just one holiday. But I knew no matter what I did, I'd never be enough to make my mother happy. We gathered for grace, blessed the food, and I grabbed a plate and sat down on the couch. There wasn't much room in the kitchen. That's when I saw my cousin walk in. My heart stopped.

They smiled like they didn't have a care in the world, like the years of abuse were just erased from their memory. But I remembered. I remembered everything. I sat there, paralyzed by fear. I had heard the rumors—that he had become more violent, that he didn't hesitate to put his hands on people, especially women. My fear was a living, breathing thing inside me. But I refused to let him have the same power over me he did when I was a little girl. Not this time. I wouldn't give them that.

At some point, I went to get a second plate, trying to distance myself. But when I returned, they had made sure to sit right next to me. Even with their girlfriend and child right there, they still found a way to violate my space. I remember them placing the baby between us, using the child as a shield to reach for me. Their hand touched me, and it felt like fire on my skin. I jumped up, heart racing, and left the room. It was happening all over again. I gave myself a pep talk in the hallway, telling myself it was time to stand up for me for the child I had once been. But how? How could I fight in a house filled with people who made me feel just as powerless, just as small, as my mother always did? I felt so out of place, so unprotected, so alone. I kept quiet, praying for the day to end.

As the night wound down, people started saying their goodbyes, and my cousin used the moment to blend in with the others, trying to hug me like everyone else. But this time, when they grabbed me and tried to touch me, I pushed them away. "We aren't kids anymore," I said, my voice firm but trembling inside. "I will never let you disrespect me again. Keep your hands off me." They just smiled that sick, devilish grin and laughed as they walked out with their child and girlfriend as if nothing had happened.

I rushed to the bathroom, my heart pounding and my chest aching. I broke down in tears, feeling trapped in a way I hadn't felt in years. I had no transportation. I couldn't leave. I was just a teenage girl trying to make something of myself, and yet here I was—stuck in the same nightmare. I knew I could call my friend, and she would have come for me without a second thought. But the shame—the overwhelming feeling of being a burden—was too much. I couldn't even bring myself to make the call. What would I say? "Can you come get me? My cousin just tried to violate me again, just like they did when I was a little girl." The words wouldn't form.

The next day, I was told my aunt wanted to see me before I headed back to campus. A family member dropped me off at her house. When I walked inside, there my cousin was—the cousin I had tried to avoid all holiday long, sitting there, waiting. I knew this was it. This was the moment where I'd either fight or flee.

I sat down, and he sat across from me, that smug grin on their face. They brought up the encounter from the night before, laughing like it was some kind of joke. "I know you liked it," they said, their smile twisted and vile. I told them that they would never place their nasty hands on me ever again and that I was ready to take on whatever came in at that moment. Deep inside, I was terrified and said to myself, "Are they going to rape me?". Call it what you want, but I call it divine intervention. Even though I wasn't thrilled to see her, and I was only making my rounds on my mother's side to keep her off my back, in that moment, I had never been more relieved to see her walk through that door. It was like a lifeline, even though I hadn't expected one. After that visit, I returned to my grandmother's house, grabbed my things, and waited for my friend to pick me up. We headed back to campus, and I felt a wave of exhaustion wash over me, but I knew I had to make a call.

    I called my mother to tell her what had happened and what I had endured. But, just as expected, instead of receiving any comfort or understanding, I was met with victim-shaming. She wasted no time. She immediately called her mother to pass along what I had shared, and the response was as predictable as it was painful. I was made out to be a liar, painted as some kind of troublemaker—someone who couldn't be trusted. And I knew, without a doubt, that my mother had added her venomous spin on things, weaving her narrative into the words of my grandmother, as she always did.

It wasn't just something that had happened throughout my childhood—this was different. This moment changed me. It marked the beginning of a deeper silence, one that would stretch through the years and seep into every part of me. My voice was stolen that day. I learned, in that instant, that speaking up didn't matter. No one would believe me. No one would care. And so, I internalized everything. From that point forward, I swallowed my pain, my truth, and the injustices done to me.

I slipped into the role that I knew all too well—defeated, submissive, surviving because that's what I had to do. I knew how to survive, even when it meant silencing myself to do it. My pain was her twisted pleasure, a source of sick satisfaction, whether it came directly from her or through others she manipulated. Her abuse knew no bounds. There wasn't a day that went by where she didn't take another opportunity to remind me that her mission was to break me—to destroy me from the inside out. This wasn't love; it was calculated cruelty. The scars she left were not just physical—they were embedded deep within my soul.

But this, tragically, is only the beginning. We're barely scratching the surface of the torment she inflicted. We will come back to this dark truth as my story unfolds. For now, we'll leave this moment here, as painful as it is, because there's so much more to reveal.

Chapter 7

As I transitioned from childhood to my teenage years, the abuse only intensified. My growing independence, my budding identity, and the simple fact that I was becoming a young woman—it all seemed to threaten her. I was no longer just her daughter; I was becoming something she couldn't control. My looks were blossoming, my voice was growing stronger, and my opinions were no longer pliable under her thumb. To her, I wasn't a daughter—I was competition, the "other woman" in her world.

One memory still burns deep: the day I got my first diary. I had saved my allowance and bought it at the elementary school book fair. It was supposed to be a sacred place for my innermost thoughts, a refuge from the storm that raged around me. I poured myself into those pages, scribbling down my day, my crush on the boy next door—innocent musings of a teenage girl.

But my sanctuary turned into a nightmare. I came home from school one day to find her sitting at the dining table, the diary in her hands, the lock broken. Another family member sat beside her, an enabler who thrived on the hate she cultivated against me. She read my entries out loud, each word a knife slicing through my dignity. They laughed and mocked, their voices growing louder as I stood there, paralyzed by the betrayal. My private thoughts—the only place where I could be myself—were turned into ammunition for their cruelty.

The more I cried, the more they laughed. My tears were fuel for their sadistic fire. "It's just a joke," she sneered, "You're too sensitive. You need to toughen up." At that moment, it wasn't just my privacy that was shattered—it was my sense of safety, my ability to trust. They turned my vulnerability into a weapon, and with that, they killed a part of me. After that day, I never wrote in a diary again.

My development into young womanhood was gradual, almost as if I was trying to resist it every step of the way. I was a tomboy through and through, not by some rebellious choice, but because it felt inevitable growing up with only boys before my sister was born (which we'll get into later). Boys were just boys to me, nothing more.

But then my world shifted. I thought it was the end of everything when I got my period. It felt like my body was betraying me, especially when my breasts started to develop, even if they were barely noticeable. I remember walking with my shoulders hunched, trying to hide the fact that my body was changing and that I was becoming something other than the carefree girl running around with the boys. I hated it. It felt like any tiny part of my development was breaking news to my mother and not the kind that should be celebrated. There was no sense of "girl code" with her. Instead, it was as if she lived for opportunities to humiliate me, to twist these moments into something ugly, only to gaslight me afterward. She'd make me feel like I was the sensitive one, like this was just part of growing up. But it wasn't. It was her cruelty masquerading as maternal care.

When it came to me, there were no boundaries—no privacy, not even in the most intimate moments of my life. My development through puberty felt like an invasion, a spectacle she believed she had every right to observe. She would barge into the bathroom without warning, catching me mid-shower or while I was drying off, always with an inappropriate remark ready to cut through my discomfort. 'Oh, look at you! The nerve to be getting some peach fuzz and little titty balls,' she'd say, grabbing at her words like they were playful, harmless observations. But they weren't. Her behavior violated me and chipped away at my sense of safety, and no amount of squirming or discomfort was enough for her to stop.

Even into adulthood, she pushed the line. If I locked the bathroom door while showering at her house, she'd pound on it, claiming she desperately needed to go and the other bathroom was occupied. I'd give in, only for her to swing back the curtain as if she owned me—no hesitation, no shame. 'Oh, you have a nice body, girl,' she'd say like I was nothing more than something to be examined. I started waiting for her to leave before I'd shower, dreading the sound of her voice just outside the door.

And it wasn't just me. I saw her eyes scan other women at stores, her comments going far beyond what's normal between us as women. Never a sweet or girly compliment, always something that reached too far, something that left me—and them—cringing. I could see it in their forced smiles, their uneasy laughter. For someone so brazen, so out in the open with her uncomfortable observations, she was quick to project evil onto me. Promiscuity.

Shame. Accusations that I had somehow become what she always saw in her twisted mind. How do you process that? Being violated while simultaneously being made to feel dirty for things you never did? It was a cruel contradiction, one that weighed heavy on my spirit.

As I write this, a memory resurfaced—a chilling moment when her obsession with branding me as a "whore" began to take root. They say hindsight is 20/20, but I say that hindsight combined with healing brings light to even the darkest moments, ones you didn't realize were dark at the time. I now see those moments for what they were.

I remember her pulling me out of school randomly for my physicals—what she called "girl appointments." She never told me in advance, always showing up unexpectedly, as if she enjoyed the control it gave her. Now, through the lens of healing, I realize it was strategic. Every time she took me, she'd make the same comment, like a broken record: "Your grandmother used to take me to my physicals, and at mine, the doctor would tell her I was doing more than holding hands." She never failed to say it, not once.

Looking back, it's clear now. She was laying the groundwork, planting seeds of suspicion, insinuating that if I was doing anything, she'd know. It was like she wanted to find something, like she was hoping to catch me in some lie, to have proof that I was exactly what she wanted me to be: the bad girl, the whore. She knew it wasn't true. I knew it wasn't true. But for her, the truth was never beneficial. She didn't want the truth—she wanted control. And with me, control always meant humiliation. One of the many reasons why I dreaded the physical changes that came with becoming a young woman.

I would braid my hair in simple cornrows, rejecting the pretty hairstyles that girls my age flaunted. I even signed up for cheerleading but barely made it through one game before ditching the pom-poms to try out for the basketball team. Baggy jeans, oversized shirts, hoodies—they were my armor, my way of holding on to the innocence I feared I was losing. The thought of wearing a skirt or capris to school made me sick. It wasn't just about disliking the clothes; it was about rejecting this new identity that I didn't want to embrace.

Looking back now, I realize that during this time, I was still safe and innocent in a way. I wasn't seen as a threat yet, not in the eyes of my mother, because I hadn't fully stepped into womanhood. I was still a girl, not someone to be envied, not yet. And maybe part of me wanted to stay that way for as long as possible before everything started to unravel. As soon as I started liking boys, everything changed. My style shifted, and I began to care more about my appearance, about embracing femininity. It was a gradual transition, but my mother made sure to weaponize it at every turn. If she wasn't busy branding me as a "baby whore in training," she was tearing me down in more subtle, cutting ways.

She homed in on every little detail, every imperfection. One of her favorite targets was my posture. I remember her mocking me with a twisted delight, exaggerating my slouch in this childish, exaggerated manner. She'd parade around with a grin plastered across her face, putting on a show as if humiliating me was some kind of achievement. She wasn't content with just saying it once—she'd perform it, make it a spectacle.

It worked. I became hyperaware of myself, constantly forcing my back straight, no matter where I was. I could be in the most laid-back environment, where everyone else was relaxed, but I couldn't bring myself to let go. It wasn't safe to let go. This fixation followed me into adulthood, to the point that even today, I catch myself doing the same thing—unnaturally sitting up straight, almost as if the echoes of her voice still control my movements.

Her words, her mockery—they seeped into me, shaping how I carried myself in the world. Even now, it's become second nature, a burden I carry, stitched into my very posture.

I never had the chance — nor did I ever feel comfortable — opening up to my mother about anything at all. Not my thoughts, not my feelings, and certainly not my discovery of liking boys. But somehow, one day, I summoned the courage to tell her about a boy who had taken an interest in me. A boy who made me feel seen, something I craved so desperately but never received at home. My siblings and I would go skating with the church every other weekend, and that's where this boy, a little older than me — maybe 16, while I was only 13 — first approached me.

Of course, we know how young teenage girls are: full of naivety, brimming with the awkward pains of growing up, and eager for affection. It's at this tender age that most girls lean on their mothers, seeking guidance and reassurance, a mother's words of wisdom to help them navigate this confusing terrain of emotions. But not me. That wasn't my story. Instead, I was met with the same cruelty I had come to expect. My mother, who should have been my protector, my safety net, seized this moment — this vulnerable, raw moment — to do what she always did best: make me feel like dirt.

Rather than step into the role of a concerned, protective mother, she saw this as an opportunity. An opportunity to weaponize my innocence, to watch me squirm in pain, to ensure I learned the "lesson" she believed I needed to. The lesson she was always so eager to teach me — that no matter what, I was never enough.

So, she allowed it. She let me go back to those skating functions with this older boy, knowing full well what he wanted. She didn't care about my safety, my well-being, or my trust. In her mind, I deserved whatever was coming. I was branded promiscuous before I even had a chance to understand what that meant. Branded the troublemaker, the girl who couldn't possibly be a victim. I was always painted as the one at fault.

I remember that one evening so vividly. After one of those skating events, the boy asked me to sit next to him on the bus. I thought nothing of it, eager to hold on to the little shred of attention he gave me. But soon enough, I realized what he was truly after. He leaned in and exposed himself, asking me to touch him. I froze in horror, my body rejecting everything I thought I knew at that moment. I moved away as quickly as I could, and with my heart shattered, I spent the rest of the ride crying, feeling violated and confused.

When I got home, I told my siblings. I told my mother what had happened, hoping that maybe, just maybe, this time she'd see me. That she'd comfort me, protect me like mothers are supposed to. But instead, she delighted in my pain. She reveled in it. She relished the fact that her daughter had been exposed to such filth that I had been humiliated. She didn't regret what happened — she allowed it, after all. She even admitted to me that she knew exactly what this boy wanted from the start. "I wanted to teach you a lesson," she said as if there was some sick justification in her decision to let me get hurt.

No lesson needed to be taught. I was already a good kid, an easygoing daughter who would have listened if she had just sat me down and warned me. I didn't need this first-hand betrayal to understand what it felt like to be preyed upon. But that's the thing, isn't it? My mother never really cared about protecting me. Watching me cry didn't stir any sympathy in her heart. Looking back now, I realize it excited her. She loved watching me suffer, loved knowing that I was being hurt and that I had no choice but to come back to her broken.

There was always gaslighting, always something to make me feel like it was my fault. My fault for being a teenage girl who dared to want affection. My fault for living in a world where boys liked me, and I dared to believe their lies. How could it ever be my fault? Especially when my home life was already a nightmare, devoid of love, devoid of warmth. Could you blame me for wanting to feel wanted, even for a moment?

I was always left drowning in shame, constantly feeling like there was something fundamentally wrong with me. As if, somehow, I could have stopped all the terrible things that happened, as if I invited them into my life. That's what she wanted, wasn't it? It was all about control. It was her way of keeping me small, keeping me crushed under her thumb, stealing away every ounce of self-worth I tried to muster within myself.

How could I ever believe I was anything but worthless when my mother made it her mission to remind me, over and over, that I wasn't? How could I believe I was deserving of love, happiness, or anything good when the one person who was supposed to build me up made it her life's work to tear me down? Every look, every word, every subtle dig was crafted to chip away at my spirit, leaving me doubting my value as a human being.

It's hard to see yourself as anything but broken when your mother makes sure you never forget that, in her eyes, that's all you are.

Chapter 8

The very first boyfriend I had as a teenager remains one of my most cherished memories. Not because of the typical teenage infatuation but because he made me feel something I never truly experienced at home: safe. In those moments with him, I felt more protected, more seen, than I ever did within the walls of the place I was forced to call "home." He became my sweet escape. He didn't want anything from me—nothing more than to simply love me for who I was. Even if people brushed it off, saying we were too young to know what love was, I knew what it meant to feel safe, valued, and adored in his presence.

I was just this shy, little teenage girl, walking around the neighborhood with my best friend, giggling and talking when he approached me. I could see it in his eyes—his mission to make me his girlfriend. He was rough around the edges, but with me, he was always gentle, kind, and respectful of every boundary I had.

He treated my parents with respect, especially my father. He'd come to the door, knock, and greet him warmly, even though my mother was usually absent, off in her world of distractions. I remember my dad would invite him in, letting him sit on the couch while he washed dishes or cooked dinner. He always had this quarter on him that he would give to me and instructed me to hold it in between my knees. He'd always say the same thing to him every time: "You see that quarter, young man? The moment that quarter hits the floor, it's time for you to go!" He'd say it like a joke, but I knew he meant it. In that strange, rare way, it was my dad's way of showing that he cared—that he wanted to protect his baby girl.

He trusted this boy so much that he'd even let him walk me down to the water if we were back before the streetlights came on. No lectures. No guilt trips. No gaslighting like my mother would constantly do whenever I was around the opposite sex. We'd sit by the water, and he'd drape his jacket over me if it was cold. We'd talk for hours about everything and nothing, and he'd listen—listen—to whatever I needed to get off my chest. For a moment, just for a moment, I felt free. Light. Like all the burdens I carried were gone. Even though I knew that as soon as I went home, they'd be waiting for me, heavier than ever.

He even brought me Christmas gifts, and it wasn't about the money—though he wasn't cheap with me. It was about the thought, the care. I remember the year he gave me a Burberry watch. He had his mother drive him over to my house just to give it to me. He was upset because he couldn't find the matching belt he'd wanted to give me, but I didn't care. I was just grateful—so deeply touched that he'd even thought of me, let alone gone through the effort of getting me something so special. I wore that watch with so much pride. It was like my little symbol of happiness, something that was just for me.

But, of course, she couldn't let me have that. My mother. I showed her the watch, and I could see the excitement drain from her face as she saw the joy in mine. It's no coincidence that the watch vanished shortly after. I had placed it in the same spot as I always did, but one day, it was gone. She confronted me, asking why I wasn't wearing it, knowing full well what had happened. I didn't dare challenge her—because she was who she was, and I knew she'd twist it, lie, and somehow make it my fault. Just like that, another piece of joy was ripped from my hands.

It was a pattern, one that haunted my life. Anything that brought me a shred of happiness was snatched away as if to remind me that I wasn't allowed to be happy, not allowed to feel good about anything. It was always her way of keeping control, her way of keeping me small. Soon, she would take him away from me completely, never to see him again.

He wasn't just sweet; he made me feel like I mattered. Yet even in that safety, I never felt I could confide in him about the dark, suffocating reality of my home life—the abuse, the neglect, the shame. I couldn't even tell my best friend the full extent of what I was going through. He was *so* protective of me. That boy didn't play about me—*honey*, I was his world, and he made sure everyone knew it. If anyone even dared to hurt me, make me cry, or cross me in any way, he was right there, ready to defend me.

I'll never forget one day when we were talking on the phone—back when cell phones weren't even an option like they are now. You had to stretch the phone cord as far as you could, praying your parents didn't pick up the other line and embarrass you by telling you it was time to hang up. I had my fair share of those moments. We were laughing, talking, just being us, and he overheard a boy in the background teasing me. I remember the boy was just playing, but when my boyfriend heard me say, "Stop," it was enough to set him off.

He immediately asked, "Who's that? Who's bothering you?" I brushed it off, telling him it was nothing, that the boy was just joking around. But he wasn't having it. He said, "You tell that boy to leave you alone. You said stop, and that means he needs to stop." I laughed and told him it was fine; everything was cool. I thought that would be the end of it. But then he said, "I gotta go,

babe. I'll call you right back." He hung up abruptly, and I thought nothing of it. But no more than 30 minutes later, I heard this loud rumbling on our front porch.

I ran up to the screen door to see what was going on, and there he was—my boyfriend, wearing that familiar jersey I knew so well. Before I could even say a word, he flew through the screen door, knocking it off its hinges, and went straight for the boy who had been teasing me. He didn't ask questions; he just threw himself into that fight, fists flying, ready to defend me. My father stormed out, furious, seeing the broken screen door lying on the floor. He was so mad, his voice booming as he turned to me and said, "Tiffany, you can tell your little friend goodbye because this is the last time he'll ever come over here. *Tabar? Tavar?* Whatever your name is, get your bike, get your friends, and get out of my yard." My heart sank.

The boy who had been teasing me looked at me, bewildered and hurt, saying, "Get your boyfriend. I was only joking with you, and he came over here and hit me in the face." It wasn't funny then. I cried, not because of the fight, not even because of the chaos my boyfriend had caused. I cried because I knew my father meant it—I wouldn't be seeing him around the house anymore. But inside? Inside, I was smiling. Because for once in my life, someone fought for me. Someone cared enough to stand up for me, protect me, and show me what it felt like to be loved that way.

I craved that from my parents. *God*, I wished and prayed for that kind of fight, that fierce love and protection to come from my mother. In all the times I needed her most, she was never there to defend me, always the bully I needed defending from, never there to stand up for me. But he was. He showed me the love and care I desperately longed for, the love I should've had from the one person who was supposed to be my fiercest protector.

He was my safe place. I don't think he ever knew how much I needed that; how much I appreciated him being one of the few good things in my life during that time. I had so little, and whenever I went to my basketball games, I was always too ashamed to admit that I didn't have money to eat after. But he made sure I never went without. He'd send me money through his sister, who was on the team, just so I could eat like everyone else. It's only now, looking back, that I realize how God placed angels in my life when I needed them most.

I would soon come to find that her twisted need to sabotage my happiness, particularly in my love life, would become a relentless pattern. Each relationship was met with increasing boldness and cruelty from her, as if my growing independence was a threat she couldn't allow. In my younger years, her goal seemed singular: to humiliate me, rob me of any remaining shred of self-esteem, and poison every glimmer of hope I clung to. If she could scare them away, she could reinforce her twisted narrative — that I was unworthy, unlovable, and insignificant. It was as if she was determined to convince me that I didn't matter.

Her devious acts always started small — subtle criticisms, passive-aggressive remarks, and silent disapprovals that seemed harmless to anyone on the outside looking in. But they pierced me deeply. As I got older, those small cuts turned into vicious, deliberate blows — each one designed to chip away at any happiness I found. No matter how insignificant her actions might have seemed to others, to me, they carried the weight of a thousand knives. With each calculated move, she reminded me that I would never escape her grip. And worse, I started to believe her.

A memory so deeply etched in my mind amongst so many others is when she snatched off my fake ponytail in front of my boyfriend, leaving me mortified. I had just come from church and had a day out with him and his family, which was always so welcoming of me as we all grew up in church together. My mother had shown up to come and get me and take me home, and he and I were outside of the vehicle conversing and doing what teenage lovers do: smiling and laughing, the puppy loves things. While wrapping up her conversation with the other adults, she approached him and me.

Creeping up behind me as if she were playing some childish game that is always in her eyes would be deemed harmless, but every move she had with me always served a sick purpose. She then snatched the ponytail off my head and ran about the yard, swinging it around and laughing with such sick satisfaction and joy at what she had just done to her daughter. I was humiliated at that moment granted, I had hair, but it was beside the point. It was the fact that my mother would do such a thing to hurt me in front of a boyfriend that I felt pretty in front of and was trying to impress. We all know as teenage girls, the evolution from childhood into young womanhood is a process, and self-esteem is so important that boys and the changes they bring about in us that turn up our femininity a little more. My mother was determined to stop it before I even had a chance to explore what it felt like for the opposite sex to make me feel better or wanted.

I remember holding back the tears at that moment and being filled with such hurt and humiliation and anger and yet not wanting others outside of the toxic home that I was in to see any part of how her actions were destroying me little by little. Once again, shame overwhelmed me at the sight of her exposing some of her devilish ways concerning me and disguising it as the playful mother when this was far from the truth. The ride home, I cried, replaying in my mind that moment and her so childishly after running about the yard, adding more salt to injury by attempting to place the ponytail back on my head in the presence of my boyfriend.

As usual, the gaslighting commenced, and I was, as always, made to be overly sensitive about something, and the words "I was just playing with you" always made their way into the conversations that she lacks accountability, which is mainly 100% of the time. She would always attempt to beat me to the punch with my father by starting conversations about her childish behavior and portraying them as her playing around with me while I became overly upset about it. My blind, loyal father would always favor her version over mine or anyone else who dared to speak against her or tell the truth about any situation. To further compound the dreadful and humiliating experience, I also had to face constant criticism from my father about my so-called sensitivity and that I needed to lighten up.

Her actions, as always, aimed to undermine my self-esteem and independence. She even weaponized my wardrobe, ensuring I looked as undesirable as possible, while she, of course, always appeared impeccable. It wasn't about whether the clothes came from a department store or the local Salvation Army; it was about what she selected for me, always a step below everyone else—even my siblings. Her hair was always done, her nails perfect, and her outfits carefully chosen, making it painfully clear that the issue wasn't a lack of resources or style. It was something far deeper: her complete lack of care for me. One morning, she handed me an oversized men's trench coat, claiming the weather was cold.

Sure, it was chilly, but when I compared what my brothers wore to the hideous coat, she forced on me, it was clear as day what her real intentions were. It wasn't about keeping me warm; it was about keeping me small. I was so determined not to wear that coat that I'd rather freeze at the bus stop than let anyone see me in it. But she never missed a chance to twist the knife. She peeked out of the house that morning, spotted me without the coat, and yelled for me to put it back on. I had no choice but to obey, standing there, suffocated in that monstrous thing while my brothers tried their best to console me.

They were always there, trying to protect me, even daring anyone to make fun of what I wore. But that didn't take away the shame, the sting of knowing my mother had orchestrated the humiliation. There were days when it got so unbearable that I started sneaking clothes out of the house. I would stuff my backpack with outfits that made me feel like myself, clothes that wouldn't invite ridicule. I'd drop the bag out of the window to my brothers, who waited outside like loyal accomplices in my small rebellion.

We had it down to a system — sometimes, I'd change in the shed, and other times, I waited until I got to school. I was a good kid, did well in school, and was the kind of child who flew under the radar, so she never thought to check up on me like she did with my brothers. But looking back, I realize that even as a good kid, it would've been nice for her to show up in class — just to see how well I was doing. Just to care. But this was *my* mother we're talking about. The only thing she ever cared about when it came to me was making sure I never outshone her, never stepped out of the shadows she forced me into.

One day, out of the blue, she decided to show up at my school, unannounced as always, lurking in the background of my life like a shadow I could never shake. I wasn't expecting her — none of us were. She came into my classroom that day and discovered that I had changed my clothes. Her face was a mask of feigned kindness as she asked my teacher so politely if she could come sit with me. My teacher, completely unaware of the devil in disguise, obliged without hesitation. My mother sat beside me, sizing me up, her eyes scanning me from head to toe, seething in silence. Then, as if it wasn't enough to humiliate me quietly, she roped in one of my friends who sat nearby. 'Did she have this on at the bus stop?' she asked, her voice coated in sweetness. My friend, oblivious to the truth, giggled and replied, 'No, ma'am.' She had no idea that her innocent answer had just sealed my fate.

My mother's grip tightened around my arm, not in a way that would raise suspicion, but in that way only I knew — the way that warned me of the storm to come. She smiled sweetly, told me she loved me, and left the room. But I knew. I knew what awaited me when I got home. The moment I walked through that door, I was beaten not just for disobeying her wardrobe choice but for daring to claim even an inch of autonomy over my life, my body, and my image. From that day forward, she checked my bags before I left the house, ensuring that whatever humiliating outfit she chose was exactly what I had to wear, whether it destroyed me inside or not.

The weddings and family gatherings on my father's side often became stages for my mother's manipulation and resentment. At one of my uncle's weddings, her behavior followed its usual pattern. While she arrived immaculately dressed, I was intentionally neglected, wearing mismatched or unkempt clothes. It was a recurring theme—her shining for the world while I was left to stand out in shame.

Yet, my aunts on my father's side, angels in disguise, always seemed to know. They never waited for me to speak about my plight; they anticipated my needs before I arrived. At this wedding, they had already prepared a beautiful outfit, complete with shoes, waiting for me. One of my aunts whisked me into the bathroom and told me to change. Tears welled in my eyes, not only from the humiliation of standing out so starkly among the other children but from the overwhelming gratitude I felt for their kindness. They saw me, they cared, and they acted.

When my mother saw me in my new outfit, her rage was palpable. She turned to my father and, in her typical fashion, framed herself as the victim. "I'm her mother," she declared. "No one is to undermine me by changing her clothes." She tried to enforce her control by painting herself as a mother doing her best under challenging circumstances. But we all knew the truth—she relished the humiliation she could inflict on me, thriving off the power it gave her.

That day, however, she was too late. I was allowed to keep the outfit on, and for once, I felt like I blended in. I joined the other children, took pictures with my cousins, and, for a moment, felt the joy of belonging.

But her attempts to sabotage my appearance didn't end with clothes; she extended it to my hair. The upkeep of my hair was another battleground for her cruelty. While braiding my hair was a task she performed intermittently, the real torture was in the in-between moments. Wash days were particularly grueling. She would command me to take out my braids, comb my hair, and wash it. Then, as if reenacting a bonding ritual common in many black households, she'd instruct me to gather my hair supplies and sit between her legs in the living room.

But unlike other black mothers who lovingly did their daughters' hair while sharing stories, laughter, or tender moments, my mother twisted this experience into something entirely different. It was never about care or connection; it was about control and asserting her dominance over me. She could turn even the simplest, most culturally significant ritual into a tool for her sadistic pleasure, stripping it of the love and nurturing it was meant to embody.

When I sat between my mother's legs on those dreaded wash days, it became less about hair care and more about performance—a spectacle designed to manipulate and torment. She would begin her theatrics abruptly, launching into what seemed like convulsions. Her body would shake violently, her eyes rolling back into her head as foam bubbled at her mouth. The first time it happened, I was terrified. I jumped up, screaming for my father, pleading for him to save her. I was too young and too naïve to understand what was happening.

The episodes never lasted long—just long enough for my father to notice and come rushing to her side. He would gently carry her to their bed, telling me she needed rest. And with a sorrowful look in her eyes, she would gaze at me as if apologizing for failing me once again. My father, always quick to defend her, would assure me that she wasn't in any condition to do my hair and that I'd have to find another solution.

But as time went on, these episodes began to feel too calculated, too convenient. They always seemed to happen when I needed her most—especially on wash days when my hair needed to be done before school. The pattern was impossible to ignore, and I began to wonder if it was all an act. Was this just another one of her ploys to hurt me? To humiliate me? Even as these thoughts entered my mind, I felt a pang of guilt. Could I believe my mother would stoop so low? Yet, deep down, I knew the answer. She had shown me who she was repeatedly.

Her so-called "illness" became her shield, her excuse for every failure, every neglectful act. She claimed to be epileptic, but the dramatics were always too exaggerated, too perfectly timed to dodge accountability. It was a performance she wielded to avoid doing my hair, sending me to school with my hair unkempt, ensuring I stood out for all the wrong reasons.

Eventually, I stopped asking her altogether. I'd rather risk damaging my hair with my clumsy attempts than endure her cruelty masked as helplessness. Her refusal to care for me wasn't about inability; it was deliberate. Another tool in her arsenal is to belittle, humiliate, and break me. And yet, despite it all, I found ways to pick myself up, to piece together the fragments of care she withheld, and to fight for my dignity—one strand at a time.

Children can be cruel—brutal, even—but nothing compared to the cruelty I endured before I even stepped onto the school bus. I wouldn't say I had it the worst at school, but I had my share of teasing and humiliation. And not because of anything I had done but because of *her choices.* My mother's choices. She had a way of sending me into the world like I was a living punchline—dressed in whatever humiliating outfit she deemed suitable for the day, my hair barely touched, messy and unkempt. It wasn't just that I didn't have the best of anything; it was the way she made sure everyone knew it.

Other kids didn't have much either, but you could tell they were *loved.* It was in the way their parents did their best to present them with care, to show the world they mattered. That wasn't my reality. My reality was walking into school, feeling like I'd been set up to fail before the first bell even rang. I felt like a walking target, marked for ridicule because of her need to humiliate me, even from afar.

Despite it all, I managed to make friends. I was outgoing and funny, and I wanted so badly to connect with people. But even with those friendships, there was a wall—a shame that I couldn't escape. I never wanted anyone to come over to my house. How could I? My mother turned our home into a trap of embarrassment. She would accuse my friends of things they hadn't done, even if they were just sitting outside on the porch. She'd scream from her bedroom, claiming they had stolen something or snuck into the house, as if the mere presence of another child offended her. The accusations were loud, humiliating, and constant. It was suffocating.

There were times when I'd rather stay inside and face her wrath alone than go back outside to my friends after one of her outbursts. The shame she heaped on me felt inescapable like it clung to my skin. And no matter how kind my friends were, I couldn't bear the thought of them seeing how chaotic and cruel my home life was.

Out of all my childhood friends, only one ever stayed over. She was different—supportive, kind, funny, and somehow, she made me feel like I wasn't alone in the chaos. She saw things, of course. She questioned some of what she witnessed, but she never judged me. Instead, she offered me an escape for the weekend, a few precious hours where I could laugh and feel like a normal kid, even within those walls.

I was ashamed of my family, ashamed of the dysfunction that screamed louder than any love ever could. But with her, I felt okay being vulnerable. For once, I didn't feel like I had to hide the cracks in my life, even though I desperately wished they weren't there. She was my little light in the darkness—a reminder that there were people in the world who cared, even if the person who should have cared the most didn't.

Chapter 9

As I grew older, the physical abuse became more frequent, but it wasn't just her hands that inflicted harm—it was her choices and the chaos she cultivated. This escalation coincided with the time my mother began yet another affair. It wasn't her first. She had a habit of entertaining men behind my father's back, inviting them into our home as though it were a revolving door. My father would leave for work, and like clockwork, the men would start arriving, one after another.

I remember their faces and names, each one seared into my memory. One day, I looked downstairs and saw my mother entertaining one of them—her clothes stripped away, her boundaries nonexistent. Later that day, I came downstairs to go to the kitchen, only to be confronted by the same man. His presence confused me, and I spoke up: "I don't understand why you're here when my father is at work." That one sentence made its way back to my mother.

She called me downstairs, her anger simmering just beneath the surface. I was ordered to apologize to him. She dismissed my concerns with a lie, insisting he was just a friend stopping by. "Stay in a child's place," she snapped. It was a pattern I would come to recognize—a relentless demand for compliance and silence, no matter how obvious her betrayal.

But one of her "friends" crossed a boundary that I could never have imagined. He violated me in my sleep, stealing not just my sense of safety but a piece of my childhood. My brothers caught him one night, standing over me in my room. I had no idea he had even been there. Yet, despite their confrontation and their insistence on his guilt, my mother kept him in our lives. She chose him over her children's safety, a decision that underscored her cruelty and self-serving nature.

When my brothers caught her and this man together in my parent's room, she scrambled to create a story to protect herself. She was a master manipulator, willing to destroy anyone to preserve her image. To her, people were disposable. They were only as valuable as their usefulness to her. The moment they threatened her narrative or her control, she discarded them, no matter the cost.

In this instance, she feared my father discovering the truth—not just about this man, but about the toxic patterns that had plagued their marriage for years. Infidelity and promiscuity had always been part of their relationship, a toxic cycle of betrayal and forgiveness. My father, forever playing the role of the betrayed husband, would act hurt but always stayed, enabling her behavior time and time again. She knew this and weaponized it, twisting every situation to her advantage.

To cover her tracks, she spun an elaborate lie, telling my father the man had raped her. She claimed to be the victim, fabricating a story of violation and despair. The man was arrested, and she groomed my siblings to corroborate her tale, ensuring there were no cracks in her façade. My father, blinded by loyalty or perhaps denial, stood by her side, believing her lies and condemning the man to punishment.

Just like that, the man went from being a part of her world to being erased from her mind, discarded without a second thought. It wasn't the first time she had manipulated someone, and it certainly wouldn't be the last. Her ability to exploit, manipulate, and destroy left a sinister trail.

She had one neighbor thrown in jail and seduced the other next door, dragging me into her tangled web of deceit as if I were her pawn. This time, I wasn't just a bystander to her chaos—I was the cover story. She used me, manipulating my innocence and my desperate yearning for her love and validation. She knew I wouldn't question her; knew I was too quiet and too eager for her approval to push back. That's who I was then—a child still holding onto the fragile hope that if I did what she wanted, maybe she'd love me the way a mother is supposed to.

But that hope was her weapon, and she wielded it ruthlessly. She turned me into her errand runner, sending me to the corner store to meet him—her lover. She gave me clear, calculated instructions about where to go and where to find him like I was some sort of courier in her twisted operation. She'd press a single dollar or a few coins into my hand, a pathetic "reward" for my obedience, as if I were nothing more than a dog performing tricks for scraps.

I hated it. Every step I took to carry out her demands felt like a betrayal of myself, like I was being swallowed by the darkness she created. But I had no choice. The alternative was worse: her rage, her fists, her cruel words tearing me down until I felt smaller than I already did. She had a way of making me feel like I was the problem like I was the one ruining her life, when all I wanted was for her to love me.

I walked to that store with shame burning in my chest, my stomach twisting with the knowledge that I was complicit in something I didn't understand and never wanted to be a part of. I told myself it was better to just go along with it, better to do what she wanted than to face her wrath. But deep down, I knew it was wrong, and the weight of her manipulation crushed me a little more each time.

Every trip to the corner store was laced with a lie, a script carefully crafted by my mother that I was forced to memorize. I became her accomplice in deceit, rehearsing the lines she fed me on the ride back home to my father. Each word felt heavy in my mouth, a betrayal I couldn't escape. I hated lying to him, but what choice did I have? She left no room for disobedience—her manipulation was as suffocating as it was cruel.

The drive from the store wasn't just a trip; it was an exercise in erasure. As I sat in the passenger seat, I tried to block out the things I had seen. But how do you erase what's burned into your mind? The car would idle behind the store, the engine humming like a bystander to her recklessness. She would step out with no regard for my presence, closing the door, and the volume in the car cranked up just enough to drown out her actions—or so she thought. But no amount of noise could silence what I knew was happening.

Her commands were clipped and cold. "Stay put," she'd bark as if I were an object to be left behind. And then she'd vanish behind the store, the door slamming shut like the punctuation on yet another secret. I would sit there, alone with my thoughts, my stomach in knots, my heart pounding with confusion and shame. I tried to make myself small, invisible, as if shrinking into the seat could make me disappear from the reality unfolding around me.

There was nothing discreet about these encounters—nothing subtle in her actions or in the lies she spun to get us there. And yet, I was the one left to uphold the facade. I was the one who had to face my father and pretend that nothing had happened, that we had simply gone grocery shopping but somehow returned empty-handed.

It felt like I was being crushed under the weight of her choices, forced to carry secrets too heavy for a child. The lies, the deceit, the blatant disregard for my innocence—it all chipped away at me, leaving me hollow and exhausted. I wanted to scream, to cry, to tell her I couldn't do it anymore. But I knew better. In her world, there was no space for my feelings, no room for my pain. She made sure of that.

After lying to my father's face yet again, the guilt would consume me. The weight of the lies she forced on me felt unbearable, like a stone pressing down on my chest. I would retreat to the bathroom, hoping the shower could wash away the shame I felt for betraying him. But no amount of water could cleanse me of what I had become complicit in. I would lie in bed afterward, curled up in a ball, tears streaming down my face as I muffled my sobs into my pillow. The darkness of the room felt like a reflection of the darkness in my heart, a heaviness no child should ever have to endure.

The burden was mine alone to carry. My siblings were blissfully unaware, spared from the sick reality that our mother had created. But me? I was her pawn, her secret keeper, her shield. And as the days went on, her boldness only grew.

She and her lover found ways to make their affair more covert and more calculated. They began using walkie-talkies to avoid leaving any trace on their phones. It was like watching a twisted game unfold, a game I didn't sign up for but was forced to play. The rules kept changing, and her audacity knew no bounds.

Then came the day her lover crossed yet another line. I didn't know that he was in our house until the doorbell rang. My siblings and I had been eagerly waiting for the pizza we had ordered, and I ran downstairs to grab it. I expected to see the delivery guy standing there, a box of cheesy comfort in his hands. But when I stepped into the living room, my stomach dropped.

There he was, sitting on our couch like he belonged there. My mother sat beside him, both relaxed and comfortable, as if their affair was no longer a secret. As if the house wasn't my father's home. As if he didn't have a wife and children, he was waiting for him somewhere else. The sight of them together made me freeze, my breath catching in my throat. The pizza I had been so excited for no longer mattered. The room felt suffocating, and all I could do was stare, trying to process the betrayal happening right before my eyes. How could she be so bold, so shameless, so utterly dismissive of the family she was tearing apart?

At that moment, the realization hit me like a punch to the chest—she didn't care. Not about the consequences, not about me, not about the family she was tearing apart. To her, I was nothing more than a pawn, a means to an end. A cover, a tool, an alibi. The pain of that truth burned deep, but what choice did I have? In her world, refusal was not an option. I swallowed the hurt, the anger, the betrayal and carried the weight of her secrets in silence.

But I couldn't keep it all in. I needed someone to share this burden with, someone who could help me feel less alone in this nightmare. One evening, I broke down in my room and shared everything with my siblings. Every ugly, heartbreaking detail spilled out of me as tears streamed down my face. I hated dragging them into the mess, hated dumping this on them, but for the first time, I felt a sliver of relief. I wasn't alone anymore. They knew. They *knew*.

That night changed everything. It was a turning point, though I couldn't yet see how it would all unfold. For a moment, the weight didn't feel as unbearable, even though I knew it wasn't fair to them. But it was the only way I could survive—to share the burden and hope they wouldn't hate me for it.

Still, my mother's manipulative games continued. She was a master storyteller, weaving her victim narratives to anyone who would listen—me, my father, whoever she needed to convince. She'd sit there, lamenting her unhappiness, painting herself as the long-suffering wife. "I've been staying for you kids," she'd say, with a dramatic sigh, as if she deserved a medal for enduring my father. But I knew better. I'd seen too much and heard too much. Her words were just another dodgeball aimed at accountability, another way to shift the blame.

She'd say things like, "One day, I'm going to leave. And I'm taking you with me." As if her escape plans were some kind of gift as if she could erase the years of betrayal and manipulation with a single promise. I didn't believe her, not really.

Then came the day her lover joined in on the charade. We were on yet another one of her "errands," which meant leaving her car at a park-and-ride and hopping into his. He drove, his hand intertwined with hers, their stolen moments playing out like some cheap romance movie. I sat in the back seat, squirming in discomfort as they gazed into each other's eyes, oblivious—or indifferent—to the fact that I was there. When the car stopped, he turned to me, still holding her hand, and with a smug smile, asked, "Your mother and I are planning to leave one day. Are you coming with us?"

The audacity of his question made my skin crawl. Who did he think he was? But worse than his words were the way my mother's face lit up at them, glowing with admiration for this man who had invaded our lives. She stared at him as if he hung the moon as if this moment were the pinnacle of her existence. And then I answered. "No," I said firmly. "I'm not going with you. I'm not going with either of you."

Her face changed instantly. The warmth, the glow, the admiration—it all vanished, replaced by the cold, seething anger I knew so well. That look, the one that made me feel like I was less than nothing, washed over her. "She's so damn loyal to her damn father," she spat, venom dripping from every word. "I swear, it's like I don't even fucking exist. And that's exactly why I'm going to get the hell on. We'll see what your daddy does for you when I leave."

Her words cut deep, but by now, they were just another wound on a body already covered in scars. Her anger didn't faze me as much anymore—at least, that's what I told myself. But inside, I was still that little girl yearning for her love, her approval, her validation. And no matter how many times she let me down, a part of me still hoped she'd see me, really *see* me, for the child who just wanted to be loved.

Shortly after that moment came an event that would shake all our lives to the core. A life-changing revelation that added another layer of chaos to an already fragile existence. I can't recall every detail—I was just a child, and the memories blur together like watercolors running down a page—but what I do remember is enough to make my stomach churn even now.

I was sitting in the back seat of the car, quiet as usual, staring out the window, lost in my thoughts. I wasn't trying to eavesdrop; I didn't need to. Her voice pierced the air, sharp and frantic, cutting through any attempt I made to block it out. "What am I going to do about this baby? I'm going to have to go out of town or something," she said, her voice trembling, rising with the kind of desperation that made my chest tighten.

Those words hung in the air like a dark cloud, suffocating and heavy. My mother—pregnant? The realization crept into my mind slowly, unwilling to settle but impossible to shake. I was just a child, but I wasn't naive. I was smart enough to catch the drift of what she was saying, though I wished I weren't. I didn't know who she was speaking to—her lover, maybe? Another man in her endless rotation? What I did know, with chilling certainty, was that it wasn't my father. Her words carried a weight that I couldn't fully understand at the time, but even then, I knew they weren't meant for his ears.

The air in the car felt thick like it was pressing down on me, suffocating me. I wanted to shrink into the seat and disappear entirely, but I couldn't. My mind raced, trying to process what I'd just heard, trying to piece together the fragments of a story that was unfolding right before me but felt too big, too adult, for me to grasp fully. Her betrayal wasn't just a wound anymore—it was a gaping, festering chasm that now threatened to swallow another innocent life. And there I was, a child caught in the middle of her chaos, forced to carry the weight of a truth I didn't even ask to know. A truth that would change everything.

She had decided to keep the child, and the delivery of the news to my father was soon to follow. When she told him, I watched as he lit up with elation, as if this was the miracle he had always dreamed of. At that moment, I couldn't help but feel an overwhelming sense of betrayal, as if my entire world had tilted off its axis. I was blindsided by this news, but I now know the truth—my father had a vasectomy after having me and my twin. I had no idea back then, and I sat there, staring in disbelief, trying to understand how she had somehow made this work in her favor once again, as always.

She had sold it to him as some miraculous gift from the universe, a child that defied medical science, slipping through the cracks of his vasectomy from 14 years ago. The audacity of it—it was as if she could make anything appear real, even the impossible, just to keep her own selfish needs satisfied. And my father? He questioned not a single word. Without hesitation, he spread the news with a glee that stung deep in my chest, as if this child—this stranger—was everything he'd ever wanted.

But even in her joy, she made sure to remind me that I didn't matter. Even with a new life growing inside her, I was still invisible, still insignificant. She continued to neglect my needs, twisting everything to make me feel small. I can still recall the time we went school shopping—she told me to pick out what I wanted, and for a moment, I felt a flicker of excitement. But that excitement was quickly snuffed out when, at the checkout, she suddenly claimed to be in so much pain that we had to leave without my things. No apologies, no explanation—just another crushing disappointment.

I wanted so desperately to be excited about the new life that was coming. I wanted to be a good big sister, to be happy for a sister who would make my heart feel full again. But instead, I was just angry. Angry at the fact that she could never make space for me—angry at how easily my heart was being let down, time and time again. It hurt more than I could put into words because I had kept trying to make room for love, trying to make room for her. But all she ever gave me in return was emptiness, and now this child—this miracle—was a reminder that I would never be enough.

My father, in his excitement, put together a beautiful Tweety Bird-themed nursery for her. Delivery day finally arrived, and the air was filled with a sense of anticipation, a mix of joy and nervous energy. My father, my siblings, and I crowded together in that sterile hospital room, waiting for her arrival. It was supposed to be a moment of family unity, a moment of joy that we could all share. But what I felt in that room was not happiness—it was a suffocating sense of displacement like I was standing in the shadow of something I wasn't a part of.

I remember a moment when my father, out of nowhere, told my siblings and me to leave the room. We were confused, but we obeyed, unsure of what was happening. As we stood there in the hallway, I could see my mother's eyes—eyes that once held a semblance of warmth but now were clouded with something darker. It wasn't guilt, I knew that much. It was something else, something I couldn't yet name—something that made my heart tighten. Her eyes betrayed a cold kind of pain, not for what was happening, but for what wasn't. She wanted her lover there. She wanted to share this moment with him, not with us.

And in that moment, it hit me: I was nothing more than a backdrop in her life, a child whose needs and emotions didn't matter. Her tears—the ones I could hear as I stood outside that room—weren't about the birth of her child or the joy that was supposed to fill the air. They were about who wasn't there. They were about the man who should have been there by her side, the one she had chosen over her own family time and time again. The tears weren't for me or for the family we were supposed to be. They were for her selfish loss—the absence of him—and I knew, with a sickening certainty, that we would always come second to her desires, to her distractions, to whatever gave her fleeting satisfaction.

Nonetheless, my father prayed over her for a healthy delivery, and they headed into surgery. We brought her home, and the air in the house shifted as a new life filled the space. For a moment, everything felt right. She was a joy for all of us, and my father, so proud, took her to church with him, just as he had done with all of us. You could see it in his eyes—the love, the pride. He was a father in his truest sense, and for a fleeting second, I wanted to believe that this time, things could be different. But, as always, that hope was short-lived, like so many other moments in my life.

The day seemed like any other as my siblings and I made our way to the bus stop. But this time, something felt different. The weight in my chest told me that something was off. As we walked out the door, my mother hugged us one by one. It wasn't the hug that unsettled me—it was how she held me, how her arms wrapped around me so tightly as if trying to pull something from me that wasn't there. "Momma loves you, you know that?" she whispered into my ear. And in that moment, I wanted to scream, "No, you don't." The words felt like a cruel joke. I had never truly felt loved by her—not in the way a child should.

Her version of love was hollow, conditional, a performance meant to control, not to nurture. She held me longer than usual, her grip tightening with each passing second as if not wanting to let go. I froze, my mind screaming for her to release me, to stop this game she played. I told myself over and over that we were just going to school, just going through the motions—nothing would change. But deep down, I knew it wasn't true.

There was something in the way she held me, something suffocating in the way her arms encircled me, that made me feel as though I wasn't going anywhere. Maybe this was the last time I would ever feel her touch without it being tainted by all the cruelty and manipulation beneath it. It was like she was trying to force something that wasn't there—something that had never been there—and in that moment, I wished I could escape, wished I could leave and never come back. I didn't want to be a part of this twisted reality she was weaving anymore.

After we let go, my siblings and I walked to the bus stop, but I couldn't shake the feeling that something was wrong. The pit in my stomach grew heavier with every step. "She's going to leave us, y'all. I feel it. Today, she's leaving us," I said, my voice trembling as I tried to keep my fears in check. My siblings looked at me like I was overthinking it, dismissing my words with confused glances. But I wasn't imagining things—I felt it deep in my bones. The way she hugged us, the way her words lingered in the air, heavy and foreboding... it wasn't normal. And though I tried to convince myself I was wrong, a part of me already knew the truth.

When we got home that afternoon, it was as if the walls themselves mourned her absence. The house, once full of life—even in its dysfunction—was eerily quiet. We walked through the door and froze. Three stories of emptiness greeted us, the echoes of her betrayal ringing louder than any sound. She was gone. Not just her but nearly everything we owned. Furniture, belongings, even the car—she had taken it all. All that remained was the weight of her absence and a suffocating silence.

My heart raced as I spotted the note on the dining table. Trembling, I picked it up, reading aloud the first line: *"Well, I guess the thorn is finally out of your side now."* Her words felt like a dagger, sharp and cruel, twisting the knife deeper into an already open wound. I couldn't bear to read anymore. My voice cracked, and tears burned my eyes as I threw the note back onto the table. As if to add insult to injury, she had left us—her children—with five dollars each. Five dollars. That was her parting gift. As though five dollars could ever compensate for the void she had left in our lives. She took our baby sister, the one thing that brought us all joy, and abandoned us without a second thought.

I dreaded what came next, telling my father. The familiar sound of his bicycle rolling into the yard reached my ears, followed by the squeak of the shed door as he parked it. My heart sank, heavy with the weight of what I had to say. Watching him stride toward the house, blissfully unaware of the devastation waiting inside, felt like a cruel twist of fate. He had no idea that his world—our world—had just been turned upside down.

My father, always the devoted husband, had spent years leaving the car for my mother so she wouldn't have to go without. Day after day, he pedaled that bike to work, putting her comfort above his own. And now, that very car, along with so much else, was gone. Taken. Just like that. She had robbed him of more than transportation—she had taken pieces of his soul, his trust, his love.

When he walked through the door, his usual cheerful greeting momentarily pierced the tension: "I said, hey, up in this mug!" His voice carried its usual warmth as if the ground beneath him hadn't already been stolen. He stood there, expecting us to come running, our usual chorus of "Daddy's home!" echoing through the house. But none of us moved. None of us could. The weight of what we had to say kept us rooted in place. I couldn't even bring myself to look him in the eyes, knowing what my words would do to him.

My father was a man of faith, a man who had spent his life shielding us from the ugliness of the world. He even replaced his curses with playful words like "mug," a small act of devotion to his role as a father. But no amount of faith or love could soften the blow waiting for him. His smile lingered for a moment longer, unaware of the storm brewing just feet away. I watched it fade as his eyes searched ours, realizing something wasn't right.

We gathered in the dining room, and he followed, confusion etched into his face. He asked why we hadn't greeted him at the door like we always did. The words caught in my throat, but I forced them out: "She left us, Dad. She's gone." I slid the note she left across the table, my hands trembling as he picked it up. He sat silently, his face a mix of disbelief and confusion, reading her words. Without a word, he stood and made his way upstairs, past the now-empty rooms, and into his bedroom. He closed the door behind him, a sign we all knew well—when his door was closed, he was in prayer. It was his way of seeking strength, of processing the unbearable. We didn't disturb him. We couldn't.

His silence on the way up spoke volumes. Each step seemed heavier than the last, weighed down by betrayal, loss, and heartbreak. I could only imagine what he was thinking as he passed the remnants of what she had left behind. When he finally called me up, I hesitated before making my way to his room. He sat me down on his lap, and his voice, though soft, carried a strength that shook me. "Daddy ain't going nowhere," he said, his eyes filled with love and resilience. "We are going to be alright. I'm not going to bad mouth your mother, but just know—we are going to be alright."

He looked at me, his gaze steady but tinged with sorrow. "I know it's going to hurt all of us, but you especially. I know what it feels like to feel abandoned, but I'm here. You're not alone, baby girl." His words wrapped around me like a blanket, offering the comfort I desperately needed. But the blows kept coming. Later that day, the next-door neighbor's wife knocked on the door, her expression grim. "Is your wife gone too?" she asked my father. My heart sank further as her next words confirmed the hunch we all had. Her husband, our neighbor, had packed up and left as well. It didn't take a genius to connect the dots.

The betrayal wasn't just personal—it was a public unraveling of the family we thought we had. My father, still reeling from the day's events, stood tall, his strength unwavering in front of us. But I knew, deep down, he carried the weight of it all, even as he vowed to carry us through it.

She disappeared without a trace, leaving not a single clue as to where she had gone. Each passing day of her absence fueled a growing hatred inside me, as if the pain of who she was when she was present wasn't already enough. Her absence was a loud declaration that we didn't matter. It didn't matter. We were nothing compared to the man she abandoned us for. The physical distance only cemented the emotional abandonment we had already felt for years.

My father took it all in stride, though I could see the toll it took on him. He carried the weight of it all—our pain, our survival—on his shoulders. With her gone, every financial burden fell squarely on him, and the cracks began to show. The cold winter came with a new level of hardship, stripping us of even the small comforts we once had. Our rooms, once private sanctuaries, became iceboxes. We pushed my siblings' beds together, huddling around a single kerosene heater to share whatever warmth we could muster. The chill seeped into everything, even our breath visible in the frigid air. The inside of the house felt colder than the world outside.

Showering was torture, a cruel necessity we all dreaded. Even getting dressed for school in the mornings felt like an impossible task. Outside of my father's room, with its kerosene heater, the rest of the house might as well have been a freezer. Yet somehow, through all this, my father's love never wavered.

He did his best with my hair, fumbling through the process with hands that were meant for hard work, not braids. Gel became his go-to, slicking my hair back in a way that was far from perfect but full of love. I never complained because even in his clumsy attempts, I felt something I never felt with my mother: care.

He worked endless overtime hours, trying to make up for her financial absence, sacrificing rest and warmth so we wouldn't go without. With no car, bikes became our lifeline. Mornings meant waking up early, bundling up against the snow, and riding to my grandmother's house. He made sure we were fed and warm, even if it meant trudging through the biting cold on two wheels.

Our bike rides became a routine. My father would lead, and we'd follow behind like a line of ducklings, each with a backpack strapped to our shoulders. At the grocery store, we'd load up on whatever we could afford, packing our bags to the brim. The ride back was brutal, the added weight of the groceries pressing down on us as the snow stung our faces. But I never complained—not once. I knew my father was doing everything he could for us, and that was enough. It was more than enough.

When the hot water ran out because the furnace was too expensive to fill, we boiled water from the basement to bathe. It was another blow, another reminder of how far we had fallen, but we adapted because we had no other choice. Bologna sandwiches became our staple meal, cheap and easy to keep on hand. To this day, the sight or smell of bologna makes my stomach turn, a visceral reminder of those cold, hungry days.

School became more than just a place to learn—it was a refuge. A warm classroom and a hot meal were enough to make the mornings bearable. I never told a soul what was happening at home. I mastered the art of smiling through the pain, a skill I had perfected long before this when surviving my mother's cruelty. I wore that smile like armor, fooling the world into believing that everything was fine. But behind that smile was a little girl carrying the weight of an absent mother, a struggling father, and the kind of resilience no child should ever have to summon.

Months had dragged by with no sign of her—no phone calls, no letters, not even a whisper of her existence since the day she vanished. Each day without her hardened my heart further, layering anger and resentment over wounds that were already bleeding. I told myself I didn't care, that her absence was a blessing in disguise. But a small, rebellious part of me still ached for answers, for closure, for *something*. Then, out of nowhere, she reappeared.

Chapter 10

It was a regular school day, uneventful and routine, until the intercom crackled, summoning me to the front office. My name rang out over the speakers, slicing through the monotony of class. I sat frozen for a moment, surprised—I never got called out of class. The curiosity gnawed at me as I gathered my things. My best friend, sensing something unusual, excused herself to the bathroom and trailed behind me, her concern silent but tangible.

We had barely made it halfway down the hall when the moment hit me like a freight train. There she was, standing at the far end of the corridor. My mother. The woman who had disappeared without a trace, leaving nothing but an empty house, shattered trust, and a note full of venom. And now, she stood there, arms outstretched as if she was some prodigal saint returning to her flock.

Her face radiated entitlement as if she truly believed I had missed her, as if she deserved my forgiveness and an embrace to welcome her back. The warped selfishness of her gesture ignited something volcanic inside me. Rage, disbelief, and heartbreak surged through my veins, tangling with the icy shock of seeing her again. I stopped in my tracks, my feet rooted to the floor, while my mind screamed a thousand questions. *How dare you?* How dare she waltz back into my life as though the gaping hole she left behind had magically healed itself? Did she think her absence would be erased with this grand display? Did she truly believe that the daughter she had abandoned, emotionally and physically, would greet her with open arms like none of it ever happened?

The hall seemed to stretch endlessly between us, her presence a suffocating weight pressing down on my chest. My best friend froze beside me, her hand gently brushing my arm in silent support. I swallowed the lump in my throat, my emotions too tangled to make sense of. She kept walking toward me, her arms still open, her smile so bold, so misplaced, that it stung worse than the coldest insult. There was no apology in her eyes, no remorse for what she had done—just the expectation that I should somehow feel lucky she had returned.

But I didn't feel lucky. I felt robbed. Robbed of peace, of trust, of the love she had hoarded so selfishly for herself and never once spared for me. My mind raced with the weight of all she had taken and the scars she had left behind. Yet here she was, striding down the hallway as if she deserved a hero's welcome. She wasn't alone. A woman I didn't recognize followed behind her, just like so many others who always seemed to circle my mother—strangers to me but props in her ongoing performance.

This one, too, seemed blissfully unaware of her role in the spectacle, probably thinking she was offering "emotional support." But I could see through it all. She was just another spectator, there to witness the next act in my mother's never-ending theater of lies. If my mother was going to return, she had to do it on her terms, with all eyes fixed on her. She couldn't just quietly slip back into our lives. No, she needed to ensure the spotlight was shining brightly, that she was the star of her warped narrative, the misunderstood victim coming back to claim what was hers.

God only knows the twisted story she had spun for this woman, just as she had spun for so many others. I could almost hear the lies—the carefully curated lines designed to paint herself as the wounded heroine, surrounded by villains who just didn't understand her pain. She was an artist with her façade, building a house of cards with her charm and manipulation, luring people in only to leave them blind to the wreckage she left behind.

And this woman, like all the others, believed her. How could she not? My mother had perfected this performance her entire life. But I wasn't fooled. I had seen the truth behind the mask too many times. As I stood there in that hallway, staring at the spectacle unfolding before me, I didn't feel an ounce of the love or longing she expected from me.

All I felt was anger. And exhaustion. And a quiet, unshakable resolve that I wouldn't be a pawn in her twisted drama anymore. But, of course, my silence wasn't enough to deter her. She closed the distance between us, wrapping me in a hug I didn't ask for, forcing a closeness I didn't want. Her theatrics never ceased. "Oh my God, he's turned my kids against me!" she said to the woman who stood by her side as if her actions hadn't done that all on their own. She couldn't even fathom being the villain in her own story—never had, never would.

The blame always had to land somewhere else, anywhere but on her. It was a talent of hers, deflecting, redirecting, dodging accountability like it was an art form. I stood there stiffly, unwilling to give her what she was fishing for: validation, forgiveness, or even a shred of sympathy. Not this time.

But I noticed something. The sunglasses she wore stayed glued to her face the entire time. Not once did she take them off. Even as she spoke, even as she hugged me, they stayed on like some kind of shield. And though I didn't know why at that moment, I had a sinking feeling the truth behind those glasses would reveal yet another chapter of her deceit when I got home.

For now, I had to return to class, to the pretense of normalcy, as if my world hadn't just been shaken again. I sat in my seat, but my mind wasn't in that classroom. My body was present, but my thoughts were miles away, spinning in endless loops of anxiety and dread.

What was waiting for me at home? Would she still be there? Would there be another scene, another performance? My heart raced with anticipation of the unknown, the unshakable fear of what new wound she might carve into me. The rest of the day was a blur. The teacher's voice faded into static. The words on the page blurred together. All I could focus on was the suffocating weight in my chest, the anticipation of stepping into that house and facing whatever storm awaited me.

I arrived home at the sight of a massive U-Haul truck parked in our backyard. In our tiny town, where everyone knew everyone, the news of her return traveled faster than I could have imagined. My grandmother had already called ahead to warn my father, but seeing that truck made it real. There she was, bringing with her all the chaos she always carried—her literal and figurative baggage.

My sister, now walking, was toddling around. It hit me like a punch to the gut—I had missed those moments. Her first steps, her first words, all the milestones I had longed to witness as a big sister, stolen. I couldn't focus on her joy, though, because there stood my mother. Once again, those sunglasses were glued to her face, hiding something, always hiding something.

Inside the house, she and my father sat in the living room, talking in hushed tones. But I wasn't a child who tiptoed around anymore. I marched in and demanded to know why she wouldn't take off her sunglasses. My patience for her theatrics had run dry. She hesitated, of course, as she always did when confronted with the truth.

It was my father who finally stepped in, cutting through her web of deceit. He told her she needed to explain herself—not just to him, but to all of us. Her children. The ones she had left behind. Slowly, begrudgingly, she removed her sunglasses, revealing two swollen, blackened eyes.

Even then, even battered and bruised, she couldn't tell the truth. Her pride wouldn't allow it. Instead, she spun one of her outlandish tales, claiming she had been on the "wrong side of the tracks" and was robbed and beaten. I knew it was a lie. I knew in my gut that the man she left us for—the man she chose over her family—had done this to her. And later, that truth would be confirmed. But at that moment, I didn't need confirmation. I could see through her, as I always had.

And yet, I felt no sympathy for her. None. What I felt was anger—deep, scorching anger. Not because she had been hurt but because, even in her return, she proved who she truly was. She hadn't come back to us out of love or remorse. She didn't return because she missed her children or realized the pain she had caused. She came back because her fantasy had crumbled. Because he turned out to be a monster, just like her.

It was infuriating, knowing she didn't care. That she hadn't thought about us once while she was gone. There were no phone calls, no letters, no small gestures to show we mattered. Nothing. At that moment, all I could imagine was her sleeping peacefully beside him, building a new life with my sister, discarding us like yesterday's garbage.

I looked at her, standing there with her flimsy excuses and fabricated stories, and I wished she had stayed gone. Permanently. I would have rather carried the pain of her absence than have her waltz back into our lives, proving again that we meant nothing to her.

My father took my mother back. Again. As if all the pain she had caused could somehow be undone with another round of betrayal. It didn't take long before she picked up where she left off, reigniting her affair with the same man. I suppose she never really stopped.

This time, my aunt—my father's sister—was the one who put the pieces together. She'd happened to see a familiar car parked behind a house out of town, right next to our family van. The car was unmistakable, distinct in its odd shape and color, and it belonged to the man who had already torn our family apart once before. My aunt wasted no time. She handed her car keys to my father and sent me and my siblings off to our weekly church skating night, trying to shield us from what she knew would unfold.

My father drove out to the house, his mind probably racing with scenarios that couldn't prepare him for the truth he was about to confirm. He arrived and saw it for himself—the car of her lover parked right beside our van. He turned off the headlights, stepped out, and crept to the back of the house. Looking through the door, he saw them—my mother and her lover, tangled together on the couch as if they had no shame, no conscience, no fear of the damage they'd already done.

My father snapped. He stormed in, breaking the door, shouting and swinging in a fit of rage and heartbreak. He demanded answers, screaming at her, asking how she could do this again. But the man—terrified—didn't stick around to answer. He bolted, scrambling out a window like a coward, and ran next door to call the cops. My father stayed, waiting for the officers to arrive. When they did, he told them everything, explaining that any man would've done the same in his shoes. Even the officers couldn't argue with that.

That night, I returned home from skating with my brother to find the house eerily still. All the lights were on, a glaring contradiction to my father's usual frugality, and it was clear something was wrong. My brothers told me to wait outside while they checked the house. Moments later, my mother pulled up in the van like a whirlwind, screaming at us to get in. "Don't ask damn questions," she barked. "Just get your asses in the van."

We climbed into the van, confused and scared, only to see a man sitting in the driver's seat with a towel pressed against his face, soaked in blood. "Your father is in jail," she snapped when we asked where he was. And then, as if we hadn't suffered enough, the driver lowered the towel from his face. It was him. Her lover. The very man who had caused this chaos was now driving us to my grandmother's house as if it were the most natural thing in the world.

The court proceedings dragged on, and death threats loomed over my father as he awaited trial. Somehow, the charges were dropped, but my mother found a way to twist even that into a mockery. She clipped the newspaper article about the incident and kept it in the glove compartment of the family van—the same van, I later learned, that her lover had bought. It was as if she took pride in the destruction she had caused.

And yet, unbelievably, my father took her back. Again. He even visited her at the same house where it all happened, this time bringing us along. Walking into that house was like stepping into a battlefield, with shattered furniture and blood-streaked walls standing as silent witnesses to what had transpired. She explained, without a shred of remorse, that the house was leased in her and her lover's name. And just like always, no one asked how we felt. No one cared. We were just dragged along, voiceless and invisible.

Eventually, my father moved us into that very house, trying to make it a home for us. He tried to keep us in the same school to preserve what little stability we had left. But, of course, my mother couldn't let that last. One day, she showed up at my school unannounced, pulled me from class, and told me to pack my things. "You're switching schools," she said flatly. There was no discussion, no chance to say goodbye to my friends—nothing. My classmates didn't even know it was the last time they'd see me. She did not explain, no kindness. She was cold and commanding, her words final. "Because I said so, now let go." That was her mantra.

I cried the entire drive to our new house, knowing I'd have to start over again. That house became a fresh hell, no different from the one before, just smaller and more suffocating. The abuse intensified as if she was determined to punish me for the truth I'd revealed about her affair and the ways she'd dragged me into her mess. My sibling had told my father first, but when I was called to confirm, I couldn't lie. I told him everything. And for that, she despised me.

Her hatred was palpable, and she made me pay for it every single day. And she did—every single chance she got, especially when my father wasn't around. She would bait me, poke at my vulnerabilities, and antagonize me relentlessly until I gave her the slightest reason to unleash her fury. It was like a sick game to her. "You're so damn loyal to your father," she'd spit at me, her voice dripping with venom. "I'm your mother. You don't go against your mother! I carried you for nine damn months, not him!" She demanded loyalty as if it were her birthright, as if the sacrifices of motherhood granted her a free pass to destroy me.

Her twisted need for allegiance was mind-blowing. No encounter ended without her hurling insults that cut deep and blows that cut deeper. She would call me out of my name, each word carefully chosen to strip away my sense of worth, and then hit me to drive her point home. But her cruelty didn't end there. She made sure to weave a narrative so convincing that my father bought every word.

To him, I was a rebellious, defiant teenager who had somehow grown too big for her britches. "She's smelling herself," my mother would say with feigned exasperation, using the phrase often heard in Black families to imply I was too bold, too confident, and too audacious to know my place. And he believed her. She had him wrapped around her finger, her puppeteer strings invisibly strong and unbreakable.

"I'm telling you now, girl—you've got to go!" he'd declare, his voice filled with frustration that wasn't even his own but hers, planted and cultivated. He'd talk about how they were looking into options to get rid of me, to send me away as if I were some kind of burden to be discarded. And there she'd be in the background, silent but smug, with a devilish smile that screamed victory.

She reveled in the power she wielded over him, basking in her ability to manipulate him into turning on his child. I wasn't his daughter in those moments—I was her target, her scapegoat, her enemy. And she delighted in every ounce of pain she inflicted, watching as my father's hands carried out her will. It was a betrayal layered on top of betrayal, the kind of hurt that doesn't just sting—it leaves scars.

Chapter 11

School and sports were my sanctuary, the only escape I had left. In those fleeting hours, I felt like I could outrun the chaos at home, leaving the weight of my reality behind. I made new friends there, teammates who felt like family in ways my blood never did. But even in that sacred space, she found a way to inject her venom. Her misery had no boundaries—it followed me everywhere, like a shadow I couldn't shake.

She showed up to one of my basketball games unannounced, a rarity that should have felt like support but instead filled me with dread. I should have known better than to hope for anything different. Her behavior spiraled quickly, an explosion waiting for a spark. She singled out one of my teammates, hurling insults loud enough to stop the game. Her voice echoed through the gym, sharp and cutting, drawing every set of eyes toward her. My teammate froze in the middle of the huddle with a coach, tears spilling down her cheeks, and stormed off the court. I sat on the bench, paralyzed, my face burning with humiliation.

"Whose mom is that?!" my coach asked, his voice laced with confusion and disgust. I didn't respond. I couldn't. I didn't dare turn around to look at her—I already knew. My heart pounded in my chest as I prayed to disappear, to become invisible. But there was no hiding from her chaos, no distance great enough to escape the shame she carried into every room.

For the first time, my father managed to attend one of my games. I wanted so badly for it to be a good memory, for him to see me play and be proud of me. But true to form, he sat silently, wrapped in his aura of enabling. All he could muster was a half-hearted tug at her arm and a weak plea for her to sit down. She wasn't going to listen—she never did.

When I couldn't take it anymore, I bolted off the court and into the locker room. There, I found my teammate trembling with rage and sobbing uncontrollably. She punched the lockers as I stood frozen, my stomach twisting in knots. I stammered out an apology, even though none of it was my fault. "I'm so sorry," I said, choking back my tears. To my surprise, she stopped and looked at me with kindness I didn't think I deserved. "This has nothing to do with you," she said. I hugged her tightly, but the weight of guilt lingered. My mother's actions had hurt someone I cared about, and I couldn't protect her from it.

There was no apology from my mother, of course—there never was. Instead, on the ride home, she rambled on about how my teammate "needed to hear" how much of a "ball hog" she was, as if her cruelty was some twisted form of honesty. She didn't stop there; she turned her wrath on me, berating me for having the audacity to console my friend. "Why would you run after her? She deserved it," she hissed. Her words were a knife to my heart, but I bit my tongue. I had long since learned that silence was safer.

From that moment on, I never wanted her at another game. I didn't care if she never showed up again. Her presence wasn't support—it was sabotage. My safe space had been tainted, and once again, she left destruction in her wake.

I was always the last kid standing in an empty parking lot, clutching my bag and forcing a smile that barely masked the embarrassment. Game after game, practice after practice, the story was always the same. My ride never showed. The sting of being forgotten wasn't even shocking anymore—it had become routine. I stood there in the dark, pretending not to care, pretending the ache in my chest wasn't there, that I didn't feel utterly abandoned by a parent who couldn't be bothered to care about my safety.

Basketball games, track meets, it didn't matter. They all ended the same way: me alone under the dim parking lot lights, waiting long after everyone else had gone home. The silence would stretch on until one of my coaches, concern etched on their face, would reluctantly ask if I needed help. I hated that question because it forced me to confront the truth.

Sometimes, I mustered the courage to shyly ask a teammate for a ride, my voice barely above a whisper. Their parents were always kind and gracious, never making me feel like the burden I felt I was. But no matter how warmly they treated me, I couldn't shake the familiar weight of shame. The guilt lodged itself deep inside me, whispering that I was an inconvenience, an unwanted obligation.

It wasn't just the car rides—it was the sinking realization that I had grown accustomed to being forgotten, to being someone's afterthought. The feeling was so familiar it felt like home, a cruel echo of the environment I had to endure. Even in moments of kindness from others, I couldn't escape the shadow of what my reality had taught me: that I wasn't worth the effort.

I was always the last kid standing in an empty parking lot, clutching my bag and forcing a smile that barely masked the embarrassment. Game after game, practice after practice, the story was always the same. My ride never showed. The sting of being forgotten wasn't even shocking anymore—it had become routine. I stood there in the dark, pretending not to care, pretending the ache in my chest wasn't there, that I didn't feel utterly abandoned by a parent who couldn't be bothered to care about my safety.

It brought me back to those younger days, back when I first found sports—not just as a pastime but as a lifeline, a way to escape the chaos of home. Stepping onto the court or the field was more than just playing a game; it was a chance to pretend, even for a little while, that I was a normal kid. A kid with a normal life, going home to a normal family. It was my ticket to be among classmates and friends just a little longer, to feel like I belonged, even if I was only borrowing that feeling.

At first, she came to those games and painted herself as the "fun mom." She put on a show—cartwheels, loud cheers, smiles that stretched too wide. The kids loved her, the other mothers enjoyed her energy, and for a fleeting moment, I let myself go along with it. I played my part because it was better than the cold, cruel version of her I faced once the lights dimmed and the audience was gone. Even if it was all an act, I soaked it in. Because when you're starving for love, even scraps can feel like a feast.

But like everything else with her, it was just that—a moment. It never lasted. The "fun mom" disappeared as quickly as she arrived, and I was back to being on my own. Catching rides to games, standing in parking lots, hoping someone would step in where she failed. My saving grace was my aunt, my "sweet lady," God rest her soul. When she was home from truck driving, she became the mother I deserved but never had. She showed up for me without hesitation, without strings attached, just pure love and care.

And then there were my teammates' parents—kind, selfless, and so willing to pick me up and drop me off without a second thought. They didn't treat me like an inconvenience; they treated me like one of their own. No judgment, just open arms. Their kindness meant more to me than they could ever know. In a world where my parents left me feeling invisible, these strangers reminded me that I mattered.

I'll never forget them. Their simple gestures shined a light in the darkness I had grown so used to. Because there's nothing more isolating than being left out in the dark—literally and figuratively—by the very people who were supposed to love and protect you.

I found love again—or at least what the elders would dismiss as "puppy love"—at my new school. But even in its innocence, it was more than just young infatuation. It was the beginning of something much deeper, much darker. Looking back now, I see it clearly: it was the moment I unknowingly began to mirror the dysfunction I had grown up with in my relationships. It wasn't intentional, but it was inevitable.

I never took on the role of my mother—her cruelty, her selfishness—but somehow, I was still carrying her presence with me. Instead, I became my father. I fell into the role of the martyr for love, the people-pleasing doormat who sacrificed herself to hold onto someone—anyone. I lacked the courage, the confidence, and the *ability* to set boundaries. My worth was tied to the love I was desperate to receive, even if it came at the cost of my dignity.

Deep down, I believed love came with conditions. I thought I had to endure pain, to suffer quietly, to prove my loyalty before I could be worthy of even scraps of affection. That was the normality in my household, the twisted foundation on which love had been built for me. And without realizing it, I carried those lessons with me, clutching onto them as if they were truth as if they were all I deserved.

This pattern—this belief that love and suffering were two sides of the same coin—followed me like a shadow well into my adult years. Every choice every relationship was laced with the echoes of my past. And though I didn't know it then, I was fighting battles that weren't mine, seeking validation in all the wrong places, trying to rewrite a narrative I never should've been handed in the first place.

Things started beautifully, as they often do in relationships, whether young or old. There's something so sweet and simple about those early moments, the butterflies, the innocent excitement of it all. We had grown up in the same church, and our families were familiar with each other. It was like our worlds had always been quietly orbiting one another. The day he discovered I was enrolling at his school, he happened to be passing by the front office. That small twist of fate sparked something new.

He gained the courage one day during a long bus ride to one of our away basketball games. A note was passed to my friend, then to me, with the question that made my heart race: would I go out with him? I said yes, and for once, it felt nice—nice to be noticed, to be liked, to be admired. It was such a foreign feeling in my world of invisibility and criticism.

From then on, we did everything that teenage couples do. Double dates at the movies, lazy afternoons just hanging out. I cherished every moment we spent together. And his family—they welcomed me like one of their own. For the first time, I got a glimpse of what love could look like and what it felt like to be treated with kindness and acceptance. In their home, I was seen. I was valued. I mattered.

But my mother—she could never stand the idea of anyone liking me, let alone loving me. It didn't matter who it was: family, friends, or even a boyfriend. Anyone who saw in me that she had tried so hard to deny, anyone who recognized the light she worked tirelessly to extinguish, became a threat to her.

It was as if she couldn't bear the thought of someone else acknowledging what she refused to see. The moment someone showed me love, it was as though it mirrored everything she wasn't willing to give, everything she wasn't capable of being. And so, she did what she always did: found ways to dim my light, to cast shadows where there was brightness.

I was preparing for my very first prom, and like any teenage girl, I was filled with excitement. Prom—it felt like such a pivotal moment, one of those milestones you look forward to where, just for a night, you get to feel special. A chance to dress up, to dance, to be carefree. For once, to feel beautiful. But with a mother like mine, that kind of joy always came with a target on its back.

She never participated in anything that brought me happiness, and this was no different. I know now that the very idea of me having a moment to shine, to feel pretty, must have made her skin crawl. It was the competition she created, the constant battle I never wanted to be in. As I started growing into a young woman, the rivalry she imagined only grew worse. This prom, which should have been mine to cherish, was just another opportunity for her to take from me.

I remember that weekend so clearly. My boyfriend had asked me to prom, and I was overjoyed. I was nervous, too, but mostly excited as I built up the courage to tell her. I found her up the street, helping a neighbor with a yard sale. It was rare for me to approach her with any hope; hope was something I had learned to keep hidden, but this time, I let it slip through.

I told her the exciting news and asked if she could take me dress shopping. In front of the neighbor, she put on her act. She smiled, feigned interest, and told me to ask my father for the money. I clung to the sliver of promise in her words, thinking maybe, just maybe, this time would be different.

I asked my father for money, and he grumbled about how tight things were and how we couldn't afford it. But still, he handed over $100. Back then, for a girl like me, that was more than enough. I clutched the money in my hand, my heart filling with hope again. I went back to her and told her I was ready to shop. She made a grand promise right there in front of the neighbor, assuring me she'd take me. I wanted to believe her so badly, but deep down, I knew better.

She never took me. Of course, she didn't. She never intended to. My boyfriend's mother stepped in instead, taking me shopping and making sure I had what I needed for my special night. But even that—someone else showing me kindness—was enough to set her off. She complained about it afterward, masking her anger as an annoyance. But I knew the truth. She wasn't mad because someone else helped me; she was mad because someone ruined her plan to sabotage me.

She tried to hide it, but I could see through her. I always could. And as grateful as I was for my boyfriend's mother, the pain still lingered. She had stolen more than just a shopping trip from me. She had stolen the simple joy of having a mother who cared, of sharing a moment I would remember for the rest of my life.

Prom night had been such a dream—until it wasn't. For the first time, I let myself enjoy the moment: the dress, the music, the carefree laughter of being young and alive. But that all came crashing down at the after-party. My boyfriend broke up with me right there, in front of everyone. His reason? "I feel ugly, and I don't know why you chose to be with me." Two teenagers, both fighting battles we didn't know how to name, let alone win. I sat there in my dress, tears streaming down my face, consoled by his friends as he drifted into the background.

When I got home, I hung up my dress carefully, almost ceremoniously, and told my parents I had a great time. I lied through my teeth. This wasn't just a one-time moment. This would become the blueprint for our relationship—love that crumbled under the weight of insecurities, both his and mine.

We will come back to revisit this relationship, as it holds a mirror to the heart of what happens when children from narcissistic, physically, and emotionally abusive households attempt to navigate love and connection. These relationships are less about the people involved and more about the reflection of the dysfunction deeply etched into the child's psyche.

It's imperative to highlight this dynamic because it reveals a painful truth: children raised in chaos often carry that chaos into their adult lives. The wounds from a toxic home become a lens through which they see people and the world. What seems like love can often be a reenactment of the patterns they've been conditioned to accept—patterns of control, fear, and the desperate hope for validation that never comes.

This isn't just about the relationships themselves. It's about how a child mirrors the trauma they endured, unknowingly perpetuating cycles of pain. And it's about how healing begins, not by erasing the past but by recognizing these patterns and rewriting them.

Chapter 12

My time at that school was painfully brief—a fleeting moment of stability stolen away by my mother's endless need to outrun her shame. Once again, she couldn't bear to face the consequences of her actions in our small town, even in the refuge of relocation. Her solution? Pack us all up and uproot our lives entirely, moving us out of the state as if distance could erase the damage she caused.

We had just started to adjust—new friends, new routines, a glimmer of normalcy. But for her, none of that mattered. She tore it all away with the same reckless abandon she wielded over our lives. My father, as always, played the role of her enabler. Whatever she wanted, she got. It didn't matter how much pain it caused or how many lives she disrupted.

Our feelings were collateral damage in her constant pursuit of control. No one's emotions ever seemed to matter to her—not her husband's, not her children's. For her, the world revolved around her desires, her fears, and her narrative. And once again, we were left in the aftermath, picking up the pieces of yet another life she destroyed before it even had the chance to begin.

As we packed up our lives yet again, loading everything we owned into storage, the familiar sting of displacement settled in. My mother and I moved in with her mother, while my father and brothers stayed with his side of the family until it was time to leave the state. Even in this brief limbo, before the next upheaval, my mother found a way to stir chaos. This time, it wasn't a lover from before—it was someone I'd never expected. It was as though I had yet to fully grasp the depths of who my mother truly was, and this moment would rip the veil away even further.

Late at night, I would hear her on the phone. The tone of her voice was unmistakable—soft, flirty, the kind reserved for someone you're enamored with. But this wasn't my father on the other end of the line. I may have been young, but I wasn't naive. I knew the difference between casual chatter and the secretive intimacy of forbidden attraction.

Even my grandmother noticed. She'd mention how my mother would sneak off late at night with the phone, her whispers trailing into the dark. My grandmother's words seemed to bounce off my mother's shield of deflection. It hurt—deeply—watching her take more pleasure in those stolen conversations with strangers than in spending time with me, her daughter. That's the cruel irony of a narcissistic mother: strangers are treated like royalty, while her children are cast aside as mere burdens.

My curiosity burned brighter with every hushed conversation, every stolen moment. Who was this person on the other end of the line? What role would they play in the wreckage of my already fractured life? It was painful to see the contradiction staring me in the face. Here was my mother—so deeply humiliated, so 'wounded' by the fallout of her actions that she insisted on uprooting us from everything and everyone we knew—yet indulging in the very same behaviors that led to our exile.

It was a vicious cycle: destruction, denial, and displacement. And once again, I was left trying to make sense of it all, caught in the whirlwind of her chaos, knowing deep down that she'd never stop. One day she received a letter from her mysterious person. I had heard their name enough over phone conversations to know that the letter was for my mother.

I opened the envelope cautiously, my cousin peering over my shoulder. Inside was a letter—five detailed pages long. The words spilled out like a tidal wave, full of passionate declarations of love for my mother. But it wasn't just love; it was romance and explicit details that made my stomach turn. Things that no child should ever have to read about their parent, let alone know. Yet, this wasn't my first time being exposed to my mother's secrets. I had seen too much before, during her last affair.

This time, the revelation hit differently. The lover wasn't a man. It was a woman. She. I guess my mother thought this would be an easier secret to conceal. At first, I was shocked, but that feeling didn't last long. By then, I had grown almost numb to her betrayals, as if my mind knew to expect more chaos. I folded the letter carefully, slipped it back into the envelope, glued it shut, and placed it on the table as if it had never been touched.

I didn't breathe a word of what I'd seen to anyone. But later that night, I cried quietly, the kind of tears that spill out when you're just too exhausted to carry the weight anymore. The anxiety of what this would mean—what kind of upheaval it might bring to my already shattered world—left me reeling. I didn't know what was coming, but I could feel it brewing.

Not long after, my mother decided we were going on a trip. She packed a bag for me and my baby sister, and the three of us hit the road to visit this woman. She told my grandmother it was just a friendship, but I knew better. The drive was long, and I had school the next morning, but as always, my needs didn't factor into her plans.

When we finally arrived, the house stood out immediately—a beautiful home in a pristine neighborhood. Standing at the top of the stairs, greeting us with a radiant smile, was Miss Tina. My mother beamed back at her, introducing us. 'This is Miss Tina,' she said, nudging me forward to shake her hand. I forced a smile, allowing her to pull me into a hug, my mind racing with questions.

Inside, the home was just as lovely. Miss Tina's life looked like something out of a dream: nice furniture, beautiful decor, and an air of comfort that I wasn't used to. She showed me to my room, a gesture that appealed to the hopeful, poor country girl in me who wished for more. I stayed there, retreating into my music and solitude while my mother and Miss Tina disappeared into the kitchen for hours of 'grown folk talk' over drinks.

I didn't mind being alone. I'd always been comfortable in my own company, and Miss Tina seemed to respect that. As the night stretched on, I showered, got ready for bed, and prepared for the early morning ride back to school. My mother popped her head in at one point, tucking my baby sister into bed with me before heading back downstairs. I drifted off to sleep, grateful for the temporary quiet.

Morning came quickly. I woke up, got dressed, and called out to my mother to let her know I was ready to leave. There was no response. Confused, I started searching the house. I checked room after room downstairs, the basement, and nothing. Finally, I made my way to Miss Tina's bedroom. I knocked lightly. When there was no answer, I peeked through the crack in the door and pushed it open.

'Good morning, Mom!' I said, stepping inside.

What I saw stopped me cold. My mother was in bed with Miss Tina. They scrambled to cover themselves with sheets, but it was obvious they had been lying there together, unclothed. I froze for a moment, forcing myself to act normal, to pretend I hadn't seen what was right in front of me. I walked over to hug her, my mind screaming with questions and disbelief.

When does this ever end? I thought bitterly. *Why does she drag me into her chaos, forcing me to witness it all?*

I wanted to escape. I wanted to run far from her world of madness. But I was just a child trapped in her web of dysfunction. Speaking up wasn't an option—it never was. I knew all too well what would happen if I tried to hold her accountable. She'd make me pay for it. And so, like always, I stayed silent, burying what I felt deep inside and pretending it hadn't happened.

I stood frozen for a moment before snapping out of it and rushing to leave the room. Miss Tina offered me a small, awkward smile as I passed her. In my head, I thought, *Yeah, lady, try being the daughter. Try being me.* I closed the door behind me, holding back the tears that threatened to spill.

I packed my bags quickly, grabbed my sister, and waited outside in the car. From the window, I watched my mother and Miss Tina at the front door, embracing like two star-crossed lovers. My mother smiled as she walked toward the car, glancing at me as if expecting me to share in her joy as if I should somehow be happy for her. I wasn't. I couldn't be.

The drive back to school was excruciatingly quiet. Not a single word was spoken about what had just happened. She didn't explain, didn't apologize—nothing. I sat there in silence, the weight of everything pressing down on me like a heavy blanket I couldn't shake off. By then, I was well-trained in what to say and do if anyone asked questions. I had been groomed for moments like this, conditioned to protect her secrets at all costs.

But this time, she seemed different. She carried herself with boldness, a smugness as if she knew she could do whatever she wanted without consequence. Her arrogance filled the car like a suffocating fog, and I could feel it sitting between us, looming large like an elephant.

The elephant wasn't just in the room—it was her companion, her pet. She treated it like a trophy, as if she was the ringmaster of a twisted circus. And if she was the ringmaster, I was most certainly the sad clown.

We pulled up to my school, and she dropped me off without so much as a glance, acting as though it was just another day. And for people like her, it was just another day. But for those of us who had to endure them, it was the worst day on repeat. A constant cycle of confusion, pain, and betrayal that felt like it would never end.

Miss Tina didn't disappear after that encounter; her presence only grew stronger, bolder. The weight of it all became unbearable, so I finally confided in my sweet lady and my grandmother. I couldn't hold it in any longer. My heart was desperate for peace, stability, and normalcy—things that felt so far out of reach.

True to the kind, protective nature of my father's side of the family, they listened without judgment. Their love was unwavering, and though they didn't voice much, their watchful eyes spoke volumes. They were always about protecting the children. My grandmother, in her quiet wisdom, chose not to confront my mother directly but stayed vigilant, holding me close whenever I felt like crumbling.

As the days raced toward our move out of state, Miss Tina's actions mirrored my mother's growing audacity. She began showing up at my grandmother's house, boldly pulling up in front of the home as if flaunting her presence. My mother would meet her outside, the two of them laughing and talking like carefree teenagers, as though my grandmother—the mother of her husband—was blind to their behavior.

I remember my grandmother shaking her head, holding me tightly. 'It's okay, baby,' she whispered, her voice trembling with emotion. 'Grandma doesn't know what to say about it all, but you need to know this—you are always loved and protected here with us, baby.' Her eyes welled with tears as she tried to reassure me, though I knew she was heartbroken. She understood, as I did, that soon I'd be taken away from her, leaving me vulnerable in a situation that was beyond her control.

The final day of our time there arrived, and with it, one last gut punch. I learned that Miss Tina wasn't just visiting that day—she was coming with us. Her belongings were packed, and she was relocating alongside us. I couldn't fathom how my mother had orchestrated this or how my father remained so blind to it all.

Miss Tina climbed into the van as if it were her rightful place, laughing and chatting, while my mother acted as though nothing was out of the ordinary. My father, clueless, sat behind the wheel, thinking he was moving his family to a new chapter. But he wasn't just driving us; he was unknowingly transporting my mother's next lover.

I sat in the van, my mind a whirlwind of disbelief and betrayal. How could my mother pull this off so effortlessly? How could she dangle Miss Tina so boldly in front of him, like a child sticking out her tongue in defiance, knowing she'd never be caught? The only person who saw her audacity for what it was—the only person who understood the truth—was me, her daughter. And yet, I was powerless to stop it.

My grandmother, in a desperate attempt to reach my father's oblivious heart, made a fuss over her house phone being left on top of our van. But I knew it wasn't about the phone. No, this was about her watching her son, my father, pack up her grandbabies, taking them away with the woman who had systematically destroyed him and them. This was her last plea, the final effort to get him to see the truth. She used the phone to lure him back in, a feeble attempt to make him question the decisions he was about to make.

'You know she's fucking that woman? She ain't no damn friend,' she said, her voice tinged with heartbreak and frustration. My father waved her off, dismissing her words as if they didn't matter.

'I swear, you are about the most ass-backward child I have,' my grandmother said, her voice shaking with emotion.

'Then Mama, I'll just have to be ass-backward then. We've got to go,' he responded, his tone resolute and final.

And just like that, he packed us up one last time, and we drove away. My grandmother's voice, the final plea for a reason, faded in the distance. I watched her home, which I had always considered one of the few safe havens in my life, disappear in the rearview mirror. It felt like the last piece of comfort I had was being swallowed up by the road.

Chapter 13

We began the long road trip to yet another new place, with new people—including my mother's lover—yet with the same old problems. Nothing ever changed. The cycle repeated, and there was no escaping it. We stayed with family there until my father landed a job. All of us crammed into a small apartment that my family was gracious enough to share with us, along with my cousin. We made it work, my father's family has always been such a joy to be around. It felt nice to be under the same roof as good-hearted people, surrounded by positive spirits.

For me, it offered a brief sense of relief, a brief escape from the constant chaos. I told myself that, at least for now, my mother would have to hide who she truly was. Even though the circumstances were far from ideal, for a girl like me, who had been dealing with so much daily, it felt like heaven—even if Satan was sitting in the midst.

Eventually, the time came to enroll my siblings and me in school there. Once again, we prepared to start over in a new state, ready to face yet another challenge. Backpacks in hand, we headed inside the school, but this moment, like so many others, would turn out to be a mind-blowing one. As we entered the building, I noticed Miss Tina picking up a backpack and slinging it over her shoulder. I thought nothing of it at first, but that changed when we reached the front office. It was then that my mother not only introduced my siblings and me to the staff and principal but also introduced Miss Tina—as if she were just another student.

At that moment, my heart sank. I was consumed by confusion and disbelief. Everything around me seemed to blur as I tried to process the harsh reality. To myself, I whispered, 'Wait a minute... so you're telling me that 'Miss' Tina... isn't Miss Tina?'

The gut-wrenching truth hit me hard. I had been calling her *Miss* Tina all this time, oblivious, while she played along. The fact that she was only a year older than me made me sick to my stomach. But what made me even sicker was the overwhelming weight of what this moment revealed about my mother—what kind of person she truly was, on top of all the other things she had already shown me. The full scope of who she was started to crystallize, and the truth felt unbearable.

At that moment, my mind transported me back to a time when my mother worked at a boys' home when I was much younger. She would pick me up from school or the bus stop in the company van, always accompanied by the same two boys from the home. It was never anyone new. Day after day, she would bring them back to her shop, which she also owned, and once they became familiar with me, she would leave me with them without a second thought, as if it were all completely normal.

One of them began making inappropriate advances, saying things that made my stomach turn and filled me with dread. I didn't know how to react, but I was scared. Later, I learned that my siblings, too, were quietly protecting me, taking the physical blows meant for me, absorbing the violence to shield me from harm.

This continued for what felt like an eternity. I noticed the way my mother acted and how unprofessional and inappropriate her behavior had become. In hindsight, with the clarity of adulthood, I now see just how wrong it was. Those boys had no business being around me, and I'm certain the staff and her employer had no idea what was going on. She was so skilled at charming everyone around her, always appearing devoted and trustworthy, so no one ever questioned her actions.

Then, one day, I remember my father and I picking her up from work. She was visibly upset. She had been fired, but she never explained. Her story to my father was always one of victimhood. She painted herself as the one wronged, and he believed it without hesitation. He never questioned what she told him; he just accepted it as the truth.

It wasn't until many years later, as an adult, that I uncovered the real reason behind her firing. My suspicions, all along, had been spot on.

I went home that day with a heavy heart as if it couldn't possibly be heavier than it already was. Once again, I was the only one burdened with this sick secret. My mother never spared a second thought about the truth I had uncovered. She always saw herself as a manipulative genius, and at this moment, I think she was so wrapped up in her own belief that she had outsmarted everyone that she forgot or simply didn't care that her daughter had been witness to all her chaos as usual.

This time, I decided to carry the weight of it all alone. My parents were finally able to get their place, so we moved into another apartment. It was just as empty as I felt, surrounded by yet another one of my mother's messes. We had lost the storage from the previous state, so we slept on the floor. No furniture. No TV. No tables. Just us and the overwhelming presence of my mother's madness.

There were only two rooms in the apartment. My siblings slept in the space that would have been the dining room, while my baby sister, Tina, and I shared one room, and my parents slept in the other. My father worked late-night shifts, and my mother, as always, took advantage of this, just like she had when we were back home with her revolving door of lovers while he was away.

One night, I was asleep, but I was a light sleeper. I always heard everything; my hypervigilance was a result of living in a hell where I was always on edge, anticipating the unexpected. Tina, in her strange way, would always slip into our closet to write in her journal and shut the door behind her. She would stay in there for a while before emerging with a note. She moved like someone certain I was asleep, and I, of course, played the part. I was curious about what she was doing up at that hour when my father was gone.

Like clockwork, she would slide the note under my mother's bedroom door, pacing around until my mother opened it and invited her in. Tina would stay in there for most of the night, only leaving when my father's arrival was imminent. It was clear what was going on—what had been happening. Tina would come out disheveled, exchanging flirtatious words at the door before my mother closed it, and Tina would slip back into our room, pretending to be asleep as if nothing had happened.

This went on for some time, each instance growing bolder and more shameless. It began to feel as if they believed they were the only two people in the house, even during the day, carrying on in the open. I started to notice how flirtatious they became, even when my father was home. When we went out to the store, what was supposed to be a "girls' day" would somehow morph into a day all about them. I was merely an accessory—an alibi for her dirty deeds.

Sometimes, when I wasn't around, my mother would disappear well into the evening, only to return with one of her trademark outlandish stories. These stories were as infamous in my mind as she was in real life—crafted to distract, misdirect, and draw attention away from the truth of her absence.

I'll never forget one night. She arrived home and promptly gathered us all as though she were a campfire storyteller—but this storyteller was Satan himself, spinning tales over her flames. She launched into an elaborate recounting of how she'd had an extraordinary encounter with a very famous celebrity. Living where we did, running into celebrities wasn't unheard of, but something about her story was off from the start. I knew, instinctively, it was a lie.

Still, I sat quietly, watching her weave her web. What started as a chance meeting quickly escalated to her supposedly being invited to this celebrity's mansion. She claimed they'd bonded, and she'd even shared my siblings' dreams of being in a music studio one day. According to her, the celebrity was so impressed that they offered to help make those dreams come true.

I watched as their eyes—my siblings' and even my father's—lit up with wonder and excitement. They were captivated, clinging to every word of her fabrication. But for me, it was torture. To sit there, the only one who could see through her lies, the only one immune to her manipulation, was a form of silent suffering.

I often likened it to being wrongly tossed into a paddy wagon—screaming for someone to hear you, to see the mistake, but knowing no one ever would. Tina sat quietly in the background, a smile faintly playing on her lips, though it felt like a mask. She knew, just like I did. Yet, there was something in her expression—an unspoken curiosity, almost as if she were a suspicious spouse silently questioning her partner's whereabouts. I could see it in the whispers that passed between them afterward, their hushed chatter betraying a shared understanding that went deeper than anyone else in the room realized.

Meanwhile, my siblings and father remained utterly captivated by my mother's story. They were lost in the illusion, their imaginations running wild with dreams of what this "opportunity" could mean. Completely distracted. Completely manipulated. Completely brainwashed. And there I sat, trapped once again in the crushing solitude of being the only one who could see the truth.

Though I'd long accepted my mother's disdain for me, Tina's presence heightened everything. My mother's loathing wasn't new, but I couldn't help but feel waves of jealousy and resentment towards both. They seemed to share a bond that excluded me entirely, deepening my isolation.

At school, the humiliation didn't stop. Tina and I shared one class, and while everyone welcomed her with open arms, I was cast into the little sister role. They adored her, not knowing the truth of who she was. I wanted nothing more than to blend in, so I buried my knowledge of her deceit far in my mind. School was my escape, and I refused to let my painful reality seep in. Survival meant keeping up appearances. But when I got home, I was emotionally drained.

Even my mother's jealousy of Tina was thinly veiled, though she tried her best to hide it. One instance stands out. Our neighbor, a kind-hearted woman, suggested hosting a birthday party for her children and for me and my twin since our birthdays were so close. She wanted to throw a casual kickback for the teenagers at her house. I wasn't thrilled about being the center of attention: it was the opposite of my shy nature, but the thought of escaping the house, even for a little while, was too tempting to pass up.

My mother begrudgingly agreed though it was clear she hated the idea. She couldn't object without exposing her possessiveness to my father, so she had no choice but to let Tina come along. The jealousy was all over her face.

At the party, I mostly kept to myself, nibbling on a slice of overly sweet store-bought cake and using it as an excuse to avoid the dance floor. But as the night went on, I was urged to stop "babysitting my seat" and join in. A boy finally asked me to dance, and though I was reluctant, I gave in. I started to let my guard down, even allowing myself to enjoy the moment. For the first time in what felt like forever, I felt a flicker of joy. After all, this was my sweet sixteen. The only truly sweet part of it was the thought that I was one year closer to escaping the nightmare I called home.

I danced near Tina, loosening up and trying to soak in what little happiness the evening offered. But the mood quickly soured. Other teenagers began nudging me away from the boy I was dancing with, their actions seeming playful at first. I thought they were teasing the shy girl finally having fun. But their movements carried urgency. They were trying to save me, and I realized it too late.

Her voice rang out, sharp and familiar, calling me by my full name. My mother stood there, her face painted with fake disappointment and righteous indignation. The performance was for everyone else, not me. She always knew how to play her role. I was her target, as always. My siblings weren't even acknowledged.

She barked at Tina too, though it wasn't because Tina had danced with someone else, it was because that someone wasn't her. The sting of humiliation burned as she dragged me back into her web of control, reminding me once again that even fleeting moments of happiness were not mine to have.

She grabbed my arm tightly, dragging me out the door while yelling loud enough for everyone to hear. "Your father is a minister, and here you are grinding all up on some boy! Let's go!" she spat, her voice dripping with self-righteousness. She loved painting me as a wild, promiscuous child, though nothing could have been further from the truth. I didn't realize it then, but this moment would mark the beginning of a narrative she would brand me with a scarlet letter she'd sew into my identity and carry well into my adult years.

Her so-called "payback" came during Bible study, where she took yet another opportunity to humiliate me under the guise of a testimony. She twisted the story of our birthday celebration into one of her self-serving sermons, proclaiming how the Lord had used her to save her children from the clutches of Satan. The irony wasn't lost on me. She spoke as if she weren't Satan herself, standing there basking in the attention, relishing every second of her performance.

It wasn't about redemption or faith. It was about her, as it always had been. And once again, I was left to carry the weight of her lies, her manipulations, and her relentless need to shine, no matter how much it dimmed my spirit. I remember sinking into the pew as I sat there mortified, my father looking on and shaking his head in agreement with the goodness of God bringing us back home. But what other choice did I have?

Having Tina around became unbearable. It was bad enough to endure my mother's mess, dragging along the chaos she was supposedly "escaping." But to see it, hear it, and live with a constant reminder of everything that took precedence over me—it was enough to make anyone mentally and emotionally sick.

One day, Tina and I were sitting in the living room, still barren and lifeless, much like how I felt inside. She was joking and laughing, her carefree demeanor grating on me. By that point, even her presence—her breathing, her blinking—set me on edge. Normally, I was a loving and kind-spirited person despite the dysfunction I'd come from, but resentment and jealousy consumed me whenever she was around.

As she tried to be playful, I couldn't take it anymore. Out of nowhere, I snapped. "You don't think I know what you and my mother are doing?!" I shouted, my voice shaking with pent-up anger. Tina froze, laughing nervously to defuse the tension. Her fear was palpable—she was desperate to play it off, to keep the ugly truth hidden.

But I was done. Done carrying the weight of my mother's in-house secrets, done protecting her lies. At that moment, I didn't care whose ears were around. I wanted it all out. My father emerged from the kitchen, his face a mix of confusion and concern. "What are you talking about?" he asked, his tone wary. And in that moment, I told him everything. The weight I'd carried for so long spilled out of me, each word freeing me from the silence that had suffocated me for far too long.

As expected, Tina denied it. Moments later, my mother emerged from her room, summoned by the confrontation. She, too, denied everything. Her denial was predictable, but it didn't sting any less. Making me out to be the unstable, lying, promiscuous one was her favorite strategy—a game she'd perfected and would continue to play for years to come.

But I refused to back down. Even as her familiar, demon-possessed glare locked onto me, a look so dark it seemed to pull the light from the room—I stood my ground. Tears filled my eyes, and my heart raced, pounding so hard I thought it might explode. I was terrified because I knew what usually came next.

The rage in her eyes was always the warning sign, the precursor to her physical retaliation. So, I braced myself for her wrath, ready for the worst but determined not to let her silence me again. As always, she managed to talk my father down, and more work was done in the privacy of their room when I was not around, just like any abuser, isolation is key to ensuring that they can do their work on that person, gaslighting.

But, as always, manipulating him wasn't enough. She needed more—she always did. When things got dangerously close to exposing her, she resorted to her usual tactic: elimination. It didn't matter how it was done or who was hurt in the process. If she covered her tracks and protected herself, the end always justified the means.

She was, without a doubt, the CEO of CYA—*Cover Your Ass*—and Tina was no exception to this ruthless strategy. What came next would pull me even deeper under the veil of her darkness, forcing me to witness yet another layer of her twisted, self-serving evil.

Looking back now, through the lens of my growth and healing, I see Tina for what she truly was: just a kid like me. Despite everything, she didn't deserve what was about to happen. She didn't deserve to be used, manipulated, and discarded like so many others in my mother's wake.

Before I knew it, my mother had taken Tina's journal and weaponized it to feed her twisted agenda. She was determined to get rid of Tina before my father could muster the courage to think for himself and break free from her narcissistic grip.

I had no idea back when I was calling her "Miss Tina" that she was a foster child—someone who had once been cared for by a foster mother. I learned she was labeled as a "troubled child" in need of guidance. But even now, it baffles me how any good mother could allow her to leave with a stranger. The only way I can make sense of it is by imagining my mother exploiting Tina's history and playing the "rescuer" card to get her to come along, all while hiding her true agenda of bringing her lover under the guise of charity. There's no way the full truth could have been presented, and the thought of it even now makes my skin crawl.

Using the journal, my mother fabricated lies and exaggerated stories, painting Tina as unstable and in need of psychiatric care. Everything moved so quickly. One moment, we were being told that Tina had been admitted to a psychiatric ward, and the next, my father, siblings, and I were preparing for what would turn out to be our only visit to see her there.

I'll never forget the look on her face during that visit—she carried a heavy heart yet stayed true to her nature, keeping her spirits high. She joked about the admission process and not being allowed to have shoelaces. But the weight of it all was undeniable. I didn't know it then, but that was the last time I would ever see her.

The one person responsible for putting her there was nowhere to be found, as usual. My mother, even after executing her vile plan, wasn't finished. When we returned home, we were led to believe Tina would be leaving the ward and returning to her original foster home. But instead, I discovered something even more sinister—my mother had already begun grooming my younger sister to perpetuate a disgusting lie about Tina. She was just a baby, far too young to grasp the weight of what my mother was coercing her into agreeing with. Her little nods were nothing more than the innocent gestures of a toddler, unaware of the manipulation at play.

She told the household that she was gone because she had found out that Tina was molesting my sister. So far from the truth, Tina adored my little sister and would never hurt her. I have been present for most of the time she has ever interacted with her, and there was not one time when she was alone, so I knew for sure that this was a lie.

When I returned to school, the questions began almost immediately. Everyone who loved her wanted to know where she was. I couldn't bring myself to tell them the truth. How could I? What could I say? That she was in a psych ward and wouldn't be coming back? That everything they thought they knew about her, about me, and the situation at home was built on lies? The words refused to form, so I told them she wasn't feeling well, that she was in the hospital but would be back soon.

The concern in their eyes was so genuine, so untainted. If only they knew the truth—knew what happened—perhaps that concern might have been extended to me, too. But I kept it all inside. Each day, it became harder to explain her absence, and eventually, I settled on a simple answer: she had to move.

I didn't want to tarnish her name or image; that was never my intention. I was just a hurt kid, longing for the love of my mother and struggling to make sense of it all. Tina had become nothing more than collateral damage in my mother's twisted world, yet I still shielded her, even when she didn't deserve it.

But in truth, I wasn't protecting her for her sake I was protecting myself. I wanted to be a normal kid, to blend in, to avoid the weight of shame that came with exposing who my mother truly was. Speaking the truth would have shattered the fragile illusion I clung to. So, I crafted a version of her that others could admire, spinning lies to make her look good.

And that's where the fundamental difference between us lay. I lied to make others like her. She lied to turn others against me, weaving falsehoods to cast herself as the victim and further isolate me from the world.

Chapter 14

As always, life continued as if nothing had changed, as if she had never existed at all. Just like she did with everyone and every situation, there was no acknowledgment, no apology. For us—those who had been directly impacted, those who were caught in the aftermath—it was a traumatic experience. But for her, it was just another day, another moment to brush off, another instance to keep moving forward without a second thought.

As time passed, each day felt heavier. I dreaded being in this new state, both physically and mentally, with the woman who had made my life a living hell. Always on edge, it seemed like every moment was just another step toward her plotting how to make me miserable. She worked tirelessly to make me feel unwanted, unloved, like a burden—always pushing me further into that darkness.

Days were filled with slaps, punches, and harsh words. I was called every name under the sun but rarely my own. In those moments, it felt like my birth name was erased, replaced by whatever insult she could throw my way in her rage. I longed for an escape, wishing I could run away—if only I dared to do so. I was still with my boyfriend from back home, and his senior prom was approaching. I wanted more than anything to be there; it was a chance for me to be away from her and around my friends, even if it was a reminder of what she didn't care that she made us leave behind.

I pleaded to go, knowing that convincing my mother and father would be a challenge. With my mother, any hint of my happiness made her sick, so I expected resistance or some manipulative move to ruin it. Convincing my father was tied to her control over him, whatever answer he gave wasn't truly his, but hers. Yet, to my surprise, things worked out in my favor. I call it luck, but I believe it was divine intervention, keeping me in the fight just long enough to break free for good. Whatever it was, I accepted it with open arms.

My mother, surprisingly, asked around about prom dresses and found someone who worked at the post office with a daughter my size. She brought a few options for me to try on. I was shocked that she even attempted something like this, and in moments like these, I clung to a glimmer of hope that maybe, just maybe, there could be some kind of connection between us. But it was nothing more than a fleeting gesture—a form of breadcrumbing, keeping me on the merry-go-round, dizzy and sick from the cycle of give and take.

I went along, but as expected, she didn't attend. She always stayed behind during family events because it gave her the space to do whatever she wanted while my father was away—something that had always been the case. I didn't understand it. Even if she did act in front of him, she could always twist it into something else, and he would be easily convinced. My father, my siblings, and I packed into the car for his prom. I could hear him grumbling the whole way, but in those moments when he wasn't under her spell, his heart shone through. It kept me close to him.

He didn't have to drive all those miles for me, but I was deeply grateful that he did. We got a hotel, and he gave me the rundown about my day, setting curfew and telling me to enjoy myself. Despite everything that would happen later between us, moments like this kept me holding on to the hope that maybe someone could be there for me. I couldn't understand how someone like him, who had done this for me, could later turn away. After all, all I had ever tried to do was make him proud.

This time, prom with my boyfriend was a great experience, unlike the previous one, where I had been left in tears. I guess the distance between us allowed us to truly live in the moment, knowing I'd be returning to my reality in just a few hours. At least, that's what my young, deprived heart wanted to believe—that things were better between us and that our bond would grow stronger. But, as I would soon learn, that wasn't the case. Remember when I said we'd revisit that relationship later?

The fun was over once I returned to the hellhole I called home. The dream was lived, and it was back to the same old routine. During that time, my boyfriend and I discussed whether there was a chance I could stay with him and finish school back home. He'd already laid the groundwork by asking his parents. He pitched the idea to them, saying he'd be graduating high school and living on campus, so they wouldn't need to worry about us, love-struck teenagers under one roof. He'd be away at college, and I would focus on finishing my senior year.

I knew it was a long shot, but I was desperate—not just as a teenager in love, but as a kid aching for a better life, for love, and for genuine people around me. I refused to let the fear of asking my parents stand in my way. The worst they could say was no; I would rather face that than live with the torment of "what ifs."

Everything about being there suffocated me. Beyond the obvious reasons, I hated the school, hated the cold and unwelcoming atmosphere, and hated how my bubbly personality clashed with the environment. It was like the area itself mirrored my family's façade—a perfectly polished surface masking an ocean of dysfunction. I wanted out. I asked, and to my surprise, they both agreed. Of course, I didn't tell them the real reasons I wanted to leave. I let my love-sick teenage heart take the lead, masking my deeper desperation.

For me, this wasn't just about young love—it was a chance to tiptoe out of an evil place that smothered my dreams and drained my hope. It wasn't freedom yet, but it was the closest thing I could imagine at the time. On the next trip home to visit family, I was packed up and dropped off. Containing my excitement the entire drive, afraid that even the slightest stench of happiness would shut the entire show down.

I had my father's side of the family, and deep down, I knew that if they truly understood the abuse happening behind closed doors, they wouldn't hesitate to fight for me or welcome me with open arms. But I also knew there was no way my parents would allow that. My mother was already brainwashing my father, slowly and methodically turning him against his family, isolating him in the way abusers often do. It was textbook, though rarely acknowledged because he was a man. It didn't make it any less insidious.

The thought of his family discovering my distress would have set off a chain reaction my mother couldn't afford. She played her role perfectly, always ensuring my father believed it was the two of them against the world—a twisted narrative that would eventually extend to include their children as the enemy. I never understood the hold she had on him, and maybe I never would.

I felt a deep pang of guilt about leaving my siblings behind, but I knew the truth: the only way any of us had a chance was if one of us made it out. If one of us could escape, perhaps the rest could follow. In my mind, I was like the Harriet Tubman of trauma—desperately seeking a way out with the hope of coming back for others. I didn't yet know how I'd do it, but I was determined. Somehow, I would find a way to free us all.

Chapter 15

When I moved in, I was enveloped by an overwhelming sense of welcome. His parents and siblings opened their arms to me, and for the first time in a long time, I felt like I belonged. The house was alive with warmth and love—a sharp contrast to the cold, fractured environment I had known. His parents weren't just present; they were *devoted*. His mother exuded the strength of a matriarch who prioritized education and their children's futures, ensuring their studies took precedence. His father, equally passionate, carried the same torch for excellence but infused it with a fiery love for sports, guiding them to excel both on the field and in life.

The standard they held for me was no different from what they held for themselves. And to be completely honest, I can't even begin to express how overwhelming it was to feel their care and concern for those things. It was something I had never experienced before. I was the child who was never checked on, the one they assumed didn't need any guidance because I always performed—always got good grades, always excelled. But the truth behind my drive wasn't just about personal ambition; it was rooted in survival.

It came from years of people-pleasing, the desperate need to stay "safe" and out of the line of fire from her rage. It came from the aching, unspoken desire to be seen, to be validated, to be loved—*truly loved*—by those who should have been my rock.

But with time, growth, and healing, I came to understand the painful truth: there was nothing I could ever do to be good enough in her eyes. Nothing would ever be enough to keep me hidden from the storm; I was always a target. My successes, my achievements—they were just more ammunition for her, a reminder of her failures, of the things she *should've, could've, would've* done. Envy would always outweigh any sense of pride or praise, leaving me in a constant state of confusion.

As the saying goes, I was damned if I did, damned if I didn't. And though it was hard to grasp at first, it became a strange, bittersweet comfort when I moved into a world where I was finally treated like more than a survivor. A place where I wasn't just trying to make it through another day, another breath, another moment. It was a gift I hadn't known I needed—this adjustment to living instead of merely surviving.

Their home wasn't perfect—no home is—but compared to the chaos and emotional starvation I had come from; it felt like heaven. They believed in balance: education, God, and family always came first, with everything else finding its rightful place. It was a household built on a foundation of love, faith, and purpose.

For the first time, I saw what stability looked like—and it left a lasting imprint on my soul.

I like to call them what I've called so many along my journey—*angels* placed by God to light my path and guide me through the darkness. One of those moments came when I returned to the very same school my mother had forced me to leave, pulling me away from my childhood friends and everything familiar to transfer before we completely left the state. Walking back into those halls felt like a strange kind of homecoming, the warmth of seeing everyone again, of reconnecting with familiar faces. It was a chance to finish what I had started and graduate with the people who had shared the same experiences before life would pull us all in different directions.

And then there was him. The one I had once thought was *my forever*, just another love-struck teenager caught up in the whirlwind of young love. But there was something about the excitement that pulsed between us when we were together—the thrill of seeing each other, of being in each other's world. We'd walk his campus together when I could make it there with his family, dreaming about the future. We talked about graduation, about me attending the same school, us graduating together, getting married, and starting a life side by side. It felt like a promise—the future was ours to build.

But as the days went by, reality began to creep in. That dream of a perfect future started to shift, and the familiar shadows of the past reminded me that we weren't immune to the same patterns. It didn't take long to see that we were falling right back into the same destructive cycle that had haunted our relationship from the beginning. It was a sobering reminder that no matter how bright the future seemed, the past was never far behind.

He was a year ahead of me in school, so he wasn't there for my senior year milestones. On the day of my high school graduation, I was surrounded by the family: my sweet lady, my parents, and my grandmother, my father's mother. It was a rare, good day. For a moment, I allowed myself to bask in their pride and joy, to hold onto the warmth of the occasion. After the ceremony, though, the teenager in me just wanted to celebrate with my classmates. My aunt, always understanding, encouraged me to go. I kissed everyone goodbye, changed in the car, and joined my boyfriend and his cousin for a night of celebration.

But as soon as we pulled away, everything shifted. Out of nowhere, he began yelling at me, his words cutting me like a knife. I sat in the backseat, tears streaming down my face, completely blindsided. Why now? Why on one of the most important days of my life? His cousin, driving the car, tried to console me and talk sense into him, but it didn't matter. By the time we arrived at the party, I was too broken to celebrate. His words weren't just words—they were echoes of my mother's cruelty, reinforcing the lie I'd been told my whole life: that I wasn't worthy of love, that no one would ever truly love me. Those words burrowed deep into my soul and stayed there, far beyond this relationship.

That summer, we both got jobs to save for school and have a little extra money. But even then, his insecurities never let up. He was jealous of any boy who so much as looked in my direction. My naturally friendly demeanor became a crime when it involved the opposite sex. One day at work, I ran into someone I recognized through my mother. We exchanged polite conversation while working, nothing more. Yet, I could feel his jealous gaze from across the room.

He said nothing about it then, but when our shifts ended, his silence spoke volumes. I searched for him, expecting him to be waiting for me as always so we could walk home together. But he was nowhere to be found. After asking around, a coworker casually mentioned, "I think he left." He had. He left me to walk home alone in the dark. That all-too-familiar feeling washed over me—abandonment.

I cried the entire way home, only to be met with his fury when I walked through the door. He backed me into a corner, shouting at me with such intensity that I felt trapped. Then, as quickly as it began, he stormed off, slamming the door in my face and locking it.

These moments of insecurity and anger became a pattern. Car rides filled with shouting, my endless people-pleasing attempts to reassure him, and his relentless need to control me. I gave him the reassurance I so desperately craved for myself.

It followed us into college, where I was noticed a lot more—something that terrified him. The safety net he once had, knowing I was confined to high school classrooms and returning home to his parent's house, was gone. The more freedom I gained, the tighter his grip became.

I was so excited to attend the same college as him, despite his mother's cautionary advice that we should focus on our paths. At the time, young love seemed like it could conquer anything. Looking back, though, I wish I had taken her advice and carved out my path instead of tethering my dreams to him.

From the moment I arrived to move into my dorm, the excitement of this new chapter was quickly overshadowed by ugly looks from a few cheerleaders. It didn't take long to find out why. He had been dating one of them before I arrived, and my presence painted me as the villain who had swooped in and stolen her boyfriend. The truth was I had no idea, not until Valentine's Day when he came to my dorm with a bear and chocolates, ready to sweep me off my feet. That same day, I discovered he had also purchased gifts for her. I was shattered but forgave him, convincing myself it was just a mistake. What I didn't realize then was that this was only the beginning.

The person I thought I knew unraveled before me as time went on. When he noticed the attention I was getting on campus, his insecurities took over. Instead of celebrating me, he began finding ways to make me feel small. We'd go to eat on campus, and he'd casually mention how he thought my shirt was 'too revealing,' showing too much arm or shoulder. Then, in front of his football friends, he'd smirk and say, 'This shirt is too much, isn't it? Arms out like that—she needs to change, right?' They'd laugh it off, egging him on, and I'd sit there, mortified, until I couldn't take it anymore. Eventually, I'd excuse myself and head back to my dorm to change, just to avoid the embarrassment.

It didn't stop there. His anger would flare up at the most unexpected moments. I remember standing outside my math class one day, books in hand, when he stormed up to me, furious over nothing. Before I could say a word, he slapped the books out of my hands and walked away, leaving me standing there, stunned. I scrambled to pick them up, swallowing back the lump in my throat as tears stung my eyes, determined to pull myself together before stepping into class.

Then came the control. When I was assigned a male partner for a group project, he couldn't handle it. He secretly followed us to the library, sitting a few rows behind the computers, watching. I wouldn't even notice him until I was leaving, only to spot him standing there, making sure I saw him. His presence wasn't silent; it was a warning—a reminder that his eyes were always on me. If it wasn't him, it was his football friends reporting back to him like sentinels.

His dorm was coed, unlike mine, and he would sneak me in whenever he could. On days when the RA was stricter, he'd leave his ID outside for me to grab. I'd throw on a hoodie, flash the badge, and slip inside. But if I couldn't make it in, I'd pay for it later. He'd call me furious, berating me over the phone until I was in tears. On the rare occasions I managed to get in, it didn't feel much better. His dorm room became the place where he unleashed his frustrations, backing me into the shower to yell at me, his voice echoing off the tiled walls.

There were nights I couldn't take it anymore, retreating to my dorm in tears, curling up in bed as waves of sadness and exhaustion washed over me. I had given so much of myself to this relationship, sacrificing my happiness, confidence, and voice to keep the peace with someone who didn't deserve it.

Eventually, I couldn't take it any longer. The weight of his control, anger, and manipulation became too much to bear. I finally broke up with him. It was one of the hardest decisions I had ever made, but it was also the first step toward reclaiming myself. Even though the scars of that relationship lingered, it was a lesson I desperately needed to learn. I deserved better. I deserved to be free.

That breakup was like a wound I never saw coming, especially since it had been the only relationship I'd ever truly known. It hurt in ways that words couldn't even begin to describe, but with the love, encouragement, and support of my friends—including my dorm mate—I somehow found the strength to move forward. I remember one night, I went out on a date, and when I returned to my dorm, he was standing there, watching, trying to see who I had left campus with. It hit him hard to see me with someone else, especially when I ended up at a basketball game in our hometown, my new boyfriend by my side, and my family talking about me. It was my way of finally, for once, standing up for myself.

But what I didn't know—what I couldn't see—was that the trauma that had been embedded in me for so long wasn't just going to vanish overnight. I had dared to escape, thinking that leaving would be my breakthrough, not realizing it was only the beginning. I hadn't even begun to understand the depth of the work that still needed to be done or the patterns that had been set in motion. I was blind to the internal mending that was essential to my healing. You truly don't know what you don't know. But even then, as lost as I was, there was one thing I knew for sure: I *wanted* to be better. I *needed* to feel better.

Chapter 16

Navigating through what love was supposed to look and feel like was a struggle I couldn't quite make sense of. No matter where I turned, I always found myself caught up in relationships with broken boys or men, all while carrying my brokenness, desperately trying to fix what was never mine to heal. It felt like I had opened a refugee camp for them, my heart the sanctuary for all their pain, their mess. Looking back now, I see that those relationships were just my countless attempts at a "do-over" with my mother, trying to win her love, trying to heal what could never be healed through others.

But instead of finding what I was looking for, I ended up dating or marrying versions of my mother—those same emotional landscapes, the same twisted patterns. I became my father in ways I never imagined, a martyr for love, validation, and acceptance. What I didn't realize at the time was that I was repeating the very cycle I had been raised in, unknowingly searching for something I had never received in the first place.

It's funny—*no, it's tragic*—how trauma will have you embodying everything you desperately want to escape without even realizing it. The very things you long to break free from, the patterns you vow to never repeat, slowly seep into your soul. You don't see it coming. You don't realize how deeply it's rooted in you until one day, you look in the mirror and see those very scars, those same toxic traits, playing out in your life. It's like you're trapped in the echo of your past, living out someone else's broken story, but this time, it's your own hands that are writing the script.

The boyfriends I had as a teen during my time at university were all just little boys themselves, fighting their demons and consumed by their selfishness. And there I was, always the caretaker. Always showing up, taking on their struggles like I was some self-proclaimed demon slayer, while I was left to wither in the shadows, never taken care of in return. I took on their battles with all the strength I had, all the while, the demons from my *real* tormentor—my mother—were on my heels, closing in on me relentlessly.

It was as if I closed my eyes to the signs of no reciprocity. I ignored the red flags, burying them under false realities I created in my mind—*potential, hope,* and the desperate belief that somehow, someday, I would be given the love I so deeply deserved after all the sacrifices I had made. Suffering in the name of love came to me as naturally as breathing. It was what I had been conditioned to believe in my heart, the message drilled into me since childhood. That if I just stuck through the hard times—those *endless* hard times, without any definition or limit—I would be rewarded.

But I didn't even know what a limit was. My father had none when it came to my mother, and she had none when it came to taking advantage of him—or me. As the saying goes, "givers need to establish limits because takers have none." But I was blind to it all. I was operating on a belief that I would endure it all, suffer it all, just so I could finally receive the love I'd been yearning for since I was a child.

Even when there were no signs, when everything around me pointed to a dead end, I kept pushing forward. I clung to that faint, fragile hope that *someone, anyone*, would finally love me the way I needed, the way I had always dreamed of. Instead, I was taken advantage of—whether it was for sex, for my kind, giving spirit, or for my willingness to inconvenience myself just to make others happy. I never gave myself away freely, but I was always caught in relationships, young and naïve, easily manipulated into believing that what I was giving was love.

It was what drove me. I would buy things for them, travel to see them, and do anything to make them happy, believing that their happiness would somehow fill the emptiness in my heart. But it always ended with me in tears, unhappy, questioning why I was never enough.

But no matter how much heartbreak, heartache, and disappointment I faced, none of it was enough to close me off. I kept my heart open, endlessly pouring out love to others, never saving an ounce for myself. I was generous with my heart—*too* generous—more concerned with the happiness of others than my own, giving until my love tank was empty just so I could see a smile on someone else's face.

The idea of anyone being upset with me was more than I could bear. I said "yes" to everything, even when my soul screamed "no." I lacked boundaries, and I had no sense of self-love. Looking back on those moments, my heart breaks. This new version of me would never tolerate what I accepted back then. But it would take time—time to heal, time to grow, time to become even half the woman I am today.

College wasn't the beginning for me, and unfortunately, it wouldn't be the end, either. Finances became a constant struggle, but I was so damn determined. Going back to that hell hole wasn't an option. Failure was *not* an option. I was going to pour every bit of my energy into finding a way to stay, to keep pushing forward. That white flag of surrender? It was nowhere in sight.

My friend, my dormmate, came through for me in ways I'll never forget. She convinced her father to open his home to me for the summer when I had nowhere to go. She was always there for me from the start of the year to the very end. She saw me. She *saw* me in ways that mattered. She funded my way to softball team events when my own family didn't, she invited me to her mom's house just to get away, and she took me out with her friends—who became mine, too.

She was, and still is, an angel in my life. She called me "Tiffsky," always with love, always with care. Even though she was just a teen herself, trying to figure out her path, she gave me what she had. She used the love she was blessed with to lift me, to make me feel seen, heard, and *accepted*. That summer was about me grinding and surviving, anything to not have to go back to that God-forsaken place.

Her father didn't just open his doors to me—he opened an opportunity for me. He got us both jobs working together, and that was a game changer. She had a car and a license, and because I was working at the same place, I finally had a way to get to and from work. Even on the days she wasn't scheduled, she made sure to take me, pick me up, and always had my back. I was a waitress at a BBQ/sports bar, and I was beyond excited.

It wasn't my first job as a teen, of course. I'd worked before, as I mentioned with my ex. But those jobs were where my "country girl" really came out. I worked outside in a hot pickle factory, wearing work boots and tossing bad pickles, snakes, and frogs off the line. And, oh, I was dating one of the many frogs I kissed in my hopelessly romantic search for something real, something I'd never gotten from those who should have loved me most.

Then there was the graveyard shift, boxing cups in a hot factory. And man, that name fits perfectly. By the time my shift ended, I was *dead*—too exhausted to even think about spending a dime. So, this new job, this new chance, felt like a blessing. And it gave me the space for my personality to finally shine. For once, I had the opportunity to show the world who I was beyond survival mode.

Aside from the handful of typical assholes you'd expect to encounter in a job like mine; I loved it. I thrived in the freedom that came with finally holding onto my own money again. But that freedom came with a bittersweet edge. My genuine, hyper-independent spirit couldn't help but feel guilty about my friend taking care of me. She had given me so much already—too much, if I'm being honest—and I was eager to stand on my own feet.

But that's when the calls started coming. My parents, of course. They had a knack for showing up in ways that drained me—not just emotionally but financially. They saw me not as their daughter but as their ATM. It wasn't long before my mother led the charge, always framing the requests as though my father was the one asking. Every single time.

Looking back, it's painfully clear why she did that. She knew the weight my father held in my heart, the soft spot I had for him. She knew she had to use him as a shield to get what she wanted because she *knew*—deep down—how terrible she had been as a mother. And that's the thing about people like her: they can't help but tell on themselves. They'll give away their hidden agendas in the smallest, most subtle ways if you're paying attention.

Her constant manipulation was just another reminder of who she was and always had been. And in hindsight, it all makes perfect sense. The best way to catch someone like her, someone with an evil agenda cloaked in false concern, is to simply listen—to their words, their patterns, the cracks in their façade. They'll always tell you exactly who they are if you listen closely. She would then place the weight of them losing things, like the storage that had never made it to the new state, on me. Making me feel that it was because of me or any other person who did not give was the reason for every outcome.

I clung tightly to whatever slivers of hope I could find because those small pieces were the only thing keeping me from slipping back into their grasp. Every ounce of me fought to stay away, to stay free. But as the new school year loomed closer, the reality of returning felt like a noose tightening around my neck. The prospect of going back to that place—the one I had worked so desperately to escape—was unbearable.

I cried—deep, soul-crushing sobs—at the mere thought of it. Tears that carried years of pain, frustration, and fear. It felt like all my hard work and my determination was slipping through my fingers like sand. Going back would mean surrendering, and surrendering was a thought I couldn't stomach. The idea of facing them again, of being trapped in their cycle, was too much.

But if there was one thing about me, it was that I didn't know how to quit. I didn't know how to back down, even when the odds stacked against me felt insurmountable. That stubborn fight in me, the fire that refused to be extinguished, burned brighter in those moments. It whispered, "You have to find another way. You *will* find another way."

And that's when the unthinkable crossed my mind. The military. It wasn't a dream of mine, not even close—it was an option born of desperation. Something I'd never imagined for myself in a million years. But in that moment, it became a lifeline, a chance to keep moving forward, to stay away from the place that suffocated me.

It wasn't an easy consideration. The thought of it both terrified me and intrigued me. But what terrified me more was the idea of losing the small piece of freedom I had clawed my way toward. I wasn't ready to go back. I couldn't go back. If joining the military was what it would take to keep that door shut and push forward, then maybe, just maybe, it was worth considering. I was at the beginning of the semester, and just as I feared, I would not be able to see it through financially.

After returning from class and settling into my dorm room, I picked up the phone to call my father. My heart raced as I rehearsed what I wanted to say. I was considering joining the Army to finish school—a decision that felt monumental and terrifying all at once. I knew how much this would mean to him. He was an Army veteran, just like his father and brothers. Military service ran in our bloodline, a legacy of discipline, sacrifice, and pride.

When I told him, his reaction was exactly as I expected. He was proud, his excitement unmistakable in his voice. But then, he paused, his tone shifting from proud to protective. "I think it's a good idea," he said, "but I want you to reconsider the branch. The Navy might be better for you. My boys, well, they're one thing. But for you... I've seen too much in the Army to be comfortable with you there."

His words caught me off guard. I hadn't anticipated the concern in his voice, the way he seemed to wrestle with his memories as he spoke. For a moment, I felt seen and cared for in a way that wasn't wrapped in obligation or manipulation. He even shared a few stories from his time in the service, and we laughed together. Those fleeting moments, filled with connection and lightness, felt rare and precious.

In those brief exchanges, I felt hope flicker—the hope that maybe I had one parent who truly cared, one parent who could support me without condition or ulterior motives. For a moment, I held onto that. It was the kind of moment I would revisit in my mind over and over long after the conversation ended, clinging to it like a lifeline in the chaos of everything else.

But even as I held onto that glimmer of connection, I couldn't shake the weight of reality. Decisions like this weren't simple for me; they were tied to layers of unresolved pain and the desperate hope that someone, somewhere, would see me, love me, and want the best for me. And while my father's words gave me a spark of comfort, they couldn't fill the void.

I braced myself to tell my classmates that I was leaving. I couldn't keep up with the financial demands of school, and the only way forward I could see was to meet with a recruiter. As I shared my plans, their reactions were a mix of sadness, concern, understanding, and encouragement. Their kindness touched me, but it also reminded me of a truth I had carried for years: not all of us are blessed with unwavering love and support.

For those of us built on survival, life is different. We do what we must do because there is no one else to save us. We find strength in the wreckage, forging paths that many can't imagine. Some might pity us, but they'll never fully understand the quiet resilience it takes to turn abandonment, betrayal, and pain into determination. For those of us who rise despite it all, we become our heroes.

This was me putting on my cape—not just for myself, but for my siblings. I knew this decision would change my life in ways I couldn't yet predict, but one thing was certain: going back was not an option. The comfort of dysfunction, as familiar as it was, held nothing for me. I refused to kick my feet up and settle in that misery. Instead, I chose the discomfort of growth, of breaking free, of stepping into the unknown, no matter how terrifying.

I was determined to see it through—whatever it took, come what may. After all, I had already stared down the devil before. This time, I would walk through hell with my head held high, determined to find my heaven on the other side. I packed up and made my way back to the people who were my reminder of why I had chosen to do so one last time. Having my father take me to the recruiting office as soon as I touched down.

Chapter 17

There was a six-month waiting period before I'd be shipped off to boot camp—six agonizing months. God knows I prayed to be on the first thing smoking, desperate to escape the hellhole I called home. Every day there felt like a lifetime, a suffocating reminder of why I wanted out. Six months gave my mother far too much time to orchestrate her next sabotage, to antagonize me into exploding so she could claim yet another false victory. But I refused to give her that satisfaction. I kept my head low, stayed quiet, and made myself scarce, even though she prowled relentlessly, sniffing out every opportunity to draw me back into her twisted games.

Her attempts were calculated, as they always were. One time, during spring break, I returned home because the school shut down for the holiday. I dreaded every second I spent in her presence. That brief visit was more than enough time for her to sink her claws into me again. She'd been waiting for this moment, lying in wait like a predator, starved of the sick pleasure she got from tormenting me now that I lived away at college.

One night, I was in the family office—the one my father had lovingly built with his skilled carpenter hands, customized entirely for her. Everyone else was asleep: my father had dozed off in the living room with his Bible in his lap and a notepad beside him, immersed in his late-night sermons. I, a teenager indulging in the joys of the millennium, was on Myspace. Music played softly as I updated my page, rearranged my friend list, and tweaked my layout—simple pleasures in a chaotic life.

And then she appeared. My mother stood in the doorway, her presence like a dark cloud invading the space. "What's the password to my side of the computer?" she demanded.

I barely glanced at her. "I don't know. I don't even live here. I'm on the family account." My voice was calm and detached. But that didn't matter to her. Logic and reason never did.

She launched into one of her infamous tirades, accusing me of changing the password to spy on her, conspiring with my father to uncover her secrets—her latest affair, no doubt. The irony wasn't lost on me. She was, once again, exposing herself in her desperate attempt to deflect blame.

And then she veered into familiar territory, dragging up the chaos she had created, the affair that had torn our lives apart. She hurled accusations at me as if I were responsible for the wreckage of her choices as if I owed *her* an apology for the mess she made. Her victimhood was a song she played on a broken violin, screeching out notes of unaccountability.

I stayed quiet as long as I could, but I was full—full of years of her misplaced rage, her relentless hatred, her lies. "I'm tired of hearing about that," I said, my voice steady but firm. "What you did has nothing to do with us."

Her face twisted into a snarl, her voice venomous. "Bitch, who the hell you think you are talking to?" she spat, standing nose-to-nose with me, her fists clenched, her breath heavy with fury. Her eyes, those familiar demon-possessed eyes, bore into me. I knew what was coming. A blow or two, maybe more. She never needed a reason to hit me, but provoking her—or, in this case, *not* giving her the reaction she craved—gave her all the justification she needed in her sick mind.

This was her chance to pour every ounce of hatred, resentment, and envy into her fists. But this time, I wasn't going to flinch. I stood toe-to-toe with her, silent but unyielding, staring down the devil herself.

"Oh, so you bucking at me now, bitch? You really smelling your fucking self, huh?" she seethed, her rage bubbling over as my lack of reaction only fueled her fire.

Damned if I did, damned if I didn't. My mere existence was enough to damn me in her eyes, a mirror of all the things she wished she could be but lacked the courage and moral fortitude to achieve. I was her target simply. I existed because I dared to embody the light she would never have.

Her slap landed with a crack that echoed through the room, stinging my face and leaving behind a fiery red imprint on her hand. My cheek burned, but I didn't flinch. I stood there, still as a statue, refusing to give her what she wanted. My heart was pounding, full of anger, pain, and defiance, but my face betrayed nothing.

That only enraged her further. She slapped me again—harder this time—her fury driving her hand like a whip. My head snapped to the side from the force, but I stayed rooted, my resolve unshaken. I refused to cry. I refused to yell. I refused to let her win.

"Do what you have to do," I said flatly, my voice even and low. "Get it out of your system like you always do. Let's just be done with this."

Her slaps weren't enough. She wanted to break me, and when she couldn't, she escalated. Her hands shot up, grabbing me by my braids. She yanked hard—so hard I felt the searing pain radiate through my scalp as if she was about to tear my hair clean from my head, scalp and all.

The pain was unbearable. My resolve cracked, and I screamed. "Let go of me!" I yelled, my voice breaking under the agony. But she didn't stop. She pulled harder, her hands twisting and tugging with a force that made my vision blur.

I hit the floor with her on top of me, pinning me down like a predator claiming its prey. Her breath was hot and heavy, her voice a low, hateful snarl. "Yeah, bitch, I got your ass now," she hissed. "Not so big and bad, not so cute now, huh?"

Her words stung as much as her hands, each one laced with venom, designed to tear me down further. My siblings heard the commotion and came rushing down the stairs, their footsteps pounding like frantic drumbeats. They tried to pull her off me, but she clung on with the strength of someone possessed, her grip unrelenting. Even as they pulled at her arms, she still had my braids wrapped tightly in her fists, yanking and twisting with all her might.

I was in agony, but even in that moment, I thought about how to end it without sinking to her level. I knew I had every right to fight back, to defend myself. God knows I wanted to. But something in me held back.

With no other option, I closed my eyes and bit down on the closest thing I could reach. My teeth sank into her flesh, and I didn't realize until she screamed that it was her breast. She finally let go, staggering back and clutching herself.

"That bitch fucking bit my titty!" she shrieked, her voice shrill and filled with shock.

I lay there on the floor, my scalp throbbing, my chest heaving as I caught my breath. Even in that moment of chaos, I felt no triumph—just exhaustion and the lingering ache of all she had tried to take from me and all I refused to let her have. Even after all of that, she wasn't finished. She stormed into the living room where my father had been asleep, blissfully unaware of the chaos erupting just a few feet away. His peaceful nap ended with her loud, venomous screams. "That bitch has to go!" she shouted, her voice slicing through the air.

Startled, my father jolted awake, his face a mask of confusion. "What in the world happened?" he asked, his groggy voice tinged with concern. He looked between us, demanding answers, but none came from her. She ignored his repeated questions, her rage boiling over into another tirade.

"She's got to get the hell out of here!" she spat, pointing in my direction.

I stood at the bottom of the stairs, my anger simmering beneath the surface. "Tell him," I said, my voice firm but calm. "Tell him what you did. Tell him how you came in there starting trouble with me."

She didn't even acknowledge me. Like clockwork, she used her fury to drown out the truth, deflecting and distracting.

"I'm leaving," I said, heading up the stairs to pack my bags. "If I'm a bitch, then what does that make you? I came from you, so doesn't that make you one, too?"

That set her off. She charged up the stairs behind me like a storm, grabbing the back of my hoodie with both hands. Before I could react, she yanked it tight around my neck, choking me with the fabric. Her grip was ironclad, cutting off my air as I clawed desperately at the hoodie, trying to wedge my fingers between the cloth and my windpipe.

I gasped and choked, struggling to free myself. My father ran up the stairs; his voice panicked as he grabbed her and tried to pull her off me. It was chaos—his attempts to restrain her, my desperate fight for air, her unrelenting grip fueled by something far darker than anger. Same thing, different day. The same evil purpose is hidden beneath the surface.

I finally fought her off and stumbled into my room, slamming the door behind me. I threw everything I could into my bags, my hands trembling as I booked the next Greyhound out of there. This wasn't new, coming back and being dragged back into her madness. I had learned to hide my bruises, both visible and invisible, from the world.

For the next six months, I lived on edge. Every day felt like walking a tightrope over a pit of fire, but I was determined. She tried her best to reel me back in, to destroy my chance at freedom, but I was too resolved to let her.

One night, I sat down and wrote her a long letter. It was my final word to her, sealed and set aside to give her on the day I left. When that day finally came, her face lit up with a fake smile, her mask of happiness poorly hiding the seething envy beneath.

The thought of me setting out to make something of myself was unbearable for her. It wasn't just that I was leaving—it was that I was doing something she had never dared to do. My choice to join the military, to find honor and purpose, was a knife to her ego. Anything that shifted attention off her and onto me was intolerable.

I boarded the plane to Chicago, excited and terrified all at once. As I touched down, a wave of nervous anticipation washed over me. This was it. My life was finally beginning. The first night of boot camp was chaos. We were allowed one phone call, just one, and I clung to that moment like a lifeline. The screaming in the background, my trembling fingers dialing the number, my shaky hand holding the phone—it was overwhelming. I called my father. The phone rang and rang, but no one picked up.

They knew. He knew. Everyone knew this was the day, and yet, just like that little girl in the parking lot all those years ago, no one showed up for me. I hung up, disappointment settling deep in my chest. There was no time to dwell on it. I got in line, joining the other recruits as we began our long, grueling first night. Sleep-deprived and thrust into a routine, I pushed through. I made it.

It was the proudest moment of my life. I had done it—I had pushed myself beyond my own perceived limits. I had faced the biggest adversary of my life, the one who haunted my thoughts and dreams, and I had won. Graduation day came, and I wondered if I would receive any letters from them. For months, I had checked and hoped, but there was nothing. Then, on that day, I finally received one—from my father.

It was the sweetest letter, hand-written and filled with little doodles of smiley faces. It may have seemed small to someone else, but to me, it was monumental. He wasn't a man of many words, and his affection was rare. Yet, here it was—a glimpse of love and pride. I cherished that letter more than anything. It was a rare treasure—a quiet beacon of love in a sea of chaos and pain. A reminder that even in the darkest storms, there were glimpses of light worth holding onto.

There had been no mention in the letter that my parents would be attending my graduation. I had sent the invitation, provided all the vital details to access the base, and waited, though I wasn't used to them showing up for things like this. Still, in my heart, I held onto a hope—not for them, but for her. There was one person in my life who had always shown up and never missed a milestone. My sweet lady. My aunt. If anyone was going to be there, I just knew it would be her.

Still, as I prepared to march into the drill hall with my division, my stomach churned with nerves. Would anyone be there for me? I prayed as we stepped into formation, heading into the hall where proud families had gathered. The crowd buzzed with anticipation, but as we entered, the command rang out for silence, a stern reminder to hold applause until the end. We marched in perfect unison, our faces stoic, our pride carefully concealed under the discipline of military bearing. But then, as we passed the sea of faces, a voice pierced the stillness—a voice I knew so well.

"That's my niece! Hey Tiffers! Whoo! So proud of you, baby!"

My heart leaped, swelling with joy and relief. My lips quivered with the urge to smile, but I couldn't break formation. Instead, I let the warmth of her words wash over me. *She's here. I knew she'd be here*, I thought to myself. At that moment, the world seemed to settle, everything aligning just right. When the ceremony ended, families rushed forward to reunite with their now-sailors. I scanned the crowd eagerly, and then I saw her—my sweet lady. Short in stature but mighty in heart, she sprinted toward me, her face lit with pure, unfiltered pride.

"Tiffers! Oh, Tiffers, my girl! You did it, baby! Auntie is so proud of you! Look at you!"

Her arms wrapped around me in a hug so tight it felt like she'd never let go, and honestly, I didn't want her to. In her embrace, I felt the love I had craved for so long—the unconditional kind that asked for nothing in return. Behind her, another familiar face emerged—a tall, bald head I knew well. My father. My mother stood beside him, both smiling. But as always, I could see the truth behind the smiles. My father was genuine, a reflection of his quiet pride and love. My aunt's, of course, radiated pure joy.

My mother's smile, though, was a mask—a performance to blend in with the others. I'd learned long ago how to tell the difference. We spent the afternoon together, and I cherished every moment. My aunt, my father, and even my mother were all joined by one of my boot camp friends. She had no family there, so I'd invited her along, and she fit right in. Her humor and warmth were infectious, a perfect addition to the celebration.

We shared stories of our boot camp experience, laughing until tears rolled down our faces. We recounted our struggles and triumphs, the moments that had tested us and the ones that had brought us closer. For a few precious hours, it felt like everything was right in the world. But time, as it always does, moved too quickly. As the sun began to set, the moment I dreaded came. Uncle Sam called, and it was time to report back. I hugged my aunt tightly one more time, letting her warmth and love fill me before I had to say goodbye. This was the start of a new chapter— one I had earned with every drop of sweat, every tear, and every ounce of determination. As I walked away, I carried a quiet but powerful pride, knowing that, despite everything, there were people who truly loved and believed in me.

Chapter 18

The Navy became my new world, and for the first time in my life, I felt like I had permission to show up as my authentic self. I adjusted quickly, making friends with ease, my social butterfly tendencies thriving in this structured but communal environment. The military brought out every facet of my personality, putting it boldly on display and gifting me the courage to fully embrace who I was. I used to joke, "If you leave the service with a shy bone still intact, you didn't do it right." But even as I flourished, my father's warnings echoed in my mind. The fears he'd spoken of—the wolves, as he called them—soon began to take shape.

It started before I even set foot on my first station. The Navy's promise of structure and camaraderie couldn't shield me from the entitlement that some men carried like a badge of honor, a belief that they were invincible and unaccountable. These wolves prowled boldly; their behavior was normalized by a culture that too often turned a blind eye.

For me, it began at the recruiting office during what should have been one of the most empowering steps of my journey. I remember the way their eyes lingered, the comments they made under the guise of humor. The recruiters took my weight and measurements, and instead of professionalism, I was met with words like, "You smell so good," or "You're going to be trouble in the Navy—with the men, I mean." They said it as though it were a compliment, as though being seen as prey was something to be proud of.

It escalated quickly. One recruiter showed up at my home unannounced on a random day, offering to "pick me up for training." My father's protective instincts kicked in immediately. He confronted the man, making it clear that his presence at our home was not only unprofessional but entirely unwelcome.

From that moment forward, my father accompanied me to every meeting. He'd wait outside in the car, watching closely, ready to step in if necessary. He didn't say much about it to me directly, but I could see the worry in his eyes, the weight of his own experiences from his time in the Army.

One day, he finally spoke about it. "They're relentless," he said, shaking his head. "Some of these men—they think they can do whatever they want. I've seen it before, and I just hope it's not as bad for you as it was back then."

His words stayed with me, a cautionary refrain that I couldn't ignore. The military gave me strength, courage, and a sense of purpose, but it also exposed me to a harsh reality. The wolves were real, and they had been waiting for me long before I arrived. They overshadowed the good guys in there, but they existed, and I was grateful for them.

There was one instructor whose boldness crossed every line imaginable. During routine inspections of the barracks, he would make it a point to linger in my space, his actions dripping with arrogance and entitlement. Each time he entered my room, he made a spectacle of himself. He'd jump onto my bed without hesitation, his voice loud enough for everyone to hear as he sniffed my sheets and said, with a sickening smirk, "I'm going to sniff your sheets and dream of you tonight, *[last name]*." His tone was playful, but the malice behind his actions was unmistakable.

It didn't stop there. One day, completely unprovoked, he grabbed me without my consent, lifting me effortlessly and placing me on top of the washer. My legs were left splayed as he winked, blew me a kiss, and sauntered away, leaving behind an air of smugness that turned my stomach. His actions weren't subtle, and his confidence was bolstered by a system that had allowed men like him to act without fear of consequence.

I was just a young sailor, new to this world, and I quickly realized how powerless I was against these wolves. The environment made it clear that their entitlement was the rule, not the exception. I'd call home and recount these stories, desperately trying to process what was happening. My mother would listen, her silence often more telling than her words. I thought she was taking it all in, maybe even feeling some kind of motherly concern for me.

But I was wrong. I couldn't have known that one day, she would take those stories—my stories—and weaponize them against me. She would twist them into yet another narrative to fit her agenda, further breaking me in ways only she knew how. But that's a story for later.

This was just the beginning. These moments weren't isolated incidents—they were part of a pattern, a culture that pushed me to my breaking point. It was here that the seeds of my eventual decision to hang up my boots were sown. The Navy, which had once felt like a fresh start, became a battlefield of a different kind, one I wasn't prepared to fight. For the next 8 years, it would haunt me, but even during it all, I felt sticking it out would be better than what I came from.

My overly submissive mindset wasn't just a result of my self-doubt—it was forged in the fires of my past. The violations I endured as a young girl at the hands of my cousin and a family friend had left scars deeper than I even realized. What made it worse was the betrayal I felt from a mother who never desired to protect me and could never bring herself to believe me. She was never there to shield me, and so I grew up in a world that taught me not to expect anyone to care enough to protect me. I became resigned to survival, believing I wasn't worthy of care or protection. I became vulnerable, in ways I couldn't even see at the time, across every part of my life.

I fought, constantly, for things I shouldn't have had to—fight for my dignity, my voice, my right to exist in peace. I had to endure more in my young years than most people my age ever would, and it wore me down. Despite how strong I was on the outside, my heart had been battered. It was broken from so many years of fighting for things that should have been given freely. The will to fight was there, but it was tempered with defeat.

When I joined the Navy, I thought things would be different, but sadly, they weren't. My first duty station became just another battlefield. From the moment I stepped on board, I was lectured (especially by the women) about my smile and my bubbly personality. They saw me as a target, my very existence a threat in a world where men, too many of them, would see my warmth as something to exploit. But I wasn't going to let anyone dictate how I should carry myself. Being who I was—a kind, smiling, social person—was not a crime. It wasn't something that should invite unwanted attention or harassment. I refused to believe that just because I was friendly, I deserved to be treated as anything less than a colleague, a fellow service member.

But reality didn't care about my boundaries, and neither did those who chose to cross them. I had learned that it didn't matter whether I smiled or kept my distance, if someone wanted to impose themselves on me, they would. The very men I trusted, those I thought of as "good guys," would sometimes be the ones to betray me. That's the hardest part: having to stand alongside the same people who should've had your back but instead treated you as less than. The military is supposed to be a brotherhood, but it often felt like a pervert's playground, with little room for accountability.

At my first duty station, I would be violated twice. The first time, it was by my mentor—the very person I looked up to. He was everything I wanted to be: polished, professional, and driven. A black man who had made it, who was doing things I aspired to do. I saw him as a reflection of what was possible, a beacon of black excellence. He was always kind and professional with me, showing no favoritism, which I respected. I had chosen him to guide me, to help me navigate this world I was now in. For me, representation was everything. It was important to see someone who looked like me, someone who had made it and was thriving.

But then, in one devastating moment, he shattered the trust I had placed in him, revealing that even those who seemed to embody everything I aspired to could wear a mask, hiding the ugliness beneath. It wouldn't be the last time I would face such a betrayal, but it was the one that would change me forever.

One day, in a shared office, he asked a supervisor if I was available to come and handle some administrative work. I went, expecting nothing more than a simple task. I sat at the desk closest to the door, as I always did, with the door wide open, a sign of transparency and safety.

He stood behind me, pointing at the screen and giving instructions. At first, everything seemed normal—he was just a superior giving clear, professional guidance. I had no reason to feel uncomfortable. I trusted him. I could tell the difference between friendly and flirtatious, and at that moment, there was no sign of anything inappropriate.

But that shifted in an instant. As he finished explaining the task, he placed his hands on my shoulders, sliding them down to my chest. My body recoiled before my mind could fully comprehend the violation. I jumped up, my fury burning hot, and I tore into him, giving him the reprimand he so richly deserved. At that moment, I didn't care about rank, authority, or the hierarchy—I didn't care about the consequences. He was wrong, and I would not let it slide.

The look on his face told me everything. He was terrified—of the repercussions, of the possibility that I would take it further, that I would report him. But I was too consumed by a searing betrayal to care about his fear. I left that office in a rush, my anger and pain bubbling over into tears. I didn't say a word more—I couldn't. The hurt and rage were too much to bear.

I confided in my best friend about what had happened, and from there, a report was made to military authorities. But when the dust settled, nothing changed. He received a slap on the wrist—a letter of reprimand. And I was summoned to my Commanding Officer's office, where I was lectured told that what had happened was unfortunate and that it had been handled. It was a hollow explanation that left me feeling just as invisible and powerless as before.

That moment, that betrayal, would be the catalyst for everything that came after. From that point on, I would go into survival mode, my spirit defeated. I just wanted to escape, to disappear into the shadows where no one could see me. The next encounter would follow a painfully familiar pattern: another man, higher in rank, another predator disguised as a protector.

He would always greet me with a casual "Hey, lil lady," his voice was a mockery of what should have been respect. And as I moved to a new office, he would follow, inching closer, his true intentions slowly revealing themselves.

I shared an office with another superior, one who made a show of being the protector of the women in his department. He ensured we knew that if we needed anything, we could come to him and that he'd always have our backs. It was a speech, a well-rehearsed line, meant to make him look good—but when the time came for him to live up to that promise, he failed miserably.

Just like the others, the superior who violated me started friendly enough but soon became too comfortable, asking me questions about my personal life and probing into areas that were none of his business. He asked about boyfriends and admirers on board—questions no professional should ever ask. His invasion of my privacy was cloaked in the guise of concern, but I saw through it. It was just another attempt to control me, to make me feel small, to remind me that no matter how many boundaries I set, they would always push against them.

He found his way into our office—a space that was supposed to be secure, meant only for my superior and me. The arrogance he carried with him was palpable, the kind that made him feel untouchable. I knew he must have finessed his way into getting the door code, though no one else was supposed to have access.

His entitlement showed in everything he did, in how he talked to others, and in how he carried himself.

I started to notice the patterns. Every time he called down to the office, his first question was always the same: "Is your superior there?" At first, I didn't think much of it. I assumed he needed to discuss something work-related. But then I realized the truth—whenever I told him my superior wasn't there, he would show up in no time. Each visit left me feeling more unsettled, his presence a constant reminder of how vulnerable I was in a place that should have felt safe. He would sit behind me, too close, making my skin crawl.

The last straw came one day when I was heading off the ship for an engagement with a fellow sailor. I passed him in my uniform, gave a polite nod, and kept walking. But I had to double back to the office because I'd forgotten something. As soon as I walked in, the phone rang. I picked it up. His voice came through the line, leering and smug: "Damn, was that you in those peanut butter? I had to do a double take." Then he hung up, leaving me feeling sick and violated by something as simple as his words.

After what had happened with the last man who crossed my boundaries and how nothing had been done, I felt defeated. But I was tired—tired of being made to feel small, tired of being ignored. So, I decided to give it one more shot. I went to the superior who had proudly proclaimed he had our backs, the one who had told us to come to him if we ever needed anything. I asked for a moment of his time and told him everything. His response? "Boy, that man sure is something, ain't he?"

I was stunned. After everything I had just shared, what was his response? It was as if this man's behavior was an open secret, something people shrugged off instead of addressing. Still, I tried to hold on to a shred of faith, giving my superior a chance to handle it. I followed the chain of command like they always preached, hoping this time it would make a difference. But whatever he did—if he even did anything at all—wasn't enough. Nothing changed. The man continued his behavior as if no one had spoken to him.

Frustrated, I took the issue outside of my department and went to the Commanding Officer's liaison, a female I hoped might understand. I told her everything: the inappropriate comments, the discomfort, how I had already reported it to my superior, and how nothing had been done. She listened, nodding as I spoke, and reassured me that this wasn't the first time she had heard complaints about him. She seemed genuine, promising me that something would finally be done. For the first time in a long time, I felt a flicker of hope.

But that hope didn't last. One day, as I was cleaning my office, I noticed an email open on my superior's screen. It was from her. In the email, she had given him a heads-up about my visit to her office, informing him that I had reported the situation to her and told her that nothing had been done. I froze as I read it, the words a betrayal that hit me harder than I expected. She had broken my trust, a trust that was already so fragile after being let down by so many others. A conversation I had believed to be confidential had been handed over to the very person who had failed me in the first place.

I printed out that email and kept it in the glove compartment of my car. I knew it was technically against policy to read or take it, but I didn't care. In my eyes, the violation of my trust, my dignity, and my safety far outweighed any rule about office emails. It was proof of how the system, the very people who were supposed to protect me, had failed me time and time again. I kept that email in my glove compartment, knowing full well it violated the policy to even read or take it. But at that point, I didn't care. The violation of my trust, my dignity, and my safety far outweighed any rule about office conduct. It wasn't just an email to me—it was proof. Proof of how the system, the very people who were supposed to protect me, had failed repeatedly. Proof of why his arrogance had grown unchecked, why his boldness would escalate even further.

That night, after my superior had gone down to rest and left the office, I stayed behind. I needed to clean up and grab my uniform for the next morning's inspection, which had been announced just before the sailors dispersed after a grueling night of flight operations. I made my way to the office, the dim red glow of the ship's nighttime lighting casting eerie shadows in the passageways—or "p-ways," as we called them. The ship felt haunting under those lights, like a red-light district in motion. It was quiet, almost too quiet, and as I turned a corner, I saw him.

The wolf.

He was there, in the dark hallway, his presence as menacing as ever. I froze, hoping he wouldn't notice me, hoping I could disappear into the shadows. But he passed by, and I quickly slipped into the office, shutting the door behind me. My heart was pounding as I tried to calm myself, thinking I had avoided him. But then I saw the light shining from the doorframe when I'd opened it—it must have caught his attention. I should've known better. Moments later, there was a knock on the door.

I sat frozen, silently pleading for him to go away. If it were my superior or anyone else who truly needed me, they would have used the code to enter. But then I heard the faint clicking of buttons being pressed, and the door opened. There he was, stepping in with that same smug smile, the one that made my skin crawl. "Hey there, lil lady," he said, his tone mocking, his presence an unwelcome invasion. He had no reason to be there, no business in that office at that hour. I could feel the tension in the air, the predatory gleam in his eyes.

I busied myself at the corner of the desk, pretending to clean, trying to ignore him. There was plenty of space behind me for him to maneuver around, but instead, he brushed up against me as he passed. His body pressed against mine, his private area brushing against me. I froze. This was the moment I had dreaded, the one I had fought so hard to prevent. My insides screamed, but on the outside, I was paralyzed. I wanted to fight, to push him away, but I felt like every ounce of my strength had been drained.

Tears stung my eyes as he moved behind me. He unzipped my coveralls, his hands sliding down into my panties. I stood there, numb, his breath hot and vile against my neck. The seconds stretched into an eternity as he violated me, his filthy hands touching what I desperately wanted to keep safe from him. I shifted my neck slightly, a subtle but defiant movement to show I didn't want him, didn't welcome this, didn't consent.

Finally, he pulled his hands out, adjusted himself, and started toward the door. But he wasn't done. On his way out, he turned back, his arrogance on full display. "Oh, and don't say anything to your best friend," he said, flashing his collar device to show his newly earned rank. The smirk on his face made my stomach churn. His message was clear—his promotion gave him power, and he wanted me to know he felt untouchable.

It wasn't just his actions that disgusted me; it was the way he wielded his rank to shield himself from consequences. I had seen it before in how he belittled others, saying, "Who do you think they're going to believe? Me or you?" That memory played in my mind as I shrank into myself, retreating into the shell I'd created to survive moments like this. He had stripped me of my safety and my voice. His arrogance reminded me of my mother's projection tactics, where blame was shifted to others to avoid accountability. "I know how you look at me when we're out and about," he said, his words a cruel and calculated twist of reality.

I stood there in silence, letting him leave, praying for it to end. But the damage had already been done. He left me broken, violated, and betrayed, not just by him but by every person and system that had failed to protect me. I gathered my uniform and the rest of my things, locked up with tears in my eyes, and headed down to my rack. Trying my best as I made my way down the p-way to my berthing to hold them back with a fast-paced walk because it would not be too much longer that I would not be able to hold them in.

I stepped out of the shower, tears still streaming down my face, and dragged myself to my rack. Exhaustion and despair consumed me as I pulled the curtains closed, trying to block out the world. I cried until I fell into a restless sleep, only to be startled awake by the sound of my best friend snatching open the curtain with her usual playful energy.

She froze when she saw my tear-streaked face. "Why are you in your rack so early?" she asked. It was late, but she knew my routine—after a shift, I'd usually hang out in the hangar bay, talk trash with the crew, and hit the gym before turning in. My absence hadn't gone unnoticed, and when she didn't see me running around as usual, she came looking for me.

She sat down beside me, concern etched on her face. "What's wrong?" she asked gently. I hesitated, but I couldn't hold it in any longer. I told her everything, every horrifying detail of what had happened that night. She listened, her expression shifting from sadness to anger. We'd talked before about his behavior, how unsettling and predatory it was, but this—this was beyond anything I could have imagined.

"What do you want to do?" she asked, her voice steady but firm.

"Nothing," I replied, my voice trembling. "No one is going to believe me. Every other time I tried to speak up, nothing happened. I did what I had to do to get him to leave me alone. Maybe it'll be enough."

But she wasn't having it. Defeat was not an option for her, and she wasn't about to let me accept it either. "No," she said, her voice resolute. "Get up. Get dressed. We're going to the chaplain. If he won't help us, then God help this ship."

Her determination ignited a spark of hope in me. I got dressed, and we went to the chaplain. Even though it was late, he welcomed us in, listened to my story, and immediately took action. He was kind and supportive in a way I hadn't experienced before. He connected me with an advocate and helped start an investigation right away.

That night, I called my parents, sobbing as I told them what had happened. I thought I was reaching out for comfort and support, but I didn't realize that my mother was already collecting this pain to weaponize against me later. It wouldn't be until much later that I understood the depths of her betrayal.

The fallout from reporting him was brutal. The backlash for being a woman daring to speak up was more than I could bear. I left that ship, but the wolves were waiting for me at my next command. The investigation followed me, but so did the same toxic dynamics. The only thing that had changed was the location.

Chapter 19

The first encounter with my new post came quickly. He called me into his office under the pretense of discussing my aspirations of becoming an officer. As I entered, another superior walked out, and I had the sickening sense that he knew what was about to happen. The man sat down, spreading his legs and grinning. "Damn, you smell good. What you got on?" he said.

I felt the air leave the room. It had nothing to do with why I was there, and I knew I needed to leave. As I turned to go, he started talking about another incident—a young female sailor who had recently reported being violated. He dismissed her claims, calling her "just a white girl trying to set up his friend." Then, with a twisted smirk, he added, "A sista's gonna ride for ya, though."

I stood there, disgusted. He had no idea why I was really at that command. He had no idea that I, the "sista" he spoke of, was there because of a "brotha" who had violated me. He assumed I'd stay silent, complicit in his sick worldview. But I wasn't going to let that slide.

"You know why I'm here, right?" I said, my voice steady despite the storm inside me. "For the same thing that happened to her." His expression shifted, but I couldn't call it humility. Maybe fear. Arrogance is still clinging on. I turned and walked out, slamming the door behind me. There would be no room for fake apologies or "misunderstandings." For the next few days, he tried to test the waters, attempting to exchange smiles in passing. I gave him nothing. Not a glance. Not an acknowledgment.

But his arrogance wouldn't let him stop. One day, on the flight deck, he approached me while I was working, holding out a small box. "Hey, are we cool?" he asked. Inside the box was a bottle of perfume. The same comment from our earlier interaction echoed in my mind. I froze, but before I could react, a friend—a sailor I trusted—noticed my discomfort. Without hesitation, he came over in his loud, comedic way, cutting through the tension like a knife. His timing was perfect, his presence a shield.

The superior had no choice but to back off, muttering something under his breath as I walked away. I felt a flicker of gratitude for my friend. There were still good ones out there, and in that moment, he reminded me I wasn't entirely alone.

The holidays were approaching, and again, it would be nothing special for me. Another holiday where I would lie to all my superiors and friends about going "home" and spending time with family, and I always said it with the biggest smile, providing the reassurance that I was loved and had somewhere to go when I truly was the one that needed that.

I lost count of the holidays and leave periods I spent alone. Banished from home by my parents, each time for some fabricated, ridiculous reason they'd conjure up. I'd watch as everyone around me packed their bags, eager to head home to reunite with their families. I pretended to do the same, putting on a brave face and acting like I had somewhere to go. But "home" for me was just a quick trip down the road to my barracks room.

Before locking myself away, I'd stop to grab snacks and comfort food. Once inside, I'd bunker down in the darkness, binge-watching shows to drown out the silence. I cried often during those moments, lying to anyone who called to wish me a happy holiday or ask how things were at home. They didn't know the truth—that I hadn't left at all.

The rare times I did go home, the memories weren't of warmth or joy but of the same chaos that had driven me away. The lights that stayed etched in my mind weren't Christmas lights—they were the flashing blue and red of police sirens. Each trip home seemed to end with bruises, not just on my face but on my heart and mind.

One Christmas, I decided to return home, hoping for something different but knowing deep down what awaited me. That day, I was upstairs in my old room, trying to escape into sleep, when I heard her voice calling my name. My mother. Her tone told me everything I needed to know. I braced myself, already knowing whatever she wanted would be something I didn't want to be a part of.

I was right. She wanted to drag me into an argument she was having with my father. She demanded to know why his family dared to stand up for him—another one of her stories spun from thin air, another attempt to shift blame. Her accusations weren't even grounded in reality; they were just another way to deflect accountability. Pointing fingers at everyone else was her expertise, but when it came to herself, that same hand went limp.

I told her calmly that I wasn't going to answer her questions. I had no interest in getting involved. It wasn't my battle, and it never would be. My father, to my surprise, agreed and encouraged me to stay out of it. But that wasn't enough to stop her. She kept pushing, digging, trying to drag me into the mess until, against my better judgment, I gave in just to get her to leave me alone.

I told her the truth—the kind of truth she didn't want to hear. I said that we, as a family, had forgiven her for everything she had done to us over the years. What if we were to hold even half of the pain she had inflicted on us? She wouldn't be able to bear it. Because of that, I felt she had no right to hold grudges against anyone else.

And just as I knew she would, she erupted. Her anger boiled over into a full-blown rage. I stood there, hurt but not surprised, and told her, "This is exactly why I didn't want to be a part of this. I told you to leave me out of it."

But to her, any words that didn't serve her, especially if they came from her children, were "disrespect." It didn't matter that I was an adult, speaking logically and calmly. To her, my words were an affront simply because they didn't align with her narrative.

The truth? It wasn't disrespectful. It was her unwillingness to face reality. My words were a mirror she didn't want to look into. So, instead of accountability, she reached for her most trusted weapon: gaslighting. Twisting the narrative, dodging responsibility, and trying to make me the villain for daring to speak the truth. It always ended the same way—with her taking a swing or two. I was conditioned to expect it, bracing myself for the inevitable. When she hit me this time, I knew I had reached my breaking point. I was fuller than I had ever been, overflowing with all the years of pent-up pain, anger, and exhaustion.

I tried to walk away, to rise above it as I always had, telling her to leave me alone and keep her hands off me. "I'm not a child or your punching bag anymore," I said firmly. "I'm a grown woman."

But my words only fueled her rage. She knocked over the coffee table, breaking and throwing everything in her path as she charged after me. My father tried to pull her back, but even his strength wasn't enough to stop her in those moments.

"Bitch, I'm gonna fuck your ass up!" she screamed as she fought against him, thrashing like a wild animal. "Get the fuck off of me!" she yelled, shoving him aside.

She lunged at me, shoving me with so much force that I fell back onto the Christmas tree. My head smacked into the entertainment center on the way down, leaving me disoriented and momentarily stunned. I lay there, trying to catch my breath and gather myself.

Lord, give me strength, I prayed silently. As much as I didn't want to stoop to her level, all the years of physical, mental, and emotional abuse were boiling to the surface. I could feel myself teetering on the edge, knowing it wouldn't take much more for me to meet her rage head-on.

I pulled myself up, my body aching from the impact. With a knot forming on my head, bruises covering my body, and blood seeping through the fabric of my pants, I still attempted to walk away. I placed the Christmas tree back upright, trying to restore some semblance of order amidst the chaos. As I walked, she came at me again, punching me in the back. Each blow landed with a force that felt more like hate than anything else. The punches to my head and back were relentless, each one chipping away at my restraint. Then came one to my face, and at that moment, something inside me snapped.

I spun around and screamed, "Bitch, if you put your fucking hands on me again, I'm gonna fuck you up!"

Her reaction was almost laughable—a look of mock surprise as though clutching invisible pearls. The audacity, as if to say, *How dare you stand up for yourself?*

She turned to my father, incredulous. "You're just gonna let her fucking talk to me like that?"

Before I could even process her words, she hit me in the face again. This time, I didn't hold back. I jumped onto my father's back, swinging instinctively. My fist caught her hoop earring, ripping it off. I threw it back at her face, yelling, "I told you, if you did that shit again, I was gonna fuck you up, bitch! I'm tired of this shit! I'm not your fucking punching bag anymore! You got away with that when I was a child, but not today. Not anymore!"

At that moment, it felt like divine intervention had guided my fist away from landing a full blow. Because if it had, I don't think I would've stopped, not with all the weight I was carrying. Years of heartbreak, anger, betrayal, and knowing she was the one who had put it all there only made it heavier. My father yelled for me to grab his car keys and wait outside, desperate to calm her down without me in the crossfire. Once again, it was clear that the chaos she had already caused wasn't enough—not for her. She didn't want the kind of attention that painted her as the villain; no, she craved the kind that made her the victim.

And so, true to her dramatic nature, she sprinted toward the kitchen, ready to stage her next theatrical display. "I'm just going to fucking kill myself!" she screamed, charging toward the kitchen to grab a knife in one of her dramatic displays. True to form, everyone scrambled to her side, rushing to stop her and giving her exactly what she wanted—attention. Meanwhile, I was left to do what I had learned to do so well: tend to my pain and wounds alone.

I walked out of the house, entirely unmoved by her antics. If she truly intended to do it, she wouldn't make such a spectacle. She wouldn't announce it to the world or stage an audience. She didn't want to follow through; she wanted control, sympathy, and the satisfaction of knowing she could still manipulate the room.

This wasn't the first time, and deep down, I knew it wouldn't be the last. She once staged a car accident, claiming her car was wrapped around a tree and that she was calling from a hospital bed. In reality, she was driving that very car out of town, laughing while my siblings cried over her. To top it off, she ordered the one sibling who was with her to never breathe a word of the truth. "It's what they deserve," she said coldly.

The objective was always the same—to punish me for daring to set boundaries, to manipulate me into feeling guilty for trying to protect myself.

Then there was the night she went to the beach back home, wading into the water, supposedly trying to drown herself. She thought no one knew, but I overheard my father talking about it late one night from my bedroom. Even as a little girl, I understood what she was doing—trying to turn her pain into a weapon, wielding it to keep control over everyone around her.

The list of these manipulative suicide threats and stunts goes on. Each one was a calculated move, not a cry for help but a cry for power. This was nothing new for me. I sat in my father's car, tears streaming down my face while trying to catch my breath. My car wasn't an option—two of my siblings had taken it and were still out. I called my best friend, crying as I told her what had happened, pouring out my frustrations and explaining that I was ready to leave, already planning to pack up and head back.

As I sat there, I caught a glimpse of headlights in the rearview mirror. My siblings were pulling into the driveway in my car. Their faces turned to confusion when they saw me sitting alone in the car, my face red, streaked with tears, and bruised, my clothes torn. That confusion quickly faded as the sound of my mother's raging voice carried through the air, loud enough to reach them even outside.

They both climbed into the car with me, their concern palpable as I explained everything through broken words and sobs. They consoled me as best as they could, their anger at her behavior clear. Then, as we sat there trying to process it all, flashing lights appeared. I glanced up and saw the police pulling into the driveway.

At first, I assumed it was the neighbors who had called the cops, prompted by the chaos of my mother's screaming in the house. But I soon learned it was my little sister who had made the call out of fear and concern for how things were escalating.

When the police arrived, we stepped out of the car to meet them. They began asking questions about what was going on. In that moment, I could have ended it all—spilled every detail of the truth. My face, marked with scars and evidence of the encounter, was hard to hide despite my attempts to fix myself up in the car. Still, I tried. And instead of speaking my truth, I lied. I told them it was just a small, typical misunderstanding between a mother and her daughter.

The officers went inside to corroborate my story with my mother. I could already predict what would happen next—another act where she played the victim flawlessly. When they returned, their tone was almost dismissive. "Your mother says you started making fun of her mental illness," one officer said, "and she felt cornered, hurt."

I wanted to roll my eyes, but I didn't. Instead, I swallowed the anger that bubbled in my throat. There I was, sparing her once again while she was quick to twist the narrative and paint me as the villain. The officer added, "You know, mommas are always right. Just take it easy on her—she might be a little sensitive. You know, we only get one mom."

In my head, I wanted to respond, *Yeah, and what a draft I got with this one. How lucky for me, right?* But I just nodded and smiled, letting them go on their way. I spared her, yet again, with my silence—something I had done for far too long.

Later, though, she would tell the world a completely different story that I was the jealous daughter, bitter about her marriage, out to destroy her. The audacity of such a statement spoke volumes—not only about how she viewed me but about her twisted perception. She saw me as the other woman, a rival, not her child.

If I truly wanted to "destroy" her, as she claimed, I could have done it years ago. She had handed me plenty of ammunition over the years. But instead of using it, I bit the bullets myself, painting her as someone she wasn't—a good person. Why? Because, again, I craved normalcy, a part of me still desired the mother I never had. But we'll get to that later.

After the cops left, I stayed in the car a little longer, trying to gather my thoughts. Hearing what the officers said had restarted the clock of frustration and exhaustion in my mind. As I sat there, I saw her coming out of the house and walking toward my window.

"Come in," she said softly, her voice laced with false sweetness. "Momma's sorry. I want to talk about it. You don't have to stay out here in the car."

I looked at her, emotionless. "Back up and leave me alone. You've done more than enough," I said firmly. "This happens every time I come here. I knew I should've stayed away. Then you lie to the cops and twist things on me, even when I'm sitting out here protecting you? Please, get away from this car and leave me alone. I have absolutely nothing for you right now. I'm leaving in a few."

My father, as always, came chasing after her, yelling, "Leave the girl alone! Just come on back inside. If she wants to talk to you, she will."

But there would be no conversation—not now, not ever. When I went back inside, it was only to pack my bags and prepare to leave the next day. Even during that short time, she managed to show her true colors again, hiding her malice under the guise of a fake apology.

I sat downstairs with my father, deciding to put it all behind me. Even though I was leaving, I wanted to spend time with him. We laughed and talked about something on TV. It was always the same in this house—pretending nothing had happened. No accountability, no genuine apologies, and no interventions. I didn't even bother trying to break my own heart further by unpacking it all. I was leaving anyway.

As we talked, she appeared at the top of the stairs, looking down at us. "Why did you turn the volume up? Y'all down here talking about me, I know you are," she said sharply.

"Nobody's talking about you," my father replied, exasperated. "We're just sitting here watching TV. The volume hasn't changed. We're not doing this today."

Her target wasn't him, though—it was me. She was always trying to get a reaction out of me, and I refused to give her the satisfaction. She had always been jealous of my relationship with my father, as I've said before. To her, seeing us laughing and getting along was intolerable, like another woman trying to steal her husband.

I kept my eyes fixed on the screen, ignoring her completely. My father exchanged words with her, which only made her angrier. She stormed back to her room and slammed the door. We didn't acknowledge her tantrum; we just resumed our conversation. I was too exhausted to give it any energy.

Minutes later, she came out again, standing at the foot of the stairs. "So, you're just not gonna come up here and check on your damn wife?" she shouted at my father, trying to bait him.

"What do I need to come up there for? It's not that serious," he said, tired of her games.

"I guess you love her more than me," she spat, her voice venomous. "So fucking stuck up her ass. I'm your wife, dammit!" She stormed off again, slamming the door behind her.

That was it. I couldn't wait any longer. I had to leave. I rushed upstairs to my room, determined to gather my things and get out.

As I passed her room, I saw her sitting on her bed, pouting like a spiteful, petulant child.

I doubled back, stopping at her door. "Why do you hate me so much, Mom?" I shouted, the pain boiling over. "What is it about me that makes you not like me? I've never done anything but be good to you, but it's never enough. It's never enough for you to just love me and treat me right. Why? What did I ever do to deserve this? Just say it! You hate me. I know you do. I'd rather hear you admit it than have you keep pretending and treating me like this."

I stormed off to my room to grab my belongings, but she followed, chasing after me. "Oh, baby, I don't hate you!" she said, her voice dripping with manipulation. "Why would you think that?" She tried to hold me, but I pulled away. I didn't want to be touched by her.

"I carried you for nine months. I'm your mother," she said, her tone possessive and suffocating. She didn't see me as an individual, someone separate from her. To her, I was always supposed to be an extension of her—a reflection of her desires, not my own. I cried as I grabbed my things and walked past her. "Oh, your mother doesn't hate you, gal," my father said, his tone dismissive, as though his words could wipe away years of damage. "Both of you just need to get along. Put all this mess behind you. You know the Bible says to honor your mother and father so that your days may be long. Sometimes, it's best to hold your tongue. You know how your mother is."

His words hit me like a slap, the familiar sting of his collaboration. He spoke as if he hadn't been the biggest fly on the wall, witnessing and hearing all her cruelty toward me over the years. Instead of standing up for me, he wielded scripture as a weapon, using it to gaslight me and help her dodge accountability—along with his own. After all, his enabling of her behavior was his betrayal.

I said goodbye to my siblings and made my way to the car, heading back on the road. As usual, I spent the remainder of the holiday alone in my barracks room, tending to my scars and bruises. The ones I couldn't hide would need an explanation, but I always found a way to manage—to heal what could be hidden and endure what couldn't.

That leave period, like so many others, was emotionally taxing. But nothing could have prepared me for the phone call that followed—a call that would once again remind me how cruel life could be, even to those who try to put good out into the world.

The phone rang with an unfamiliar number. When I picked up, it was one of the investigators handling my case. They started by wishing me a happy holiday, but the words that followed shattered me. They told me that the investigation wouldn't see a trial. Their reasoning? They didn't want me to relive the trauma since it would be "hard to prove" because he had used his fingers and not his member, as if my suffering wasn't enough. As if the repeated trips to their office, answering their probing questions, and participating in their setup phone call with him—all of it—wasn't enough.

He denied everything, even claiming he wasn't near the office that night, but somehow, I wasn't worth defending in court. I had wanted to be the voice—the person standing in that courtroom holding him accountable and ensuring he couldn't harm another. But that never happened. And as I later learned, he did move on to violate others.

I knew my mother celebrated my tears. Later, her true feelings about what happened would come to light in ways I never expected. One day, I picked up one of my siblings from the bus station to live with me as he considered joining the service. That morning, she'd called me, planting yet another sick seed of manipulation. This sibling, like many, had their quirks—he sniffed a lot and cleared his throat often, something we, as kids, found annoying but knew was just part of him. But she twisted it into something sinister.

"Do you think they're using cocaine?" she asked, feigning concern.

"No," I replied, exasperated. "He's been doing that since we were kids. You know that."

But she knew what she was doing. She always did. She lived to stir the pot, to triangulate her children, to envy the closeness we shared despite her constant efforts to divide us.

When I picked him up, I joked, trying to brush off her toxicity. "You won't believe what your wonderful mommy said today," I told him, laughing as I relayed her absurd accusation.

He sighed, disappointed but not surprised. "Why is she always starting stuff?" he asked. "But, speaking of which... do you want to know what your momma's been saying about you?"

I braced myself, already knowing it wouldn't be good. "Lay it on me. What now?"

"She told us all you were a prostitute," he said.

My stomach dropped.

"She said you fly around the world, sleeping with men for money, and that's how you afford all your clothes and nice things."

I asked, stunned, "Who did she tell this to?"

"Me, Dad, and the rest of your siblings," he replied. "She gathered us all in their bedroom one day, pretending to be so concerned about you."

It felt like the air was sucked out of the room.

He continued, "She said you called home crying hysterically—about that part, she was honest. But she told us it wasn't about being violated. She said you were crying because you were ashamed of being a prostitute. She claimed you admitted to selling your body while in uniform and needed to repent for your sins."

Tears filled my eyes as he spoke.

"She told us you lied about being violated, that it was a cover because you were ashamed of your real lifestyle. She told the whole family that you got what was coming to you—that you deserved it."

I couldn't even respond. Her words—her lies—cut deeper than anything I'd experienced before.

But he wasn't finished yet. As if the previous revelations weren't devastating enough, he told me that she had gone even further. She had spread a vile rumor that I had an inappropriate relationship with my father.

There were multiple versions of this disgusting lie. One version claimed that, while I was home from college, she had come back from grocery shopping one morning and found me taking too long to come downstairs to open the door for her. According to her, it was just my father and me in the house. She told people that when I finally opened the door, my hair was disheveled, I was sweating, and I was out of breath, insinuating the unthinkable.

The other version of her story was even worse. She claimed that she walked into the house from grocery shopping to find me on my knees in front of my father while he sat on the couch, receiving oral sex from me.

I sat there in disbelief as my sibling recounted these vile fabrications.

And still, there was more. He told me about another lie she had spread—this one at my great-grandfather's repast. I had stepped inside the house to use the restroom while everyone else sat outside at the picnic tables, eating and mingling with her side of the family.

At some point, my little sister had taken my modeling portfolio out of my bag and was walking around with it, showing it off. She looked up at me, and I didn't mind her carrying it around. My mother had seen the portfolio before, but that day, she used it as an opportunity to spread another malicious rumor. She told her father—my grandfather—that I was a call girl and that I used those modeling pictures to gain clients.

I sat in the car, stunned, as my sibling recounted all of this. Piece by piece, the truth unraveled, and I finally began to see the full extent of the web she had spun. That day, at the time of her lies, I had been completely unaware of the poison she was spreading behind my back, manipulating and twisting narratives to turn the family against me.

All I could do was cry. My sibling leaned in, hugging me, trying to console me. But how could I be consoled? Here I was, thinking I was out in the world making them proud, proving myself through my hard work and independence—and yet, she had found another way to throw a grenade on my name and destroy everything I had built. Every ounce of my progress, every milestone I had achieved starting at just 17 years old, fueled by my determination to escape her toxicity, now felt tainted by her envy and malice.

Her hatred seeped into every rumor she spread, her envy dripping from every lie. She couldn't celebrate me—she despised me for stepping out into the world on my own, for thriving without her. The family on her side had heard it all, every despicable fabrication she could muster. But she never dared to spread her lies to my father's side of the family. She knew better than that. They had seen through her long before I ever did. They would have gone to war for me—for any of us children—if she had tried to harm us in that way.

I sat there in the car with my sibling, still parked at the bus station, as anger and heartbreak surged through me. I picked up the phone and made a call to a particular family member. I placed the call on speakerphone, needing my sibling to hear what I was about to confirm.

I hadn't spoken a word of what I already knew—I wanted to let them tell me unprompted so there would be no doubt.

"So, what did my mother say to you about me?" I asked, my voice steady despite the storm brewing inside me.

Without hesitation, they replied, "She said you were fucking your dad and out here whoring. I was about to come down there and beat your little ass too."

None of it was true—none of it ever happened. Yet here I was, caught in the storm of her lies once again. The family member decided to confront her about it, calling her and putting me on a three-way line.

"Oh, who said that? I didn't say no mess like that now," my mother's voice slithered through the line, dripping with false indignation. "I would never speak about my daughter like that," she added, turning to my father as if expecting him to vouch for her innocence.

And, of course, he did. As if he didn't know the woman he married. As if he hadn't already heard these same vile lies from her mouth. His complicity sickened me.

But more than anything, I was disgusted with the people who entertained her evil in the first place. The ones who gave her lies oxygen, who listened and believed, or at least pretended to. They revealed their own envy and ill intent in the process. Some of them didn't even know me—had never met me in their lives—but were more than willing to believe her venomous fabrications.

I wasn't fooled by this family member's sudden righteousness. I knew whose side they were on. My mother's side of the family was filled with toxic flip-floppers, people who smiled in each other's faces while plotting and gossiping behind closed doors. Their confrontation with my mother wasn't about defending me—it was just another moment of personal agenda, of using my pain to get back at her for whatever slight rumor she had spread about them.

I knew this person's attempt to put my mother in her place wasn't an act of loyalty to me. It was a charade, a fleeting moment of supposed allegiance designed to serve their purpose. This was the same family member who had treated me poorly since I was a child, just like the rest of my mother's flying monkeys. They hated me, too—always had. My mother, enraged at being exposed yet again, abruptly hung up the phone, cutting off the conversation. I ended the call with the other family member and started driving back to my place. But I didn't make it far.

The weight of it all came crashing down on me, and I had a nervous breakdown right there in the car. Tears streamed uncontrollably down my face as I sobbed, my body trembling from the sheer intensity of my emotions. It wasn't just her cruelty that shattered me—I had long accepted the depths of her malice. What broke me was the realization that no matter how far I thought her evil could go, she always found a way to exceed it.

I pulled over to the side of the road, needing a moment to breathe, to gather myself before I could continue the drive. I couldn't let her consume me entirely, but in that moment, it felt like she already had. The betrayal was everywhere, hiding in plain sight behind familiar faces, all complicit in her sick, twisted game. Those same faces that smiled at me and pretended to love me were the ones taking from me, piece by piece, feeding into her madness. From the moment I escaped that house at seventeen, she made it her mission to carry out her hatred for me even from afar.

She couldn't stand that I broke free of her suffocating grip, that I dared to choose survival over submission. So, from the shadows, she plotted, venomous and relentless, trying to poison everything I had built. Every ounce of pride I carried, every accomplishment I clawed my way toward despite her abuse—she was there, the biggest crab in that barrel of dysfunction, determined to drag me down. It wasn't enough that she tried to break me when I was under her roof; she wanted to destroy me from a distance, too.

When the investigation results landed in my lap, and the weight of my mother's endless lies compounded the injustices I faced—both in the Navy and the world I had fought so hard to escape—my heart shattered. It wasn't just full; it was bursting, overflowing with pain I didn't know how to release. I internalized it all the way I always had until it felt like there wasn't a safe corner of my soul left. No safe space. No one to turn to.

And that's when her voice crept back in. The voice I had worked so hard to silence, whispering all the venomous things she'd planted in me: that I deserved every ounce of evil in my life, that I was unlovable, that I was nothing more than a body to be used—my pockets and my flesh were my only value. Her words slithered into my thoughts, wrapping around my self-worth and choking it, convincing me that nothing I achieved would ever outrun the shadow of her projections.

In those moments, I was stripped bare, completely vulnerable—as if I hadn't already been. I craved love. Not the shallow, surface-level kind my bubbly, social butterfly persona drew in, but something real. I wanted to belong, to feel understood. But instead, my brokenness became a beacon, attracting others who were just as shattered. My smiles masked the gaping holes inside me, but those holes acted as a magnet for men who saw me as a refuge. The cycle repeated—another round of giving everything I had until my cup was bone-dry, leaving me used and discarded.

This time, though, the pain was sharper. This time, his face blurred into hers. My mother's shadow loomed large over this relationship, a cruel reminder of the wounds I carried—wounds I had spent a lifetime trying to heal. It was as if my heart, desperate and relentless in its pursuit of love, had decided to relive the agony with her all over again, trying to fix in others what I could never fix in her.

Looking back, I grieve for that version of me—for the heart that refused to give up, that took every betrayal as a challenge to prove it was worthy of love, all while silently screaming for its worth. My heart didn't know how to stop fighting, even when it should have. Jaded, but not enough to quit. Broken, but still reaching. I wish I could go back and hold myself, year after year, through every heartbreak. I wish I could tell her she was enough, just as she was.

Chapter 20

It was an ordinary workday for us sailors, pushing through tasks, counting down the hours until we could leave and catch a moment of peace. I was still finding my rhythm at my new command, trying to learn the faces around me, figuring out who everyone was beneath the uniforms. One face, though, stood out—his. There was something magnetic about him. He was friendly, like most of the people I worked with, but different. Goofy in a way that matched my humor, with a heart so genuine it mirrored mine. Kind, caring, and quietly brilliant, he was one of those rare souls who seemed to excel at anything he touched. He took pride in his work and was always willing to lend a hand, even to me.

Some days, though, he was distant, retreating into his world. It was my nature to notice, to want to make sure no one felt left out. Around the holidays, everyone buzzed with plans to visit family. For me, it was just another year of putting on a brave face, smiling as I left for my barracks, pretending I had somewhere to go, just so no one would worry. When I asked him about his plans, his answer stopped me cold.

He told me he wasn't welcome home.

My heart clenched. He didn't know my story, but I knew his pain all too well. I would never wish my experiences on another soul. For a moment, I let my guard down, sharing my understanding, and hugged him. Even in my loneliness, a solitude I had grown numb to, I couldn't bear the thought of someone else enduring it. I offered to spend the holidays with him if he needed company. No one should have to be alone, even if I had resigned myself to that reality long ago. He smiled, thanked me, and reassured me he'd be fine.

But that moment stayed with me. It was a turning point, the beginning of something I couldn't have foreseen. He grew on me, drawing me in with a gravitational pull I couldn't resist. We started hanging out more, and one thing led to another. Our first date was a double date to Busch Gardens. He was a gentleman in every sense of the word. No ulterior motives, no hidden agendas—just laughter, fun, and the kind of carefree joy I hadn't realized I was starving for.

He refused to let me touch my purse that night. It might seem small, but for someone like me—a woman who had always taken care of everyone else, who was so used to being taken advantage of—it was foreign. It was more than a kind gesture; it was a glimpse of what it felt like to be cared for, truly cared for. On the ride home, I fell asleep on his lap, lulled by the comfort of his presence. He gently draped his jacket over me, trying to mask his nervousness with a sweetness that only made the moment more endearing. It was the perfect ending to an amazing day—the kind that felt like the beginning of something beautiful and full of promise.

We came from different races different worlds, but our hearts spoke the same language. At that moment, none of those differences mattered. It was just us, two souls finding solace in each other, believing that maybe, just maybe, this could be the kind of love we both had longed for. With him, everything unfolded naturally. It felt inevitable, like trying to hold back the tide. He was crazy about me, and I couldn't help but fall, too. But beneath it all, there were cracks we both tried to hide. His love for me was real—I knew that—but it was his lack of love for himself that loomed like a shadow, mirroring my battles. Our demons didn't just coexist; they collided, threatening to consume the fragile connection we had built.

Once again, my heart took up the challenge—a relentless need to silence the cruel words my mother had planted in my head about my worth. Loving someone became my way of proving her wrong, of proving to myself that I could be enough. I threw myself into it with everything I had. I planned surprise birthday parties for him, inviting all our Navy friends to celebrate with him and show him how worthy and loved he was. Little arguments were resolved with playful trash talk and races at the indoor go-karting track, where kisses went to the winner—or the loser, depending on the mood.

Everything I did was deliberate, an effort to break the cycle of dysfunction I came from. I wanted to create something healthier, something opposite of the chaos I had known chaos, that had left me with physical and emotional scars I still carried. I was trying so hard to rewrite the script.

But it wasn't long before his demons started to show. At first, they were subtle, slipping out like whispers in the dark. He had tucked them away so neatly, so kindly, and I don't believe it was out of malice. Knowing him, loving him, and eventually mourning him, I truly believe his love for me was genuine. He wanted to keep, protect, and shield me from the darkness he carried.

But those demons were stronger than his love, stronger than the man who had the talent and drive to master anything he touched. They clawed their way to the unstoppable surface, leaving us to face the weight of a battle he had been fighting long before I met him. A battle he couldn't win—not for himself and not for me.

One afternoon, we were out running our usual errands, enjoying each other's company. We decided to end the day with lunch at one of our favorite spots, soaking in the simplicity of the moment. As we sat there, my phone buzzed—a social media message from an admirer. I chuckled and showed him as if I had nothing to hide. My heart was his, and I wanted him to know that.

But his reaction blindsided me. He went off, his voice rising, anger flaring in a way I had never seen before. Embarrassed and shaken, I left the table and made my way to his car. As I closed the passenger door, a sudden, violent blow rattled the vehicle. He had punched it, the force of it reverberating through the metal and into me.

I froze. Fear took over, tears streaming down my face as I sat silent and trembling. When he got into the car, I didn't dare speak. I didn't know what to say, and I certainly didn't want to risk making things worse. We drove in silence, my mind racing, my heart pounding.

When we reached my place, I finally mustered the courage to talk about what had happened. His reaction caught me off guard. He was immediately apologetic, almost desperate as if the outburst had shocked him as much as it had me. His remorse seemed genuine, tinged with embarrassment. I accepted his apology but told him I needed space to process what had just happened. I wished him a good night and retreated to the safety of my home.

Alone, I tried to rationalize it. It had been so sudden, so out of character—or at least I thought it was. His immediate regret was convincing, almost enough to make me believe it was a one-time lapse. But deep down, something didn't sit right. I tried to tell myself that it was just a moment, an isolated incident, and we moved on.

Reflecting now, I see how my response was conditioned by my childhood experiences. Growing up with a narcissistic parent teaches you to dismiss your feelings and to prioritize maintaining harmony over addressing harm. They groom their children to accept blame, even when it's undeserved, and to tolerate mistreatment because they equate love with endurance and sacrifice. In those moments, I wasn't just trying to save the relationship; I was reliving the dynamic I had grown up with—absorbing someone else's pain and chaos, hoping my love could fix what was broken.

For a while, things went back to normal, and the memory of that day faded into the background. He was the man I had fallen for again—loving, attentive, and sweet. He couldn't wait for me to meet his family, practically bursting with excitement as he told his mother about me. I listened to him speak of me with such pride, telling her how happy I made him, how special I was to him, how deeply he loved me.

Hearing those words filled a void I didn't even realize I was still carrying. My own family had never spoken of me with such affection or pride. For once, I wasn't fighting to be seen or valued. But that hunger for validation—planted and nurtured by my upbringing—was also my Achilles' heel.

Those same words that lifted me would later become the chains that held me down. I clung to the idea of what we could be, even as the cracks in our relationship deepened. If only I had loved myself the way I loved him, if only I had shown myself the care and devotion I so freely gave to others, I would have known when to let go.

But growing up under the weight of narcissistic manipulation leaves you with a broken compass. Love becomes a battlefield where you fight to prove your worth, to make someone stay, to rewrite a past that was never your fault. I stayed, believing my love could save us, but a broken and yearning heart knows no limits. And mine was willing to fight a war it never stood a chance of winning.

This moment was a blend of excitement and anxiety, yet it highlighted how differently we were raised and how those differences subtly shaped our relationship. Meeting his family was monumental for me—something that felt foreign but also incredibly healing. It was an opportunity to glimpse what it felt like to be surrounded by genuine love and acceptance, a stark contrast to the guarded and often manipulative environment I had grown up in.

The meeting with our chain of command was nerve-wracking, not because we had done anything wrong, but because my mind automatically defaulted to expecting trouble. I was always in a head space to brace for conflict or criticism, even when none was warranted. Sitting there, facing their speculation about our relationship, I was reminded of how much energy I had spent in my life trying to avoid being noticed for the wrong reasons. But their response wasn't punitive. They commended our professionalism, praised our work ethic, and allowed us to continue dating under the condition we maintained the same respect for our roles if the relationship didn't work out.

That moment, however small, felt significant. For once, I wasn't being punished or criticized for a choice I had made. Instead, we were treated with respect and trust. It made me reflect on how different the world could be outside the shadow of narcissistic control, where judgment is always harsh and love is always conditional.

As we packed our bags for the trip to meet his family, I was filled with hope. His mother, whom I had spoken to several times on the phone, was the epitome of warmth and love—traits I had craved my whole life. When I finally met her, she exceeded my expectations. Her kindness and genuine interest in me were so refreshing that it felt almost surreal. She didn't just accept me as her son's partner; she embraced me as the daughter she had never had.

Her excitement about me and her love for her son was palpable, and I couldn't help but envy the nurturing relationship they shared. Unlike my mother, who viewed me as a competition or a tool for her benefit, his mother celebrated him and supported him unconditionally. It was a bittersweet experience—both heartwarming and a reminder of the void in my own life.

Meeting his father, though different, carried its own set of emotions. My boyfriend's relationship with his dad mirrored the type of surface-level connection I had seen play out in my own family—detached and reserved, with deeper feelings left unspoken. His pride in introducing me was genuine, and the admiration in his eyes felt overwhelming. But even as his father made a casual joke, offering him a beer before driving, the unease was apparent. My boyfriend handled it gracefully, laughing it off, but the moment spoke volumes about the complexities in their bond.

Reflecting on it now, I see how much of our relationship was shaped by the wounds we carried. His parents, though vastly different from mine, had still left their marks on him in ways he hadn't fully reckoned with. And while I was experiencing what it felt like to be part of a loving family, my heart remained caught in the cycle of trying to rewrite the script my childhood had given me.

Growing up under such conditions causes you to question what love looks like and makes you hyperaware of what's missing in relationships. It teaches you to seek validation externally because you were never taught to validate yourself. Meeting his family allowed me to see what healthy love could be, but it also made me realize how unprepared I was to embrace it fully. My heart was still healing, and while I had found someone who genuinely loved me, I was still learning to love myself enough to accept it, and so was he.

This chapter of my life was a stark reminder of how the wounds from my childhood left me vulnerable to tolerating pain and confusion in relationships. Meeting his family was an incredible experience—it filled me with warmth and belonging I hadn't known before. Their love and acceptance overwhelmed me in the best way, as did the moments of laughter, shared culture, and genuine connection. Teaching his family the electric slide and hearing his grandfather's endless jokes were memories I'd cherish.

Yet, even amid joy, the shadows of my past and his demons cast a foreboding presence over our relationship.

When we returned to the hotel that evening, the person I fell for seemed to vanish. The alcohol from the celebration seemed to unleash a version of him that terrified me—a stark contrast to the man who had just paraded me around with pride. His shift was sudden and harsh, and while I didn't understand it, I knew I couldn't sleep beside him. Instead, I cried myself to sleep on the floor, too hurt and confused to process what had happened.

The next morning, he didn't even recall what transpired. His apology was heartfelt, laced with shame, and he promised to make it up to me. "I love you, mama. I'd never want to hurt you," he'd say, and for a time, I believed him. But these episodes became more frequent, escalating into verbal attacks that cut me deeper than any blow could.

He started using the most vulnerable pieces of myself—the traumas I had trusted him with—as weapons. The words he hurled at me weren't just cruel; they were calculated to inflict maximum damage. It was as though the safe space I thought I'd found was collapsing, and the walls of my childhood wounds were closing in on me.

Hearing him mock my abortion—a secret I had carried for years with shame and pain—broke me. It wasn't just about the words; it was the betrayal of someone I trusted with my story, someone who was supposed to protect my heart, not use it as ammunition. His cruel remarks about my mother, someone I had tried so hard not to become, only added salt to the wound.

This behavior was bewildering. It wasn't consistent with the man I had come to know and love, which made it harder to separate who he truly was from the version of him that hurt me. I started to question myself, wondering if I had done something to provoke this or if it was a reflection of my worth.

It's a cycle familiar to those who have grown up with narcissistic parents. Their love is conditional, their affection manipulative, and their cruelty disguised as concern. They gaslight you into questioning your reality until you believe you're the problem. Even though I had escaped my mother's clutches, her influence was still present in the way I viewed myself and in my tolerance for being treated this way.

In hindsight, I see how my upbringing primed me to accept behavior I should have walked away from. My relationship with him mirrored the unpredictability and volatility I had experienced growing up—one moment, I was adored and cherished, and the next, I was discarded and wounded. My heart had learned to cling to the moments of love and overlook the moments of pain because that was all I knew.

But there's a lesson here for anyone who's been in a similar situation: just because you've experienced love that hurts doesn't mean it's the only kind of love you deserve. Recognizing the patterns that bind you to toxic relationships is the first step in breaking free. I was still learning this lesson, but the seeds of awareness had been planted. And with time, I would learn to nurture those seeds and grow into a version of myself that demanded and received the love I truly deserved.

This part of my story was one of the most painful chapters in my life—a whirlwind of betrayal, violation, and emotional devastation. At the time, I was already navigating the complexities of loving someone who had slowly revealed his darker sides, yet I still held on to the hope that things could be different.

I'd walked in on betrayal—him in bed with another woman, a scene I can still picture vividly. It wasn't just the act itself but the series of events that followed. Instead of remorse, he added insult to injury by calling the cops and fabricating a story to paint himself as the victim. Standing outside, waiting for my best friend, I felt stripped of everything—my dignity, my safety, and even the car he'd bought to symbolize some twisted version of love.

Yet, this wasn't even the worst of it. Long before that, he'd committed an act I had buried deep inside, too ashamed and confused to process at the time. He had forced himself on me in one of my most vulnerable moments, ignoring my protests and my tears. That experience left me broken in ways I couldn't articulate, and its aftermath compounded the pain—an unplanned pregnancy.

Motherhood had always been something I dreamed of, but not like this, not under these circumstances. The joy I should have felt was drowned out by fear, shame, and heartbreak. I didn't know where to turn or what to do, but I decided to terminate the pregnancy. That choice, while mine, wasn't born from empowerment but from desperation and survival.

The experience at the clinic was isolating and agonizing. Walking past the protesters with their accusatory signs and loud voices made me feel even smaller. Inside, the silence was suffocating, except for the laughter of a few girls who didn't seem to grasp the weight of the moment. I felt so alone, sitting there with my heart in turmoil, wishing for a different life, a different partner, a different outcome.

When it was over, I didn't have time to process or grieve. Hours later, I was back in uniform, heading out to sea, expected to perform as if nothing had happened. That's the thing about trauma—it doesn't wait for you to catch your breath. It follows you, demanding to be carried even when you have no strength left.

Adding insult to injury, my vulnerability was betrayed. The person I confided in leaked my story to someone onboard who was jealous of me for reasons I couldn't understand. The news spread like wildfire, and the shame I carried privately was now public knowledge. Confronting her in a fit of rage, I decided to own my truth in the only way I knew how—to shout it for everyone to hear. "Yes, I had an abortion!" I screamed, my voice breaking with the weight of it all. In that moment, I reclaimed a small piece of myself, even if it was born out of pain and anger.

But the weight of that secret never fully lifted. I carried it quietly, never sharing the why or the how until now. That's why the words my boyfriend used against me hit me so deeply—they were calculated to wound me in a place I had worked so hard to bury.

In hindsight, I've come to understand that his cruelty wasn't about me. It was about his internal battle, his inability to deal with his issues, and the projection of his pain onto me. But at the time, it didn't feel like that. It felt like a continuation of the betrayal and abandonment I had experienced my whole life, as if I had been marked for suffering.

This experience was another harsh reminder of how the echoes of my childhood—the betrayal, the invalidation, the lack of safety—continued to shape my relationships. It's a pattern so many of us who've been wounded by narcissistic parents recognize. We confuse pain for love, mistaking the chaos for passion or normalcy because it's all we've known.

For anyone reading this who's been through similar trials, know this: your worth isn't determined by what others have done to you or the choices you've had to make to survive. Healing starts with owning your truth—not out of shame, but out of a recognition that your story, no matter how painful, deserves to be told. This chapter of my life was devastating, but it was also a turning point, pushing me to confront my pain and ultimately find a path to healing.

Chapter 21

This chapter of my life was an unraveling—both of his hidden struggles and of the hope I had clung to that we could build something solid and lasting. His habit of wearing hoodies in sweltering heat was the first red flag. At first, I chalked it up to his quirky personality, but the erratic behaviors that followed made it impossible to ignore. He would leave for the gym but never actually be there when I drove past. When I confronted him about it, he'd insist I had just missed him. His excuses were thin, yet I clung to them because I wanted so badly to believe him.

One evening, as I prepared dinner, he claimed he was off to the gym again. But I'd forgotten my bank card, which was with him, so I decided to catch up with him. When I arrived at the gym, his car wasn't there. I called, and he lied, telling me he was just leaving. I knew he wasn't. By the time I got back home, he was there, and when I pressed him, he continued to lie. I'd had enough. I told him I couldn't keep doing this unless he was willing to tell me the truth. I turned up the music in the car to drown out his denials, but in my peripheral vision, I saw him—sweating, fidgeting, hiding in that same hoodie despite the heat. My heart sank further.

When we stopped to grab food, he jumped out of the car to use the restroom. That's when my phone rang. A mutual friend called to share her suspicions about his involvement with drugs, mentioning she'd seen him hanging with people known for dealing. My stomach dropped. I felt nauseous and devastated. All the pieces started to fit—the lies, the behavior, the hoodie.

He came back to the car, and I tried to compose myself. As we went through the drive-thru, I reached for my wallet to pay, but he stopped me, pulling out a wad of cash from his hoodie. My heart shattered again. We never carried cash like that. I asked him where it came from, but he dodged the question. By the time we got home, I was furious, heartbroken, and overwhelmed. I needed answers.

While he was in the shower, I checked his phone. I'd never felt the need to invade his privacy before, but this wasn't about suspicion anymore; it was about survival—ours. The messages I found confirmed my worst fears. He was buying drugs. My heart broke for him, for the bright man I loved who was now consumed by something so dark. But I also felt like a failure. Was I not enough? Could I have done more to save him?

Drunk and high, he walked out, and I followed, desperate to pull him back. I grabbed at him and begged him not to go. "You're better than this! Please, don't do this to us," I cried, my voice cracking under the weight of my despair. He pushed me away so hard that my shirt and bra tore. I stood there, exposed, not just physically but emotionally raw and broken. I fought to take his keys, to stop him from driving off, but he grabbed my phone and smashed it against the curb.

"This is the problem!" I screamed, throwing a beer can he'd been holding. "This and the damn pills! Really? This is what you've come to?" The can hit him, splitting his nose. I froze as he turned and stormed off, leaving me standing in the parking lot—bare, bruised, and beaten by the realization that I couldn't save him.

It was a mindset I knew all too well—one rooted in my childhood, where I had learned to take responsibility for others' pain. I thought if I just loved him enough and fought hard enough, I could bring him back to the man I knew he could be. But this was bigger than me. As I stood there under the dim, flickering streetlights, my chest heaved with silent sobs, tears carving tracks down my face. The ache in my heart was unbearable, a throbbing pulse of desperation that drowned out my pain. I couldn't stop the overwhelming need to save him—even if it meant sacrificing pieces of myself I might never get back.

I felt stripped of everything: my pride, my safety, my voice. The night air pressed heavily against my exposed skin, the remnants of my torn shirt clinging to me like a cruel reminder of how far things had spiraled. It didn't matter that I was standing in the middle of the parking lot, vulnerable and humiliated; all I could think about was him, driving off with his demons, further away from me, further away from himself.

I wanted to scream at the stars above, to beg for something—anything—to bring him back to me whole. But all that came out were muffled cries of "Please... please, don't do this to us." My voice sounded foreign, hollow, and cracked, a faint echo swallowed by the night.

I hated what was happening to him, but even more, I hated what it was doing to me. My spirit, once so full of hope and fight, felt like it was unraveling thread by thread, and yet I clung to the frayed edges, desperate to weave him back into the light.

There were countless moments after that, each one a fresh wound on my already scarred soul. I remember being dragged out of his car in the middle of traffic, my knees scraping the asphalt as bystanders watched, their faces a mix of pity and discomfort. No one stepped in. He left me there on the road, humiliated and abandoned.

There was the time he gripped the steering wheel with white knuckles, his foot pressing the gas pedal to the floor as we sped down the highway. "I'll end us both," he hissed, his eyes wild and unrecognizable. The speedometer climbed to a number meant to kill us. I clutched the seat, praying for mercy—not for me, but for him, because I believed I was already beyond saving.

He called me out of my name so many times that I started to forget my own. The slurs, the insults, the venom laced in his voice—they played on repeat in my head like a tape I couldn't eject. Spit flew from his mouth, sometimes landing on me but always soaking into the fragile pieces of my self-worth.

Each moment chipped away at me, but I clung to the belief that I deserved it all. My mother's words echoed louder than my thoughts, haunting me like a ghost I couldn't exorcise. *If your parents don't love you, why would anyone else?* She had said. And I believed her. I let her words shape my worth, reducing me to nothing more than what they told me I was.

I clung to him as if he were the only lifeline keeping me from drowning, even as he was the very weight pulling me under. I thought I had hit rock bottom so many times, but each time, I discovered there was still further to fall. Rock bottom wasn't a place—it was a state of utter emptiness, and I wasn't even there yet.

A broken and deprived heart doesn't let go easily. It holds on with trembling hands and desperate hope, believing that if it just tries harder, loves more, and sacrifices more, it can somehow fill the void. I didn't see that in trying to save him; I was slowly losing myself. I was pouring what little I had left of me into someone else, all the while starving for the love I was so desperately giving away.

The Halloween party was supposed to be fun—a moment of escape, a chance to embrace the holiday I loved so much. I had begged him to go, pouring my excitement into planning the perfect costumes: Austin Powers and Foxy Cleopatra. We nailed it. He was hilarious, fully in character, and basking in the compliments from our friends. For a moment, it felt like everything was right. He was so proud to have me on his arm, like a prize he couldn't stop showing off.

But good moments never lasted long with him.

When he disappeared to the restroom, I thought nothing of it. But when he was gone longer than usual, I went to check on him, laughing as I asked, "Are you okay, baby?" His response was a slap of reality that echoed through the house. "Get off me, bitch!" he snapped, his face twisted, his voice laced with venom. The room froze. The demon in him had surfaced, and everyone saw it.

Friends rushed to smooth things over, insisting he didn't mean it, that he was drunk and just needed to cool off. They didn't know the truth. They didn't see the shadows of what I endured behind closed doors.

I didn't argue. I just wanted to leave. I grabbed my things and stormed out. But before I could make it to safety, chaos erupted on the lawn. He was in the middle of a fight, and the cops were on their way. I cried, apologizing to the host, just wanting to disappear.

I made my way to his car to collect my belongings, but as I leaned in, he jumped behind the wheel and took off, the engine roaring and tires screeching. I barely had time to pull my legs inside. "Stop the damn car! Let me out!" I screamed, banging on the dashboard. He didn't even flinch.

Instead, he grabbed the back of my neck with one hand, the other still on the wheel, and smashed my head into the parking brake. My face was buried in his lap, and I could hear his cruel, mocking voice above the chaos. "You done yet, bitch? Huh?! Are you fucking done?"

Tears streamed down my face, but I fought back. When I managed to lift myself, I lashed out in desperation, punching and clawing, trying to get him to stop the car. But he was too far gone—drunk, high, and unfeeling.

Somehow, he drove us back to base. I stayed quiet, trembling, my body throbbing in pain. I just wanted to get to my car and escape. The rain was pouring when he parked, and I thought maybe it was over. But then he snatched my phone and stormed out of the car.

I scrambled after him, pleading for my lifeline. He turned on me in the darkness, grabbing me and slamming me into a puddle. My head hit the asphalt with a sickening thud. Everything went black.

When I came to, the rain was soaking through my clothes, pooling around me as I lay helpless in the cold. I saw him standing above me, but not to help. He stepped over me, slammed his car door, and walked inside without a glance back.

I was alone, drenched and broken, struggling to lift myself from the ground. Then, as if by divine intervention, I saw his phone under my car. My shaking hands grabbed it, a small victory in the wreckage of the night.

I crawled into my car, barely able to see through my tears. I dialed the number of a close friend who lived on base. My voice cracked as I tried to explain, the words coming out in broken sobs. "Where are you? Meet me," he said, his voice steady and urgent.

I drove to his barracks, my body trembling and my mind unraveling. When he saw me, he didn't ask questions. He just pulled me into his arms, holding me tight as I cried into his chest. For the first time that night, I felt safe. He drove to gather more of our friends to help me collect my things. My chest was tight with dread and humiliation. The thought of them seeing the chaos I had been living in made me sick, but I had no other choice.

When we arrived at the room, we found him sprawled out on an empty mattress, unconscious, as if the destruction he had caused didn't exist. The sight of him there, so careless and detached, sent a wave of fury through me. I stormed in, tears already burning my eyes, and in my hurt and rage, I grabbed the edge of the mattress, trying to yank it from under him to wake him up to the mess he'd made—not just in the room, but in my life.

He stirred, disheveled, and out of it as if he didn't even recognize where he was. The guys tried to talk him down, their voices calm but firm, asking him to give me space and hand over my phone. He sat up slowly, his face unreadable, and reached for it.

"He's going to break it, like he always does," I whispered, half to myself, my voice shaking.

True to form, he dangled the phone in front of me, teasing me like a child begging for a toy. Then, with one swift motion, he slammed it against the edge of the dresser, over and over, until the screen shattered and the pieces fell into his hand. He extended the ruined phone toward me, smirking as if to say, *Here's your prize.*

The sight of it—the broken phone in my trembling hands, the mocking look on his face—made my stomach churn. Before I could react, he turned his rage on the flat-screen TV, slamming his fist into it with such force that the screen split in half, jagged cracks webbing across it.

I couldn't hold it in anymore. I screamed, my chest heaving with sobs, and ran for the door. On my way out, I grabbed the nearest thing—an innocent plastic cup filled with red juice—and slapped it against the wall with all the force I had left. The juice splattered everywhere, crimson streaks marking the white walls like a silent scream.

I couldn't take it anymore. My heart, my mind, my spirit—I was completely and utterly broken.

Things began to unravel at work when he didn't show up that morning. His absence sent waves through the crew, and naturally, they came to me, the closest thing to him. Questions bombarded me—*Where is he? What happened? Did you hear from him?*—their concern sharpened my already frayed nerves. Others had even called all the hospitals in the area, desperate to locate him, but still, there was no word.

Then whispers began to filter through: he had made it aboard, but his face was a mess. Some crew members, who likely had seen more than they let on, joked under their breath, "She finally snapped on you after all you've done to her, huh?" My stomach churned hearing their remarks, the mix of relief and shame nearly suffocating me.

But I didn't know he had made it to work, not at first. By then, I had already been pulled into the office for questioning. As I sat there, my mind raced—fear, guilt, and anger intertwined in a chaotic dance. But something in me broke open at that moment. I couldn't keep hiding anymore. The weight of it all was unbearable, and I found myself spilling everything. Every bruise, every scream, every shattered piece of myself—I laid it all out.

A military protective order was issued, not just against him but also for me, to keep me away from him for my good. It should have been a lifeline, a chance to reclaim some part of myself. But the heart is a stubborn thing, and despite the legal barriers and the whispered warnings from friends, he reeled me back in repeatedly.

The cycle continued. He slashed the tires on my brand-new car, a petty retaliation in one of his drunken, rage-filled fits. He came to harass my roommate, pounding on the door and demanding keys he accused me of stealing—only to find them misplaced once he sobered up from yet another high.

My roommate, my best friend, tried so hard to talk sense into me, to remind me of my worth. But how could she when I couldn't see it myself? Her words bounced off the hollow shell I had become; her hope was a painful contrast to the hopelessness I felt.

Then came the day I found out I was pregnant. Another moment in the toxic whirlwind of making up and breaking up, another layer to the chaos. I wanted to be excited. I *should* have been excited. But instead, I was overwhelmed by heartbreak, by the deep disappointment in myself and how far I'd fallen.

When I told his mother, his reaction surprised me. He was thrilled, determined to keep the baby, and, for once, seemed genuinely committed to getting himself together. "You deserve to be excited about this," he told me, his voice filled with rare tenderness. "You've wanted this for so long, to be a mother. You've just been waiting for the right person."

I wanted to believe him, but fear wrapped itself around my heart. This time, though, I promised myself something different. No man, not even him, would dictate my decision about the life I carried. I would see it through, with or without him.

As the weeks passed, I began to embrace the idea of becoming a mother fully. He was scheduled to deploy, and I was to be transferred to another command due to the pregnancy. Before leaving, he planned something grand—something I never expected.

He gathered our families together at his home, including my parents. I had no idea what he was planning, but the moment came when he dropped to one knee, ring in hand, and asked me to marry him. I cried, overwhelmed by a mix of emotions: hope, fear, and a cautious flicker of belief that maybe, just maybe, this could be the turning point.

The room erupted in celebration. My father had even been asked for his blessing, and in a fleeting moment, I felt a glimmer of possibility. Maybe this child, this fresh start, could bring out the man I had always hoped he'd become.

But even in that moment of joy, my mother found a way to steal the spotlight. Her fake tears of happiness felt hollow, her theatrical announcement of her crying nothing more than a ploy for attention. "Oh, stop crying, stop crying," she said, her voice loud enough for everyone to hear. It was as if she needed to remind everyone that *she* was a part of this, too. I saw through her façade the same way I always had, and yet, I let it slide. There was too much chaos already.

It was a beautiful day of celebration, one that felt like a rare glimpse of happiness amidst the chaos. I told myself I owed it to the life growing within me to try—to give this new chapter a chance to work. My fiancé had planned a continued surprise: a trip to the mountains with my parents to keep the celebration going. The serene beauty of the scenery, the crisp mountain air, and the laughter we shared made me feel hopeful, if only for a moment.

But with my mother, nothing peaceful ever lasted long.

The joy of the day unraveled when her infidelities made yet another grand appearance. We had decided to do a courthouse wedding back home—a practical decision since he was due to deploy soon. The financial benefits for newlyweds in the military offered a small relief, and we told ourselves we'd have a proper wedding later.

As we prepared, I asked my mother if I could use her laptop to look up courthouse details and requirements. What I found instead was a flood of things I didn't want to see, as usual. This time, though, my fiancé bore witness to it all. My embarrassment was unbearable.

Had it just been me, I would've quietly closed the laptop and moved on. My father's cycle was predictable—he would find out, rage, and then take her back. The same toxic pattern I had subconsciously inherited in my relationships. But now my fiancé was seeing it, and I couldn't hide it from him.

This is the hallmark of narcissistic parents: their actions rarely stay hidden forever. In time, their manipulative and self-centered behavior inevitably leaks out, leaving their children to clean up the mess or carry the shame. Narcissistic parents are notorious for undermining boundaries, demanding loyalty, and creating chaos. Their children often find themselves in impossible situations—either complicit in protecting their parent's façade or ostracized for exposing the truth.

Questions followed, and I tried to explain. He had some idea of who my mother was, but I had always craved normalcy—especially in his presence. He came from such a functional family, with an incredible mother who radiated warmth and care. I had longed for that kind of example my whole life. We talked it over and tried to let it rest, but I knew it wasn't over.

Hours later, while stopping at a gas station on the way home, it resurfaced. He was pumping gas, and my father was distracted, busy washing their car. My mother came over to my passenger-side window with a sly grin, acting as if nothing was amiss. She handed me a piece of paper, a phone number scribbled across it.

I froze.

It was the number of a man I'd seen explicit photos and videos of earlier on her laptop, a lover she'd been entertaining while my father remained oblivious. She had no idea I already knew, and now she was dragging me into her mess.

"Can you text him for me?" she whispered, pressing me with urgency. "Just send him a picture of me, you, and your fiancé to prove I'm not with your father."

I stared at her in disbelief, my stomach turning. *Not again.*

"No," I said firmly, anger surging in my chest. "I want no part of your nonsense."

It wasn't just her request—it was everything. The way she could never let me have my moment. Here I was, pregnant and newly engaged, and somehow, she had to make it about her. She handed me a small box with a gift from her lover—earrings meant to sweeten her twisted ploy. I threw them aside, disgusted.

Narcissistic parents often undermine their children's milestones, whether intentionally or subconsciously, because they cannot tolerate being outshined or out of control. They create drama, redirect attention, and insert themselves into the narrative as if they are the stars. This can leave their children feeling robbed of joy and, worse, guilty for wanting to protect their boundaries.

I didn't say a word to my father at that moment. What was there to say? I had spent my entire life watching him ignore her betrayals, taking her back as if it was his duty to endure her lies. It felt pointless to stir the pot, especially on a day meant for celebration.

I smiled, hugged everyone goodbye, and climbed into the car with my fiancé. As we drove away, I stared out the window, feeling the weight of it all pressing down on me. The exhaustion of constantly trying to rise above her chaos. The sadness of knowing she would always find a way to steal joy from my most precious moments.

But this time, it was different. I wasn't just carrying the burden for myself anymore—I was carrying it for the life growing inside me.

We spent our last hours together before his deployment in a hotel, freshly married from the courthouse ceremony. It was bittersweet, but I was content, even through the sickness that had me weak and nauseous. He doted on me, tending to my every need as if trying to ease the weight of the baby growing inside me and the life we were stepping into. For a brief moment, I let myself believe we might be okay.

He slipped out, saying he needed to grab a few things to help my morning sickness. I didn't think much of it; he was thoughtful like that when he wanted to be. But as time ticked on and exhaustion took over, I fell asleep, expecting to wake to the comfort of him beside me.

When I woke and found the bed still empty, my heart began to pound, each beat screaming louder than the last. I told myself not to panic, not to jump to conclusions. But I couldn't shake the memories—the demons that clung to him like a shadow, always waiting to resurface.

I grabbed my phone and checked his account, a move I hated but had learned was sometimes necessary. A large withdrawal glared back at me, its weight crushing my chest. My mind raced, my stomach churned, and all I could do was pray. *Please, God, not now. Not when I'm carrying his child.*

When he returned, I said nothing. But my tears betrayed me, pooling in my eyes, begging for answers my lips couldn't form. He saw them, and his face twisted into a mask of guilt and panic. His excuses came quickly—too quickly. Something about running into someone or being delayed by the line at the store. But the store was just down the street, and I knew. Deep down, I already knew.

He bolted to the bathroom, escaping behind the shower curtain as if it could shield him from the truth. I wasn't having it. I stormed in after him, ripping the curtain aside with all the fury and heartbreak I felt.

"Now there's nothing to hide behind!" I screamed, my voice breaking under the weight of my pain. "I won't let you lie to me. I am your wife! I am the mother of your child! Tell me the truth. Where were you? Where is the money? Please don't tell me you used it for pills. *Please!*"

My voice cracked as I sobbed, every word tearing through me. He couldn't lie anymore. His shoulders slumped, his face crumbled, and he confessed. The weight of his words hit me like a freight train, and I collapsed into myself, weeping from a place so deep it felt endless.

He dressed quickly, shame hanging over him like a storm cloud, and left without another word. That was how we ended our time together before he deployed—broken, raw, and unsure of how we'd ever piece this back together.

In a way, his deployment was a relief. It meant he'd be far from temptation, far from the demons that consumed him. Maybe he could heal. Maybe he could come back as the man I knew he could be, the father our child deserved. But it also meant I'd be alone for the pregnancy, carrying the weight of it all on my own.

Outside of his mother, who showed me nothing but love and support, I would face this journey alone. Yet even her kindness couldn't prepare me for what was coming in the months ahead. Nothing could.

Chapter 22

I waited for his calls while he was away. Every ring felt like a lifeline, a tether to the man I hoped would come back better, stronger, and ready to face the life we were building. I was so desperate not to miss a single moment with him that I tied my phone to my headscarf at night, letting the vibration stir me from sleep. Anyone who's been on this side of things—whether in uniform or as the spouse of someone serving—knows the weight those calls carry. They become everything.

But with each call came the heavy baggage of his stress, and it wasn't long before even those lifelines felt suffocating. I had poured myself into making a home for us, a cozy space where we could finally find some peace. I even dedicated a room to him, crafting it into a man cave he could be proud of. Late into the night, I would paint and decorate, imagining the smile it might bring to his face when he returned.

But instead of joy, I was met with suspicion. Every ounce of happiness in my voice became a target for his insecurities. "Why do you sound so happy? Why are you still awake?" he would ask, his tone laced with accusation. And yet, I tried to brush it off, chalking it up to the distance, the stress, the demons I was so used to accommodating.

I kept busy, careful not to push my body too far as my pregnancy progressed. But nothing could prepare me for the day I went to the doctor and heard the silence where my child's heartbeat should have been. That sound—or rather, the absence of it—shattered me in ways I can't even begin to put into words.

Grieving the loss of my child without my husband by my side felt like a punishment I couldn't escape. I was alone, completely and utterly alone. I picked up the phone and called my parents, choking out the words through sobs that felt like they were ripping me apart.

My father, as always, tried to comfort me. He was the spokesperson for my mother's silence. "She can't come," he said, trying to sound sympathetic. "You know your mother can't be on the road. She has a heart problem, and it isn't what it used to be, and I have to work. She wants to be there, but she just can't."

I knew better. I always knew better. My mother had all the time in the world for her chaos, her selfishness, her endless excuses. But when her daughter needed her most, she somehow found a way to turn her absence into another cruel stab. She wasn't coming, not for me, not for her grandchild.

I called my mother-in-law, breaking the news to her through my tears. Within hours, she was on the road, driving across states to be by my side. No excuses. No hesitation. Just love.

"My son would kill me if I wasn't there for you, sweetie," she said, her voice a balm to my shattered heart. She even offered to pick up my mother on the way, driving through her state, just to eliminate any barrier. I hesitated but agreed, thinking maybe—just maybe—my mother would rise to the occasion.

But, of course, she didn't. She never did. Instead, she drove the knife in deeper, choosing to abandon me once again when I needed her the most. It wasn't just her absence that hurt; it was her choice. A choice to leave me drowning in my grief, knowing full well that she could have been the lifeline I desperately needed.

I walked into the hospital that day alone, my heart heavy but holding onto a sliver of hope. I knew my mother-in-law was on her way, and she had assured me that my so-called mother would be with her. But when my mother-in-law finally arrived, the truth hit me like a blow: my mother had ditched me. Again.

In my mind, I knew why. It was always the same. She had likely found some man to occupy her time, to feed her endless need for validation, and had chosen that over her daughter. It wasn't surprising, but it still hurt. Yet, despite her absence, my heart swelled with gratitude when I saw my mother-in-law step into the room. And right behind her was my twin brother.

He hadn't come as a replacement for my mother—he had planned to be there regardless. When my mother bailed, he took the opportunity to ride with my mother-in-law, ensuring he could still be by my side. That selfless act, that unwavering support, was everything I needed in that moment.

Getting to the operating room was one of the hardest things I've ever done. Every step felt like I was dragging the weight of a lifetime of disappointment and grief. A pastor came to sit with me, prayed over me, and tried to comfort me in a way that felt genuine, even if my pain was too immense for his words to fully reach.

I don't remember much after being put to sleep. But waking up to the faces of my mother-in-law and brother, full of love and concern, was the only comfort I could cling to. My brother, ever the quiet protector, watched over me nervously, his presence steady and grounding. They say twins can feel each other's pain, and at that moment, I knew it was true. He wasn't just there physically—he was carrying this pain with me, sharing it in a way only he could.

But the comfort of their love was tainted by what I would learn later. My mother, in her predictable cruelty, had spread vile rumors about me. She told people that my fiancé had punched me in the stomach and caused me to lose my child. Worse still, she said I deserved it. That God doesn't honor disrespectful children—her twisted interpretation of my setting boundaries with her. That I would never be a mother. That I was reaping exactly what I deserved.

This was more than just abandonment; it was an attack on the most vulnerable moment of my life. Narcissistic parents like her thrive on control, and when they lose it—when their children dare to break free—they retaliate in the cruelest ways imaginable. For them, boundaries are not a healthy assertion of self but a personal affront, a challenge to their fragile egos.

This behavior is classic narcissistic abuse: gaslighting others to control the narrative, weaponizing your pain against you, and projecting their flaws and insecurities onto you. It's about power, about ensuring that even in your most broken state, they can still claim dominion over your emotions.

For anyone who has faced this, let me tell you: their actions are not a reflection of your worth. Their cruelty stems from their brokenness, not yours. You have every right to set boundaries, to demand respect, and to grieve your pain without their shadow looming over you. And though they may never admit it, your strength in breaking free is proof of their ultimate failure to control you.

Chapter 23

The loss of a child broke me in ways I never thought possible. Delivering the news to my husband, who was deployed and unable to come home, made the pain even more unbearable. I felt like a failure as a woman, convinced that my inability to carry a child full term was somehow my fault. It shattered him, too—I could hear it in his voice, the silence that lingered after I told him. And as I sat with my pain, I wondered if this loss pushed him further into his downward spiral. The guilt consumed me as if I hadn't already been carrying enough of it.

Deep down, I blamed myself. I thought something was wrong with me, as though I were defective. I beat myself up endlessly, but life offered no reprieve. There was no space to sit and grieve, no time to process. Uncle Sam demanded I keep moving forward, and I was well accustomed to shoving my feelings down. My upbringing had already conditioned me to believe my emotions didn't matter. Growing up with my evil mother and our dysfunctional family dynamics taught me to suppress my needs and always prioritize others.

I couldn't sit with my pain—it was too much, too loud. Instead, I tried to channel it into action, fixing things as I always did. I became obsessed with making it up to my husband, even though the loss wasn't my fault. I wanted to make him happy, to fill the void that we both felt but couldn't quite name. So, I threw myself into planning a wedding ceremony for when he returned. Maybe, I thought, if we had that moment—if we drew closer together—we'd be able to heal. Maybe we could try again for a little one.

My mother-in-law, ever the loving force in my life, was on board from the start. She was ready to help in any way, as always. But I wanted to take it all on myself. I coordinated everything, from the decorations to my bouquet to the invitations. Every detail was a labor of love, a desperate attempt to make things right, even when there was nothing to be fixed.

Yet, as I poured my heart into the preparations, I should've known it wouldn't go smoothly. The cracks in my plan started to show, beginning with the one person who always seemed to steal the spotlight: my mother.

The loss of a child is an unimaginable grief, and for women, it often comes with a heavy layer of societal expectations. Many feel pressure to internalize the loss, blaming themselves for what is, in reality, beyond their control. For those with a history of growing up in dysfunctional families, this grief can be compounded by unresolved wounds. Narcissistic parents teach their children that their emotions don't matter, conditioning them to put others first while neglecting their own needs.

This dynamic often leads to a pattern of overcompensation—working tirelessly to "fix" situations or people to earn love, approval, or a sense of worth. But healing doesn't come from perfection or sacrifice. It comes from allowing yourself to grieve, to feel the depths of your pain, and to acknowledge that your worth isn't tied to anyone else's happiness.

If you're carrying the weight of a loss like this, know that you are not alone. Grieving is a necessary part of healing, and it's okay to take time for yourself. You don't need to fix everything or everyone. You just need to honor your feelings and give yourself the grace you so freely offer others.

The anticipation of my husband's arrival was almost unbearable. I had planned everything to perfection—his tux, the house, the wedding itself. All that was left was my dress, the one detail that was supposed to make me feel like a radiant bride. I brought my mother along, naively hoping for even a sliver of support from her on this important day.

Excited, I stepped into my first choice. I walked out of the dressing room, praying for her approval, her smile, and her acknowledgment of how beautiful I felt at that moment. Instead, her eyes betrayed her. She didn't look at me with pride or joy; she looked through me, cold and detached, her gaze fixated on another bride in the store who was surrounded by her supportive entourage.

When I asked for her thoughts, she didn't even respond to me. She complimented the other bride instead, the envy dripping from her voice. My heart shattered right there. As if to add insult to injury, she began complaining about a sudden headache, saying she didn't know how much longer she could endure sitting through this.

I felt the sting of humiliation and disappointment wash over me. I rushed back to the dressing room, where the consultant, a stranger, gave me the kindness my mother couldn't. She embraced me as the tears I had been holding back fell freely, her words of reassurance cutting through the fog of pain. "You look beautiful," she said, apologizing for the actions of someone she didn't even know but could somehow understand. She suggested I return with a close friend instead, someone who would celebrate this moment with me.

I pulled myself together, and we went home. I did come back, as the consultant suggested, but it wasn't the same. The magic was gone. I didn't want to try on another dress or sift through options. I just wanted to get it over with. I bought the same dress I had tried on before, my heart too heavy to care about finding "the one."

It should have been a joyful, unforgettable moment. But like so many others, it was stolen by my mother's envy, her inability to allow me even a moment of happiness without making it about her. I didn't feel like a bride that day. I felt small, insignificant, and unworthy of the joy that should have been mine.

This moment is a painful example of how narcissistic parents can turn even the most joyous milestones into sources of hurt and invalidation. Their envy and inability to celebrate their child's happiness often stem from their deep insecurities. For a narcissistic parent, attention directed anywhere other than themselves feels like a threat. They lash out, whether subtly or overtly, to regain control or shift the focus back onto them.

For children of narcissistic parents, these stolen moments can leave lasting scars. It's easy to internalize the message that your happiness isn't valid or that you're undeserving of love and support. But here's the truth: their actions are not a reflection of your worth.

If you've experienced this, know that you're not alone. Lean on those who truly celebrate you, even if they're not the people you expected them to be. And remember, your joy and milestones are worth protecting, even if it means excluding those who can't show up for you in the way you deserve.

The day he came home was supposed to be the kind of moment they write about in love stories. My heart raced as I waited at the pier, surrounded by my girlfriends, who were just as excited as I was to welcome him back. The emotion hit me like a wave the moment I saw him step off that ship—love, relief, and the unresolved grief of the child we lost. My tears fell freely as I threw my arms around him, holding on like I'd never let go.

When we arrived at our new place, I was filled with pride. Every detail, from the decorations in the front yard to the door, screamed that the man I loved was finally home. I wanted the world to know, even if he wasn't one for attention. He didn't say much, but I saw it in his eyes—that he loved how loudly I loved him, even if he didn't know how to show it back.

But as much as I wanted to believe this was a new beginning, the shadows of our loss loomed over us. He never spoke about it—not the sonogram on the nightstand that I couldn't part with, not the nights I cried myself to sleep beside him. He carried his grief in silence, letting it fester alongside the pain and demons he'd been wrestling long before I ever met him.

At first, it was subtle. The nights he'd fall asleep next to me, and I'd wake to find his side of the bed soaked with sweat, something that was so unlike him. He started getting sick—on and off, nothing I could pin down, but enough to leave me restless, staring at the ceiling, worrying while he slept. I couldn't shake the feeling that something was wrong, something much deeper than what I could see.

And just as always, life had a way of forcing the truth to the surface—sooner and harsher than I ever could've imagined.

The week of our wedding should have been filled with love and joy, but instead, it turned into a nightmare I'll never forget. Our family gathered at our home—everyone but my father and his stepfather. My mother-in-law, with her calming presence, balanced out the tension my mother brought into every room she entered. The excitement I felt quickly turned into dread that night.

After everyone settled in, my husband and I went to our room, but something shifted in him. The mood changed so fast that I didn't know what hit me. An argument erupted out of nowhere, and before I could even piece together what was happening, he stormed into the closet, slamming the door behind him. I heard shuffling, cursing—then silence. When I opened the door, my world stopped.

There he was, a gun cocked and pointed at my face.

"Get the fuck out!" he screamed, turning the gun to his head.

I froze. My heart pounded so loud I could barely hear his words. Fear gripped me so tightly I could hardly breathe. Somehow, I found the strength to run, bolting to his mother. I couldn't go back in there, but she did—fearless and full of love. She talked him down, disarmed him, and locked the gun away. For a moment, I felt like I could breathe again. But deep down, I knew this was only the beginning.

Nothing about our wedding week or day went right. Losing a child and dealing with my toxic mother—already felt unbearable. How could things get worse? But life found a way to show me.

The night before our wedding, we went our separate ways to celebrate with friends. I spent the night laughing with my girlfriends, feeling like maybe I could have one night of normalcy. I had no idea what awaited me.

I woke to water splashing on my face, my friends shaking me awake, their panicked voices telling me my husband was dead. The words hit me like a freight train. My heart shattered, and I fought to sober up, tears already streaming down my face. They got me into the car, but when we reached the hospital, I couldn't take another step. At the entrance, I collapsed, crying and broken.

My father-in-law caught me before I hit the ground and carried me inside. He brought me to my husband's room, where wires and machines surrounded him. I stared at him, alive but fragile, and all I could do was ask, "What is going on with you?"

Later, I would learn the truth—he had overdosed on heroin and flatlined twice, I never read the discharge papers that night. I was too focused on caring for him, and at the time, I thought it was a suicide attempt, another cry for help I didn't know how to answer. My mind spiraled, blaming myself for everything. No matter how much I tried to love him, to hold onto our world, it all felt like it was slipping away. I had nothing left for myself—not love, not grace, not forgiveness. Just the overwhelming sense that I was drowning in a life I couldn't control.

From the moment trouble started to creep in that week, I should have called it all off. But I didn't. I was too busy trying to please everyone else. I cared more about the effort people had made to come together, to show up for us, than about the wreckage I was walking through inside. I put on that mask I'd perfected over the years and forced myself to go through the motions, even when every part of me screamed to stop. The night I lost my husband twice—the night that should've been mine, our day—was the night I stayed awake, watching over him in bed. I was physically there, but my mind and heart were miles away.

I dozed off, then woke to find he had left, slipping away to church alone. I wanted to believe it was him trying to make up for his past, but now, looking back, I see it wasn't just the addiction; it was his guilt, his demons. And nothing about that day felt like mine. I was empty. I was hollow. I was there, but not really there—drained, depressed, struggling to breathe.

I looked at the dress I had picked out hanging in front of me. Beautiful, sure. But it felt wrong. Everything felt wrong. I had chosen that dress, but even the way I'd chosen it was drowned in regret. It wasn't what I deserved. I thought it was, but now I know it wasn't. I forced myself up and realized my mother had gone to the salon—the same one she was supposed to go to with my sister the day before. Because of her, my father had to drive me to the church, picking her up first. And my sister? Her hair was still undone. The one person I needed—my mother—had me waiting for her, making me hours late for my wedding.

The phone calls came, people were leaving the church, and I couldn't blame them. My father, trying to lift me, held my hand as we drove, but his efforts felt useless. When she wasn't around, it was like a spell had lifted, and I could breathe again. But the moment she walked out, she was all smiles, as if nothing was wrong. And then, as if she couldn't let me have anything, she took flowers from my bouquet and shoved them into my sister's hair. I had paid for them both to have their hair done, and I was speechless, lost in that betrayal.

I dreaded pulling up to the church. In my heart, all I wanted was to run away, crawl into a dark corner, and cry. But I couldn't. I had to keep that mask on for the people who had shown up for me. The thought of letting them down—of showing them my brokenness—was just too much to bear. Even if by trying to make them happy, I was killing myself inside.

The front doors of the church were already closed when we arrived, just like they'd been instructed to. The only way in was through the crowd, with my father holding his jacket over me, trying to shield me from their eyes. I was mortified. I was humiliated. But I didn't let it show. I kept it together, walked in, and heard later that I never looked up. I couldn't. My father, who was supposed to be standing by my side, wasn't even in his tux. He didn't agree with this wedding—after finding out about the gun incident but had no clue about all of the other things I had kept from him all this time. And there he was, at the end of the aisle, my husband, smiling like nothing had happened, as if everything was fine.

And then there was my mother-in-law, too tired and too sad to even wear her dress. I should've been planning a funeral, but instead, I was forced to pretend, to celebrate like I was happy, when all I could feel was this overwhelming sadness, this ache.

And even in the middle of all that pain, my mother had to steal the spotlight. As my husband and I exchanged vows, she grabbed the mic, went to the front, and pretended to be choked up. But then, out of nowhere, she started shouting, falling to the ground as if the Holy Ghost had overtaken her. I couldn't even look at her. I was boiling with rage, my grip on my husband tightening, tears burning in my eyes. The pastor asked me if I was okay, but I was so far gone in that moment, the only thing that made me crack a smile was a baby crying from the chaos she caused. It was the only thing that snapped me out of my trance.

Later, we had some time before the reception, and my husband wanted to parade me through the mall, proud of his bride. I knew it was a genuine gesture, his way of trying to make me smile. We were beautiful, they said. People thought we were models walking through the mall, advertising some bridal stores. For a brief second, I forgot the weight of the day, the pain gnawing at me from the inside. But then, I remembered. And the smile I had put on for everyone else faded.

At the reception, I threw myself into every conversation, every laugh, every smile, trying to mask the pain, trying to make sure no one felt what I felt. But my mother—she couldn't leave it alone. The daddy-daughter dance—she couldn't stand to see us happy. I was the other woman in her eyes, and she came to the dance floor, pretending to share the moment with us. And to top it off, she wore white. The same as me.

I was suffocating. And yet, I smiled.

She had laid her groundwork from the beginning of the word wedding. To include the night before the wedding, before things took a fatal turn with my husband that night. She invited the cousin who had molested me since a little girl to my house to top it off while I was out with my girls. I got wind from my husband, who had never met him but asked their name and immediately told him to get out. My grandmother, standing with him, left too and left me hanging for my wedding.

I would later come to find that it was my mother's doing through one of my cousins who said that my mother told them that I insisted that he'd come. My mother told them to come and that I would need to eventually get over it because we are family. That famous line kept me in mental bondage for so long and created the self-harming people pleasing martyr for love. So I was over her just as much as I was today and ready to leave, and I did just that, away for our honeymoon.

Chapter 24

The honeymoon was as nightmarish as the wedding—I was sitting alone in a cramped cabin on a ship while my husband drank himself into oblivion every night. I was draped in the beautiful dress I'd picked for this special time, yet I lay sobbing on our bed, drowning in heartbreak, as he turned the bar into his sanctuary. When we returned home, he spiraled. His health plummeted, and in desperation, I called his mother, who confirmed my worst fears—he was using heroin.

The morning she came to help, my world cracked open. I was pulling myself together to head to base when she told me he had been shooting up *ten times a day*. He'd even stolen our wedding gift money to feed his addiction. Her words burned through me, but I didn't even have time to process them. I had to leave for work. The weight of it all hit me like a freight train when I got there. Alone in the bathroom, I collapsed, wailing into the tile, my screams echoing off the walls. "OH GOD, MY HUSBAND IS A FUCKING HEROIN ADDICT!"

Coworkers rushed in, lifting me from the cold floor, their arms warm and comforting. Still, the truth I'd hidden for so long now lay bare before my superior as I sobbed out my reality, peeling back the smile I had worn like armor every day. My life was unraveling.

I came home later that day to find our door marked with a sheriff's eviction notice and realized our bills hadn't been paid. Worse, he'd drained our bank accounts, leaving me with nothing. He disappeared, leaving me to wonder if he was alive, the only hint of his survival being the occasional "read" receipt on my frantic texts.

My workplace became my lifeline. My superiors and colleagues wrapped me in their compassion, holding me together when I couldn't do it myself. One day, they handed me an envelope full of cash they'd collected for me. I sat in my car afterward, sobbing in gratitude, unable to believe people could care so deeply for someone so broken. My therapist would later tell me, "People show up for you because you've shown up for them." But at that moment, I felt like a ghost undeserving of love or kindness.

When he eventually returned to answer for his absence in the military, the final threads of our lives unraveled. I came home to find heroin needles, burnt spoons, and aluminum cans strewn across our dresser. Our kitchen was a disaster zone; our possessions were sold off one by one. My home, my sanctuary, was a drug den, and I was living out of my car, bathing at friends' houses.

One night, I returned home to grab a few things, unaware that rock bottom awaited me there. He came in shortly after. He tried to be sweet, but I wasn't in a space to accept it. When I rejected him, his threats escalated, culminating in a promise to jump out of a window. Exhausted, angry, and hollowed out, I told him, "Go ahead." The words were cruel, but I was at my limit. I didn't mean it, but the pain and resentment surged like venom.

When I grabbed a knife—not to harm him, but to protect myself—everything spiraled. I placed it on the ground, and he then struck me in the throat. I fell to the floor, my ring finger shattered, but adrenaline dulled the pain. I blacked out, waking to find myself fighting for my life. He called the cops, spinning a web of lies that painted me as the aggressor.

By the time the officers arrived, his injuries looked worse than mine. I was the one arrested. I—a woman who'd never even had a speeding ticket—was cuffed, paraded through a hospital, and chained to a bed like a criminal. My pleas fell on deaf ears, and humiliation clung to me like a second skin.

I called my parents. Of course, they didn't answer. My mother-in-law picked up instead, apologizing as she told me that after my arrest, he returned home, used my bank card, and brought another addict into what used to be *my* home.

I sat in that cell, staring at the cold, hard floor, reflecting on how far I had fallen. My life, once full of hope, was now a pile of ash. I had loved fiercely, given everything, and it had nearly destroyed me.

Sitting in court, dressed in my uniform, I felt like a spectacle. The knife I never used was on display, painting me as a criminal, while the real criminal—the man I loved—was absent, arrested for the same addiction that had brought me to this moment. The judge, perhaps seeing the truth behind the façade, wished me well and dropped the charges. I was free to go. But freedom was fleeting.

I tried to start over, moving to a new place, yet he found me. One day, he waited on me, came out of nowhere, snatched my keys, broke into my home, and pinned me to the floor, holding me captive in what was supposed to be my sanctuary. Exhausted, I retreated to my room, my spirit as battered as my body. I was desperate to escape, yet the cycle kept dragging me back.

Desperation led me to the magistrate, where I fought to make charges stick. For my freedom—and his safety—I risked my life. One night, I lured him into a trap, knowing it was the only way to save us both. Looking back, my recklessness in the name of love terrifies me. I walked into drug dens, begging him to come out, surrounded by danger, unsure if I'd make it out alive.

Even when he was locked up, he found ways to manipulate the system. He charmed bondsmen into believing his lies, leading them to my door. One even posed as a DEA agent, his interest in me was less about justice and more about being inappropriate with me. It was relentless. Eventually, I broke free—but at a devastating cost.

Years later, I laid to rest the man who had lost his battle with addiction. The call from the detectives shattered me. Grief overwhelmed me, not just for myself but for his mother, who had endured this nightmare alongside me. Despite everything, I showed up for her and him, wearing our navy flight deck uniform instead of the traditional black dress. It was what he loved, and I wanted to honor him as the man he was—not the addict.

I stood before the congregation, delivering my message and singing from the depths of my soul, uncaring of how it sounded. It was my final act of love for him, a goodbye to the man I had once adored. That day, I found closure, not just for myself but for everyone touched by the devastation of his addiction.

In the end, the anger faded, the wounds began to heal, and all that remained was love. Love for the person he was beneath the addiction, the man who shined through despite homelessness, mental illness, and despair.

The pastor spoke of how remarkable it was that he had experienced love, even at his worst. At that moment, I smiled through my tears. Even in my brokenness, I had poured love into him when he needed it most. I felt he needed it even more than me, and for that, I found peace.

Chapter 25

Life moved on, and I began making peace with pieces of my past—yet the foundation that shaped all the pain I endured remained untouched. Because of this, the cycle repeated itself. Though none of the heartbreaks matched the dramatic agony of the past, they still whispered the same haunting truth: my mother's toxic legacy lingered. Each heartbreak perpetuated the narrative that I was unworthy of love and that no one ever truly could or would love me.

One thing I've learned about trauma is that it doesn't just live in the past—it creates patterns. Unresolved wounds often lead us to seek out what feels familiar, even when it's harmful. For me, it meant falling into the arms of my mother in different bodies repeatedly. Narcissistic abuse teaches you to normalize chaos and dismiss red flags, leaving you vulnerable to repeating cycles of pain.

Time and again, I found myself drawn to men who mirrored her manipulation, cruelty, and betrayal. Yet, somehow, she inserted herself into even those relationships. My mother had an eerie obsession with keeping the phone numbers of the men I dated, flirting with them, bad-mouthing me behind my back. Once, she even groped one of them in front of me, commenting on how sexy he was while provocatively perched on the arm of a couch. Leaving the bathroom door open on purpose as she sat on the toilet, hoping he would pass. The same one she and my father would later house, all while banning me from their home and even maintaining contact with them.

She had been doing this since I was a teenager—collecting pictures of my boyfriends, admiring them in ways that felt violating. I remember the time my father caught her scrolling through photos of my boyfriend. Though he questioned her, as usual, he didn't push the issue. She went further than admiration; she actively sabotaged me. Planting seeds of doubt in their minds, spreading malicious lies about me. Claims of poor hygiene that I had this "problem" since I was a child, and even fabricated stories of STDs—all framed as "concern." And always triggered in her by someone complimenting me, which should be a compliment to her, you'd think.

People who heard her lies would eventually come to me, prefacing with, "I can't hold this in any longer; you need to know." These confessions were heartbreaking. Some mothers pray for their children, who fight for them even in the darkest times. But my mother? She PREYED on me. She reveled in tearing me down, tarnishing my name. I could have been perfect or flawed, and she would find a way to twist it into ammunition. I was damned either way.

When confronted, she gaslit me in the cruelest ways, belittling my intelligence. "I thought I smelled you the other day. Are you sure it wasn't you? Sometimes we need to bathe a little more often," she'd say, dripping with condescension. Her envy seeped through everything, even my red lipstick—something others loved and complimented me on. She'd lie and say that my grandmother thought I looked like a clown. When I confronted my grandmother, it turned out she'd fabricated the entire thing. My mother always hid her venom behind the guise of others, but her bitterness was unmistakable.

This is one of the hallmarks of a narcissistic parent: their ability to project their insecurities onto their children, turning them into scapegoats. Narcissistic mothers, in particular, often view their daughters as competition rather than as extensions of their legacy. They work to undermine, belittle, and sabotage their daughters, driven by envy and the need to maintain control. Understanding this dynamic doesn't erase the pain, but it provides clarity. Their behavior isn't about the child—it's about the unhealed wounds and unmet needs of the parent.

Some of my breakups ended with men throwing my pain back in my face—reminders of the abuse I endured from my mother or even my deceased husband. Their parting words were aimed to hurt, to wound me further for daring to walk away. But walking away itself was progress, something the younger me could never have done.

I became a workaholic, burying myself in books and degrees to keep my mind occupied. Out of sight, out of mind—that's what I told myself. But unresolved pain has a way of forcing its way to the surface, no matter how deeply you try to bury it.

One day, after another falling out with my mother, my father called. Pretending to be oblivious, he asked why I didn't like her. I had just come home from a nine-to-five followed by night classes and was beyond exhausted. Yet, I sat in my car and gave it to him straight—from beginning to end. Every lie, every betrayal, every moment of abuse. I held nothing back. He sounded concerned, as though he might finally have a real conversation with her. For once, I thought he might acknowledge the truth. I couldn't have been more wrong.

The next evening, he called me back around the same time I usually left class. His words hit me like a ton of bricks: "I talked to your mother, and I'm just going to tell you now what I think about all you said, girl. I think you're lying. You made it all up. You've got some kind of mental illness about you! You're demonic! And something ain't right with you, girl, I'm telling you now. How can a daughter treat her mother the way you do? In my day, we'd never do and say the things you're saying, girl!"

It was clear—his distorted view of me setting boundaries was shaped entirely by her lies. My father, the man I once looked up to, had reduced me to a demon with a mental illness. My heart couldn't take it. Out of nowhere, I screamed, "FUCK YOU!" before bursting into tears and hanging up.

In that moment, I felt like I couldn't breathe. My heart, already broken, was completely shattered. It was the last blow, and I felt I had no reason—no desire—to live anymore. The once optimistic, smiling, kind, hopeless romantic who never gave up on love or life had vanished in an instant.

My mother managed to turn everyone against me—my siblings, the people who believed her lies, her side of the family, and even people who didn't know me. And now my father. In my eyes, she won. I didn't care to fight anymore. I was willing to let her have it all and give her what she seemed to want so badly: my death.

I fell into a deep state of depression, functioning just enough to work and attend school. But I always went straight home to sit in the dark with nothing but the four walls closing in around me. Every day, I entertained death more, thinking of ways to end my life painlessly. Slowly, I danced with the reaper, ready to make peace with it all.

This is the insidious nature of narcissistic abuse—it isolates you, drains you of your identity, and can even rob you of your will to live. Narcissistic parents thrive on creating division, manipulating those around them to believe their lies. They weaponize relationships, turning allies into enemies, leaving their target feeling utterly alone.

The psychological toll is profound. Victims often experience depression, anxiety, and a skewed sense of self-worth, questioning their value and sanity. They internalize the blame, believing the false narrative spun about them. When support systems crumble under the weight of the narcissist's manipulation, victims are left feeling as though there is no escape.

But there is. The key lies in recognizing the patterns, seeking external validation of your reality, and reaching out for help—even in moments when it feels impossible.

My downward spiral led me to my last desperate cry for help—a turning point I never thought I'd reach. I remember lying lifeless on my couch in the dark, my phone in my hand. I hadn't eaten in days, and my eyes burned from endless tears. My mind was foggy, but I managed to Google names, searching for people or organizations to reach out to for help—anyone who might hear me.

I didn't think much of it as I wrote emails to TV shows and prominent figures known for mending broken lives and helping people heal. I poured out the truth, raw and unfiltered. It didn't take much effort to make it stand out. I had an evil, abusive mother, but I knew I was just one in a billion. I barely held onto hope, but I prayed. I prayed that if it was God's will for me to live, to keep fighting, that He would give me a sign—because I wasn't looking for one anymore.

One evening, while driving to school, I received an email from a show. My heart raced. No one knew I had reached out, and no one knew the depth of my desire to cut ties with my parents. The thought of them being involved in this process terrified me, and I never wanted them to be. This was about me—about my mind and heart crying out for help.

But who wouldn't want to read about a mother like mine or witness firsthand the twisted, dysfunctional dynamic I grew up in? And who wouldn't want the one woman who was the topic of it all to be on the show, front and center? After all, being the center of attention is what she lives for. Stories like mine aren't everyday fare, especially in my culture. And therein lies the problem.

My story isn't unique, not in the way you might think. The taboo around speaking out and the unwritten rules of loyalty to blood keep victims silenced while abusers are protected and allowed to thrive. In many cultures, including mine, family loyalty is treated as sacred, even at the expense of an individual's well-being. There's an unspoken rule that says, "What happens in this house stays in this house." This silence creates a fertile ground for abuse to flourish unchecked, as speaking out is often met with shame, blame, or ostracism.

For survivors of narcissistic abuse, this cultural loyalty becomes a double-edged sword. On one hand, it reinforces the façade of the perfect family, shielding abusers. On the other, it isolates victims who are left battling their pain in silence, fearing they'll be accused of disloyalty or madness for exposing the truth.

Challenging these norms is not easy, but it is essential. Speaking out does more than break the cycle for the individual; it creates ripples of awareness. It invites others to question these rules and consider the damage silence can do.

By sharing my story, I aim to shine a light on this dark reality and encourage others to embrace the courage to speak their truth. Breaking these cycles starts with breaking the silence.

At that moment, I was a woman on the brink, desperate for a lifeline. When everyone around you is calling you crazy because of the lies your parents tell, and when no one believes your truth, it feels like your sanity is slipping away.

Narcissistic abuse thrives on isolation, gaslighting, and manipulation, leaving victims feeling as though their reality is distorted. This tactic, known as "crazy-making," is intentional. It's designed to discredit the victim's perception and diminish their voice. The victim is left questioning themselves, feeling unworthy, and often believing they are mentally unstable.

In such moments, reaching out for help—whether to a trusted friend, therapist, or even an external resource like a hotline or support group—can be a lifeline. It's common for survivors to feel hopeless or hesitant, doubting whether anyone will believe them. But seeking help is the first step toward breaking free from the cycle of abuse and reclaiming your sense of self.

Support can come from unexpected places, as it did for me. Even when hope feels faint, taking that small step to ask for help can open doors you never imagined. You are not alone, and your truth matters.

Chapter 26

It's one thing to live through dysfunction—it's another to have it all laid bare in front of an audience. My family's life was already complicated, filled with secrets and pain, but when the opportunity to appear on the show came up, it exposed everything in ways I couldn't have anticipated. The cameras, the lights, reliving our trauma—it was all so surreal. But it wasn't just a moment in time; it was a confrontation with my family's darkness that played out for the world to see.

I remember feeling both terrified and exhilarated in the lead-up to that appearance. Part of me wanted to believe that speaking out on national television would somehow bring justice or, at the very least, some form of clarity. But deep down, I feared the fallout. The world would now see the dysfunction, the lies, the cruelty that had shaped my entire existence. And yet, as much as I dreaded it, part of me was desperate for the truth to come to light.

Didn't know what to expect when I walked onto that stage to lead the show. Just before stepping out, the last thing I heard was my mother calling me a bitch. That moment solidified why I was there—not just to stand up to my biggest bully and speak my truth, but to save my life and fulfill my purpose. I was there for everyone who hadn't yet found their voice, to break the silence and shatter the chains of secrecy.

With my chin held high and the confidence my mother had spent years trying to beat out of me, I stepped onto that stage in front of the entire world. The nerves I had expected didn't consume me. Instead, there was a sense of calm resolve because I knew this moment had been a long time coming. This was my time to take back my power, and I wasn't about to let it slip away. My mother was at the center of it all, as she always had been. The driving force behind the family's dysfunction, the architect of the lies, and the one who controlled the narrative. But now, under the glaring lights and in front of the cameras, her manipulations were exposed for all to see.

When she walked out and took her seat, I avoided locking eyes with her. It wasn't out of spite but for self-preservation. I knew that if I looked at her, the tears would start—tears of disbelief that even in front of the entire world, she was willing to sacrifice me.

And then there was my father, my greatest heartbreak in that moment. I had warned the producers that he would try to take the stage to defend her and begged them to keep him seated in the audience. But it didn't take long for him to rise and make his way up. Not to defend me but to protect her.

On that stage, my father, who had always played the calm counterpart to my mother's chaos, revealed a side of himself I had never fully seen. He stood there, spewing lies about me being a prostitute, claiming all his children had mental issues, and painting my mother as the victim. His enabling mask fell away, revealing someone who had been complicit all along.

I watched in anguish as she directed him like a puppeteer, her subtle glances and head nods guiding his words. It wasn't just heartbreaking—it was soul-shattering. This man, whom I had once called my protector, had become a clone of the very person who had caused me the most pain.

Sitting there, I realized I wasn't just losing my mother. I was losing both parents. The grief of mourning two people who are alive as though they are dead is a pain I wouldn't wish on anyone. It's a void that feels endless, a sorrow that cuts deeper than words can describe.

The Double Loss

When a child of narcissistic parents comes to terms with the truth, it often involves a double grief. First, there's the loss of the idealized version of the parent they wanted to have. Second, there's the devastating realization of who the parent truly is. For those with enabling parents, the pain can be compounded by the discovery of their complicity—whether active or passive—in the abuse.

This kind of grief is unique because it doesn't stem from physical death but from the death of a relationship that never truly existed in the first place. It's grieving the loss of what could have been while confronting the reality of what is.

The moment we sat down, I could feel the tension in the air. My mother immediately began to play her part, presenting herself as the victim, the misunderstood mother who had only done what she believed was best for her children. She weaved her version of events with such conviction that, for a moment, I doubted myself. Had I misremembered? Was I overreacting? But then I would catch a glimpse of my father's face or hear my siblings' words, and the truth would come rushing back—this wasn't just about a family with minor dysfunction. This was about abuse, manipulation, and years of emotional scars.

Watching her on that stage was surreal. The woman I had grown up fearing was now speaking to a studio full of strangers, spinning her story in front of an audience that had no idea what she was truly capable of. It wasn't the first time I'd seen her lie, but it was the first time I saw her lie so publicly, without shame. And in that moment, I realized just how deeply her control had affected not just me but everyone in our family.

The Fallout: A Family Torn Apart

The fallout from our appearance on the show was immediate and intense. For days after the taping, the phone calls began. Some relatives were outraged, unable to believe what they had seen. Others sided with my mother, unwilling or unable to confront the truth of her behavior. Social media posts surfaced, targeting me with baseless accusations.

"Dr. Phil was some bullshit today, wouldn't even let my aunt even talk," one read. (She did all the talking—so much so that they had to split the show into two parts because she ran into someone else's segment.) "Tiffany lies so damn bad, it's just sad. I think she's just in love with her own damn father. I said what I said. Her ass needs help."

The public exposure of our family's dysfunction had caused irreparable damage. Relationships were strained beyond repair, while others shifted in ways I hadn't anticipated. The aftermath was painful. My mother's ability to manipulate wasn't limited to just the people in the room that day; it extended to our extended family and friends. She reached out to those who still supported her, painting me as the villain who had betrayed her. As always, her lies were convincing. They weren't just about what had happened; they were about who she was and how the world should see her. She started her attempt at damage control way before the airing of the show. Starting with a public social media post to her followers and family.

"Family and friends, I went on the Dr. Phil show to mend old wounds with my twins, they humiliated me and made me look like a monster, as they call me. They took it there, so many lies were told by my twins. All of you guys on here know who I am; you know my character. The things they said about me on that show about me was so humiliating and very hurtful. I should have walked off, but I didn't. I thought we came to mend and I'd get my family back, and instead, I was told I needed help. The whole show was to humiliate me and try to make me look bad. So, I just want you all to know when it airs; I'll let y'all know. Tell me if it was fair. I haven't been on here in a while. Because my heart is heavy, she even got her Aunt to write something about me, and her so-called friend, that don't even know me, got on there and said I contacted her. I don't have her phone number she was a friend on Facebook, which I now deleted her. Watch out, guys, your kids are not like we were. So I'll let you guys be the judge when it airs and let me know what the hell was going on. They never put any of my proof up. The bank statements were doctored, and I gave my bank statement and said I stole 3900.00 from my daughter. She was out for blood. They did not use one shred of proof I had to react. You guys look at it and tell me what was going on and what child would get on national TV and say all kinds of bad things about her mother. My heart is heavy. Some of the things she said was a surprise to me, she never spoke to me about you guys, why would I be jealous of my own children? I brought them into this world"

Before the taping of the show, for the first few days there, I saw posts of pictures of my parents walking about Hollywood as if it were a free vacation. Pictures of her smiling. As if she was not there for the abuse that led her suicidal daughter to desperation. We had not been paid to be on the show, we were accommodated for our rooms, eating, and transportation to the studio and airport. No check would make me sell my soul for lies in entertainment at the expense of my family and myself. She had plenty of time to back out, and as I had stated, I never wanted either one of them on the show to begin with. This was about them, but it wasn't about them, I was fighting for my sanity.

The post was riddled with lies. The producers had done their due diligence, ensuring only facts and evidence were presented. The bank statements were from my account, proof of the theft she denied. Her story fell apart under scrutiny, but her audacity knew no bounds. She constantly attempted to insult the intelligence of all by assuming she was the smartest in the room.

The comments from those who read the post and dared to still even support it here were quite telling and exposing them as well. The lengths that she went to try to destroy me even after the show, as always, had no limits. This time, reaching further than I had even begun to imagine.

The Narcissist's Damage Control Playbook

Narcissists often resort to a set of predictable tactics when their image is threatened. This includes:

- **Playing the Victim:** By framing themselves as the wronged party, they gain sympathy and deflect attention from their actions.
- **Smear Campaigns:** They attack the credibility of their accusers, often with outlandish lies, to isolate and discredit them.
- **Recruiting Flying Monkeys:** Narcissists enlist others to advocate for them, further isolating the victim.

For victims, these tactics can feel overwhelming and isolating. It's crucial to understand that these behaviors are not about the victim but about the narcissist's desperate need to maintain control and protect their image.

At the end of the show, we were all escorted by producers separately back to our dressing rooms. As I sat there, trying to collect my thoughts, I heard the screams and destruction coming from backstage—my mother's fury unleashed. It was at that moment I knew I had slain my dragon. This wasn't just a victory for me but a beacon of hope for so many others who had endured the same pain in silence.

Backstage in my dressing room, I was surrounded by love and support from those who understood my struggle. People shared how brave they thought I was, recounting their own stories of pain and wishing they possessed the courage to speak out as I had. It was overwhelming yet humbling, knowing my story resonated with so many who felt unseen and unheard.

The truth is, it's not easy to do what I did. The weight of silence often feels safer than the unknown of speaking out, and the fear of backlash can seem insurmountable. That's why so many stay silent—some for years, others for a lifetime. But I was ready. Whatever my mother or anyone else had to throw at me, I was prepared to stand firm.

Standing alone isn't easy, but sometimes it's necessary. It takes courage, strength, and an unshakable resolve to choose yourself when no one else will. And in that moment, I realized that my choice to stand up wasn't just for me—it was for everyone who needed a reminder that the truth, no matter how heavy, can set you free.

For me, the fallout was equally painful but necessary. It forced me to reckon with the truth of my own experiences and gave me the space to stop hiding behind the façade I had built around my family. The public exposure allowed me to start unburdening myself, to speak the truth without the weight of secrecy holding me back. But it also left scars—scars that I would have to confront for years to come.

Revelations About My Mother's True Nature

What struck me most in the wake of our appearance on Dr. Phil was the way my mother's true nature came to the surface in the most unexpected ways. Before, I had always seen her manipulations as a necessary part of survival, as something I could avoid or endure. But after the show aired, I realized just how deep her ability to control others ran and how much of our lives had been spent in service of her image.

In the weeks following the taping, her behavior grew even more erratic. Her facade cracked, and what I saw behind it wasn't the woman I had once feared but something darker. She no longer tried to hide the depth of her manipulation, the way she twisted people's emotions to get what she wanted.

It became clearer than ever that her need for control wasn't just about her—it was about her inability to allow anyone to have their voice. She couldn't stand the thought of someone seeing her as imperfect, as flawed, or, God forbid, as wrong. She needed to be the center of attention, the one who controlled the narrative, even at the cost of her children's well-being.

Her true nature had always been there, lurking beneath the surface. The show didn't create it—it merely exposed it.

She went on a rampage in retaliation, and once again, watching my father go along with whatever evil she wanted to bestow upon her daughter was always sickening. She had gone and filed a police report with pages of lies in an attempt to have me arrested and thrown in jail. She had a few of the family members who stood with me during the show, being witnesses and just in general the loving and supporting family I needed that stood for right, she had them all served court papers to appear in court. The paperwork was a clear display of her emotional immaturity, starting with her writing of the complaint in between lines where it didn't belong, like address input or name.

Exposing not only her immaturity but also, in writing, her ill intent, using descriptions like "fat" or "ugly" to describe a family member and once again in between lines where they didn't belong. She started out talking about things that had absolutely nothing to do with the show, but it was clear as day that it was retaliation for the fool she made of herself on national TV and now attempting to blame and punish me for her behavior and anyone who supported me. The show was mentioned several times throughout the letter and also mentioned the airing of the show. It had not aired yet, so once again, she was attempting to do damage control but all the while exposing herself. The letter ended with "The need time in jail they all destroyed my life, and I will be bringing more proof to court" and "They all got together to attack me for yrs.. 36 years"

We all lived in different states, and my state, including others, was appalled that hers would even entertain such foolishness. Sheriff told me that there was no way this would be entertained and that the letter would have been tossed out along with her from their office for wasting time. But it made it to court, and for that reason, I paid and hired an attorney for representation. She had no clue what my new address was, so she was unable to serve me, the one she wanted there so badly. So badly that she walked up to the bailiff to inform them of my absence. I was on the docket as well but never was served; the attorney assured me I would be fine. I sat by the phone for what seemed like hours while at work. He called and explained to me that he had never seen a mother like mine, as the judge said to, never having seen a mother and father be so evil to lie to have their daughter thrown in jail.

He told me that she hung herself with the documents and her desire to be the star, that in which the judge allowed herself to talk herself into a corner. He said that the only focus she had in conversing was me, the one that was not there but her only true target.

In the end, the judge informed her that there was no way that her report should ever even have made it into his courtroom and that he was upset at the idea that she would come in with my father as well and waste everyone's time. He told her he would have her locked up instead if he ever got wind that she was around me, causing problems.

But she wouldn't stop there. I would start receiving death threats to my phone while on my job. So much so that I changed my routine in what direction I came and went home, the time, etc. I pulled up the private listed call on my phone bill and saw that the number was from my mother's phone. She had stood next to the flying monkeys she recruited to do her dirty work and told them what to say in the death threats. She meant every word of what she relayed through them, too.

She would go on to recruit others to make a fake social media profile to call me every name, shoot down all of my accomplishments, wish me death, and say everything she wanted to say to me but never dared to do. She put up a trespassing sign after I had come to collect my military belongings, being that she had taken them down to include my pictures and thrown them in a closet the answer I got for that, in the long run, she was "because you made me hot, that's why I threw it in the closet, I didn't want to see your face so yeah I took it down." Once again, her immaturity is on display. To try to lure me in to call the cops and get me in trouble by lying and saying I was trespassing. Not to mention also that she had her family gathered at the house against her daughter in an attempt to ban me from my sister's graduation. Putting on a show at the ceremony, stealing yet another show from now her youngest, who she went on to abuse as well and I had made reports against.

She showed up unannounced at my house one day, dragging my father behind her like some puppet on a string. The only reason she made it past my front door was because she brought one of my nieces, using her as a human shield against the anger I felt boiling inside me. She stood there, bold as ever, and asked for a minute of my time. My father sat quietly, obediently, like he always did when it came to her.

What came next should have felt like vindication, but it was anything but. She admitted it—all of it. Every accusation I had ever made, every truth I had spoken, every lie she had ever told to smear my name, every dark, twisted thing she tried to bury. She even confessed to the sick relationship she had with that underage girl, a truth so vile that I could barely think about it, let alone speak it out loud. Hearing it come from her mouth made me want to vomit. For years, I danced around it in therapy, unable to fully acknowledge that I was tied by blood to someone capable of such depravity.

She went on and on, her words like venom. My father just sat there, silent, absorbing it all without a word of protest or shock. For hours, she confessed until she dropped the final dagger.

"You know why I don't like you, Tiffany?" she asked, her eyes dark and soulless, her mouth curling into that demonic smile I knew too well.

I froze. After all the years of denial, after all the abuse, after all the gaslighting, she finally admitted it—she didn't like me. She actually said it. But instead of the answer I had chased my whole life, the one I thought might give me some peace, I felt nothing but rage. Her reasons, whatever they were, didn't matter anymore. No explanation would ever make sense of the hell she had put me through.

"Stop," I said, my voice steady but my heart in pieces. "Wrap it up." I couldn't take any more. Her confessions didn't cleanse her soul—they dumped all her sins onto me. This wasn't something for a daughter to hear; this was something for a priest.

I turned to my father, hoping for something—anything. For years, he had stood by her, defended her, lied for her, and gone on national TV to call his own daughter a liar. And now? Now, the truth was laid bare, years of lies, abuse, and manipulation exposed.

What would he say?

His response gutted me in a way I didn't think was possible anymore.

"See? Your mother had the answers all along," he said casually as if her confession was some minor inconvenience. "If she had just come out with it, we wouldn't be here today. You see, gal, now I see. All you wanted was your daddy's love."

That was it? That was all he had to say? No apology, no acknowledgment on his part, no outrage for the years of torment she inflicted on me while he stood by and did nothing. Nothing but excuses and an attempt to pull me into his arms like that would fix decades of betrayal.

I stood there, my heart shattered into pieces too small to ever put back together. He wasn't sorry. He never would be. He was no better than her. He was complicit, a coward, and just as responsible for the pain that had shaped my entire life.

This wasn't closure. This was just another wound, another betrayal, another reminder that neither of them would ever be what I needed them to be.

As I showed them to the door, she threw out an offer for lunch, her voice dripping with false cheer. Then came the gut punch, delivered with a casual laugh like it meant nothing.

"I'll pay for it," she said. "I've stolen enough of your money; I'll start paying it back to you."

She laughed. Like it was a joke, like she wasn't talking about the same money, she denied stealing on national TV, the same money she told the world I had lied about, claiming I had doctored statements to make her look bad.

But it wasn't just the joke about the money that hit me—it was everything tied to it. It was the lies, the betrayal, the humiliation. It was the weight of that story, the one she twisted and weaponized against me, turning her wrongs into my supposed sins.

Her laugh rang in my ears like a cruel echo, dragging me back to that time in my life when the world seemed to implode around me. When everything I thought I knew crumbled under the weight of her deceit. That joke wasn't funny—it was a dagger wrapped in a punchline, reopening wounds I was still trying to heal.

Around that time, I had finally broken free from my husband—a man who had become a ghost of himself, running from responsibility, homeless, in and out of jail, and with a child on the way by another woman. He was supposed to be with his mother, "cleaning himself up" to repair our shattered relationship. Instead,

I learned through a casual phone call at work that he had abandoned even that flimsy pretense of trying.

I was drowning in the chaos of my life, desperate for escape. Deployment, usually dreaded by many, became my lifeline. For me, it wasn't just leaving—it was survival. The only way to start healing was to get far away, where I wouldn't be tempted to chase his broken pieces and lose myself in the process.

Before leaving, I tied up every loose end. Updated my life insurance policy—my mother, predictably, was angry that she wasn't the beneficiary. Her audacity to prioritize cashing out on me over my life was sickening. She would later encourage others to take out policies on their troubled loved ones like it was a family tradition. It was vile.

As always, my hyper-independence took over. I hated asking for help. Years of conditioning left me feeling like a burden. So, despite my better judgment, I left my affairs with my father. Not my mother—never her. My brand-new Camaro, my beloved dog—everything I couldn't carry with me went into his care. A flicker of that little girl inside me still hoped, trusted, that he'd keep them safe.

My deployment gave me moments of solace. Traveling the world, making memories with friends, and, for the first time, really leaning into therapy. But even from a distance, my mother found ways to poison my peace.

One day, in between flight operations, I decided to check my finances. My heart sank. My account was being run through—large, daily withdrawals that I didn't authorize. Rage burned through me. This wasn't carelessness. It was entitlement. Theft. I knew in my gut it was her. And I was right.

When I confronted her over the phone, she denied it, of course, dragging my father into her lies. "I didn't take any money, did I, Daddy?" she asked, her voice dripping with manipulation. And as always, he nodded along, complicit. But I wasn't bluffing. I let her know I would find out exactly who did it when I got home.

And when I did return, it wasn't just my account waiting for me. It was a nightmare.

My beloved dog, the last piece of my broken marriage that I cherished, was dead. My mother, cold and detached, casually lied about it over the phone. "I gave him away," she claimed. But my sister, bless her heart, couldn't let the lie slide. She called me back, sobbing, and told me the truth: my dog had starved to death. Tied under their deck, neglected, until he tried to escape and hung himself.

I could barely process the cruelty of it. But it didn't stop there. My sister, in tears, told me how my mother was now abusing her, dragging her to strange men's houses, banging her head against car windows, and whispering murderous threats—promising to kill my father in his sleep and smother her with a pillow next.

I redirected my flight immediately, fueled by rage and heartbreak. When I arrived, my father met me with my car, keys deliberately damaged by my mother in a petty tantrum. My brand-new Camaro has already been vandalized. His excuse? "You know how your mother is. Just don't say anything to her."

Inside, the house felt like a battlefield I never wanted to return to. My mother avoided me, locking herself in her room, seething with anger that I had survived deployment. She wasn't glad I was home. She was angry I was alive. Not to mention, her name was written all over every single bank withdrawal while I was away. No surprise there. It was as blatant as daylight—her signature, her theft, undeniable proof. But just like she had done before, even with evidence sitting right in front of her on national TV, she denied it with a straight face. The audacity of her lies was as sickening as it was predictable.

I couldn't stay silent. I reported her to social services, desperate to save my sister. But my mother's reign of terror was absolute. She scared my sister into recanting, leaving me powerless. My father, ever the enabler, called my sister a liar, crushing her spirit further.

In the backyard, I found my dog buried alongside countless others—innocent lives discarded like trash. My mother treated animals the same way she treated me: disposable.

I was hell-bent on staying in the military, determined to fight for custody of my sister. But without her cooperation, I had no case. My mother won again, her evil unchecked.

The weight of it all—the betrayal, the loss, the futility—was crushing. I wanted nothing more than to go back overseas, far away from this suffocating nightmare, and never return. But the scars she left behind would follow me wherever I went.

So, you see, that statement alone was more than just words—it was a calculated and intentional strike meant to wound me deeply, and she delivered it with precision, fully believing it would go over my head. But it didn't. When I escorted her out of my home that day, I wasn't just closing the door on her physically; I was closing the door on her access to me emotionally and spiritually. Still, her power lingered as even my father—who had heard the ugliness of it all—fell right back into calling me a liar and the devil.

I can't help but believe she convinced him to come to my home in the first place as part of her elaborate damage control strategy. Her aim wasn't reconciliation—it was control. To paint me as some unhinged, demonic child needing to be pacified to keep quiet about her evil deeds. But the moment they left, the switch-up was immediate. He took back any semblance of accountability he pretended to own in my presence, and the narrative shifted once again to protect her and vilify me.

Even now, I hear the venom they continue to spew about me, always laced with the same disgusting lies. My mother told my siblings never to utter my name in their home, labeling me a demonic witch who practices voodoo—using the same aunts who nurtured me as the scapegoats in her twisted narrative. She's gone as far as calling me an "ugly witch bitch" at the mere mention of my name. She's told anyone who will listen that I'm a prostitute, a liar, a whore—declaring that God will punish me for the ultimate crime of "bringing my parents" on national TV.

Never mind the fact that it was her free will and decision to participate in that show or that the only embarrassment she endured came from her own words and actions. No, in her mind, it's all my fault. Poor mom, burdened with such an "evil" daughter. The scapegoat yet again.

What's even more gut-wrenching is how she turned my siblings against me, feeding them the same poisonous lies until they, too, began to parrot her narratives. And she stood by, reveling in the chaos, wearing a mask of innocent martyrdom while watching me endure the pain she orchestrated. Nothing has changed but the years on their faces and the height of their hatred for me.

"She's not my daughter," they say, as if that declaration strips me of my worth. For a long time, those words were a knife in my chest. But now, in my healing, I see them for what they are: projections of their ugliness. And for once, I'm okay with whatever they want me to be—because what I've chosen for myself is something they can't take away. Peace. Freedom. The joy of no longer being around to hear their hatred

The Truth That Couldn't Be Denied

Watching the episode again after it aired was difficult. I saw myself on screen, speaking truths that had been buried for years. I saw the pain in my eyes, the way my voice trembled as I spoke about the abuse, the lies, and the manipulation. I saw the people I had once tried to protect—my siblings and my father—sitting in the shadows, each of us carrying our scars. And I saw my mother, still clinging to her version of events, her story so convincing that it made me doubt my memories for a brief moment.

But then, something clicked. I realized that the truth didn't need anyone else to validate it. It wasn't about the audience on Dr. Phil or the family members who had their version of the story—it was about what I had lived through, what I had endured, and how I had survived.

For so long, I had feared that the truth would destroy me, that speaking out would only bring more pain and more rejection. But in the wake of that public airing of our family's dysfunction, I realized that speaking out had given me a voice I hadn't known I needed. It wasn't just about revealing the truth—it was about setting myself free from the chains that my mother's control had wrapped around me for years.

The Path Forward

After everything had aired, I found myself at a crossroads. The fallout had left deep emotional wounds, but it also gave me clarity. My mother's true nature had been exposed for all to see, but the real work—healing from years of manipulation, rebuilding relationships, and confronting my pain—was just beginning.

The Dr. Phil episode didn't fix anything, but it forced me to reckon with the truth in ways I hadn't before. It made me realize that I couldn't keep hiding from my family's dysfunction. I couldn't keep protecting her, even at the cost of my well-being. The truth had set me on a path toward healing, but that path was going to be long, painful, and filled with challenges.

The Road to Healing

Healing is not linear. It is not a straight path, nor is it an easy one. For me, it has been a long and winding journey—a series of small steps forward and, sometimes, painful steps backward. The road to healing began long after the scars were formed, long after the trauma had etched itself into the very fabric of who I was. It began when I realized that I could no longer live in the aftermath of my mother's abuse and that I had to take control of my own life and my narrative.

Confronting the Past

The first step toward healing was confronting the past—looking at what had happened without the haze of denial or the fog of fear that had shielded me for so long. For years, I had pushed the pain down, convinced myself that if I didn't acknowledge it, it would somehow disappear. But the truth never disappears. It waits, buried in the corners of your soul, ready to emerge when you least expect it.

The moment I began to face the full extent of the abuse I had endured was a moment of terrifying clarity. It was painful, raw, and often too overwhelming to bear. But in that pain, there was also a sense of power. I was no longer running from it. I was choosing to confront it, to own it, to let it be a part of my story without letting it define me.

This process wasn't easy. I had to untangle the lies my mother had woven into my sense of self. I had to look at the ways her manipulation had shaped me—how it had affected my ability to trust others, how it had instilled in me a deep fear of rejection, and how it had left me questioning my worth for so long. The road to healing required me to face those painful truths head-on.

Finding My Voice

For years, my voice had been silenced—not just by my mother's control but by my fear. I had been conditioned to believe that my thoughts, my feelings, and my desires didn't matter. But as I began to heal, I realized that reclaiming my voice was a crucial part of this journey.

I started small. At first, it was just writing my feelings down, expressing them in private, away from the scrutiny of others. Then, it was sharing those words with a therapist, someone who could hear my truth without judgment. As I slowly opened up to the people who mattered most, I found that speaking out, even about the darkest parts of my past, didn't make me weak—it made me stronger.

The more I spoke, the more I realized how powerful my voice was. I wasn't just speaking for myself—I was speaking for the child who had been silenced, for the person I had been too afraid to become. Every word I shared was like breaking a chain, loosening the grip my mother's control had on me.

Forgiving Myself

Healing isn't just about forgiving others; sometimes, it's about forgiving yourself. For so long, I had carried around the guilt that, somehow, I was to blame for the dysfunction in my family. I believe that if I had just been better, quieter, and more obedient, my mother's behavior would have been different. I blamed myself for not being strong enough to stand up to her, for not finding a way to escape sooner.

But in the process of healing, I learned that none of it was my fault. I wasn't responsible for her abuse, for her manipulation, or for the toxic dynamics she created. It wasn't my job to protect her or to shield others from the truth. And letting go of that guilt was one of the most freeing parts of my healing.

I began to understand that I had done the best I could with the tools I had been given. And that was enough. Healing required me to release the burden of self-blame, to forgive myself for the things I couldn't change, and to permit myself to move forward without the weight of guilt holding me back.

Building Healthy Relationships

Part of my healing was learning to trust again—to open myself up to others without the fear of being hurt or manipulated. This, too, was a slow and difficult process. For years, I had kept everyone at arm's length, afraid that they would see my vulnerability as a weakness to be exploited.

But as I worked through my healing, I began to realize that vulnerability was not a weakness—it was a strength. It was through vulnerability that I began to build authentic, healthy relationships. I started to surround myself with people who saw me for who I truly was, not who my mother had made me believe I should be.

Trust, I learned, is not about perfection. It's about opening up to others despite the fear of the past. It's about giving people the space to show up for you and allowing them to be part of your healing process. Slowly, I started to rebuild relationships with friends and family, reconnecting with those who had been there for me, even when I hadn't known how to let them in.

Learning to Let Go

Healing also required me to let go—not just of the past but of the hold my mother's actions still had on me. For years, I had been living in the shadow of her abuse, carrying her lies and manipulations as if they were part of my own identity. Letting go of that weight wasn't easy, but it was essential for my healing.

I began to understand that forgiveness wasn't about condoning her behavior—it was about freeing myself from it. Holding onto anger and resentment only gave her more power over me, and I had no intention of giving her that control anymore. Letting go was about taking back my power, about refusing to allow her toxicity to dictate the course of my life.

A Journey That Continues

Healing is not a destination. It's a journey—one that I am still on and likely will be for the rest of my life. There are days when the past feels distant and days when the weight of it all feels too heavy to bear. But each day, I grow stronger. Each day, I take one more step toward reclaiming the person I was meant to be—whole, independent, and free.

The road to healing has been long, painful, and filled with obstacles. But it has also been beautiful. It has taught me that even in the darkest moments, there is hope for transformation that even the most broken parts of us can heal with time, patience, and love. And as I continue on this path, I know that I will find peace, that I will continue to reclaim myself piece by piece until I am finally whole again.

Acceptance and Letting Go

There comes a point in every person's healing journey when the realization hits: the person who has hurt you, the one whose actions have shaped your pain, will never change. It's a hard truth to accept, especially when that person is your mother. For so long, I held onto the hope that things could be different—that if I just tried harder, if I was better, if I could show her how much I loved her, she would finally see me and change. But over time, I came to understand that the change I sought in her wasn't possible. She was not going to be the mother I longed for, and in that painful realization, I had to find a way to release myself from the chains of expectation and move toward peace.

Recognizing the Truth

For much of my life, I had clung to the belief that my mother's actions were a result of something I could fix. I tried to rationalize her behavior, blaming her childhood, her own unresolved pain, or the stress of life. I thought if I loved her enough if I endured enough, I could somehow help her become the nurturing, loving mother I had always wished for. But the more I gave, the more it was never enough. The deeper I sank into her world, the more I lost myself.

The truth was hard to swallow: my mother would never change. The woman who had spent years controlling, manipulating, and hurting me wasn't going to magically transform into someone who could give me the love and care I deserved. That truth was a bitter pill, one I didn't want to swallow. But as much as it hurt, it was the key to my freedom.

I spent so much time hoping that she would change—hoping that she would see how much her actions hurt me and that, one day, she would finally understand. But change is something people have to want for themselves, and she didn't want it. My mother's world was one built on control, and in her eyes, there was no room for the kind of love and accountability that would have healed the rift between us. It took years of heartache and disappointment to finally accept that I couldn't fix her. The power to change, to heal, had to come from me, not from her.

The Pain of Letting Go

Letting go wasn't just about accepting the truth—it was about mourning what I had lost. I had lost the idealized version of a mother, the one I had held onto for so long in my dreams. Letting go meant acknowledging that this was the reality, not just for me but for our entire relationship. It meant that I had to stop expecting her to be something she could never be, and in doing so, I was freeing myself from the emotional weight that had kept me tied to her for so many years.

The pain of letting go was raw. It felt like cutting away a part of myself that I had carried for my entire life. I had wanted so badly to have a mother who loved me the way I deserved to be loved, but for years, I had been chasing a ghost—a mother who existed only in my hopes, not in reality. Letting go meant giving up that dream, but it also meant making room for my dreams.

I had to stop pretending that I could "save" her or that I could somehow become the perfect daughter who would finally make her proud. I realized that the only person I could save was myself, and the only person I could change was me. In letting go of the hope that she would change, I gave myself permission to heal.

Finding Peace in Acceptance

The true peace came when I stopped fighting for a relationship that wasn't healthy and started building one with myself.

Acceptance wasn't about giving up; it was about finding a way to live in truth without being consumed by the pain of wanting something that wasn't possible. I stopped blaming myself for her inability to change and stopped waiting for her approval. Slowly, I began to realize that my peace could not be contingent upon her. It had to come from within me.

Acceptance was a process. It wasn't a one-time event where I woke up and suddenly had no more pain or anger. It took time—years. But with each step, I began to feel lighter, as though a weight had been lifted off my shoulders. I could think about my mother without the crushing feeling of hope that she would change. Instead, I began to see her as she was—flawed, broken, and incapable of the love I had always sought. But I no longer needed her to be anything more.

As I accepted that my mother would never change, I started to release the hold she had on my life. I no longer felt tethered to her whims or her moods. I could make decisions for myself without the constant fear of her judgment or anger. For the first time, I started to live for myself, not for her approval. And that freedom was the beginning of my healing.

Building Boundaries

Acceptance didn't mean that I had to accept everything about her or everything she did. What it meant was that I needed to start building boundaries, healthy lines that would protect me from the damage her behavior could still inflict. I couldn't continue to let her control me, even from a distance.

At first, setting boundaries felt unnatural. I had been trained to comply with her, to prioritize her needs over my own. But as I learned to recognize my worth, I began to see the importance of protecting myself from her toxic influence. Setting boundaries was not about punishment or rejection—it was about self-preservation.

I finally decided to cut them off completely—no contact, no more games, no more lies. I stopped answering her calls, those calls that were nothing but emotional manipulation dressed up as a concern. For me, this was the only way out—there was no other choice. It may look different for others, and I don't judge their paths, but for me, it was the only way to find peace. Real peace. The kind you can't buy or fake. It was the only way to stop drowning in the toxicity they poured into my life, to stop feeling like I was suffocating under the weight of their dysfunction.

Letting go of them felt like I was shedding a dead weight I had carried for too long. That weight had been holding me back, keeping me from living my life the way I was meant to, the way I deserved to. I couldn't be the best version of myself while they had their claws in me. I owed it to myself to let go of the chaos they kept throwing into my world. This wasn't just about cutting ties—it was about survival, about taking my life back piece by piece.

That was my first real step in reclaiming my power. Not just for me but for the person I could finally become without them dragging me down anymore.

The more I set boundaries, the more I realized how much control she had had over me. But as I enforced those boundaries,

I began to feel a sense of peace, a sense of ownership over my life that I had never known. I was no longer at the mercy of her whims. I was free to define my relationships, my time, and my emotional energy.

The Ongoing Process

Acceptance and letting go aren't things you do once and then forget about. They are ongoing processes that require constant attention. Every time I feel myself slipping back into old patterns of hoping for her change, I remind myself that I have already chosen to let go. Every time a piece of guilt creeps in, I remind myself that I deserve peace.

This journey of acceptance has not been easy, and it won't be over anytime soon. There are still days when I feel the loss, when I wish things had been different when I ache for the mother I never had. But more and more, I find peace in knowing that I am enough without her. I don't need her approval to be whole.

Letting go was the hardest thing I've ever done, but it has been the most liberating. It has opened the door to a life that is mine, to relationships that are based on love and mutual respect, and to a future that I can create on my terms.

Breaking Generational Curses

The most difficult part of breaking free from the past wasn't just healing from my trauma—it was recognizing that I had inherited a legacy of dysfunction, manipulation, and pain. For years, I had believed that the brokenness in my family was just our problem, that it was confined to my mother and me. But as I began to heal, I started to see that the patterns of behavior, the toxic cycles of control and abuse, weren't just limited to her—they had been passed down through generations.

Breaking generational curses is not something that happens overnight. It's a slow, intentional process of unraveling the behaviors and thought patterns that have been ingrained for decades, even centuries. It means confronting the way that trauma has been passed down through the family, acknowledging the cycles that perpetuate pain, and then taking steps to stop them from continuing.

The Weight of the Past

As I looked back on my family's history, I began to see the signs of this generational cycle—my mother's manipulation and abuse were not isolated behaviors. They were learned, passed down from her own experiences, from a history of unresolved trauma and pain. The more I learned about her upbringing, the more I realized that the patterns of control, emotional neglect, and fear she had imposed on me were the same ones she had inherited from her mother. It was a vicious, unbroken cycle, and I was trapped in it.

Understanding this truth was both heartbreaking and empowering. It made me realize that my mother's behavior wasn't just a reflection of her—it was a reflection of a much larger, deeper issue that spanned generations. And while that didn't excuse her actions, it helped me begin to release the guilt I had carried for so long. I wasn't just fighting against her; I was fighting against a cycle of trauma that had been passed down to me.

But once I understood this, I knew I had to stop the cycle. I couldn't continue the pattern of dysfunction that had been woven into my family's fabric. If I didn't break it, it would continue into the lives of future generations. That realization became my catalyst for change.

Steps Toward Healing and Reclaiming Your Life

The first step toward breaking the curse was healing myself. I could not change my past or undo the trauma I had experienced, but I could change how I responded to it. I could choose to no longer let it define me, to no longer live under the weight of my mother's actions. Healing began with forgiving myself for the pain I had suffered, for the ways I had let it control my thoughts and actions.

Healing meant addressing the emotional and psychological scars that had been left by years of abuse. It wasn't just about letting go of the past; it was about actively reprogramming the way I viewed myself and the world around me. For so long, I had believed that I wasn't worthy of love, happiness, or success. I had internalized the negative messages my mother had given me, allowing them to shape how I saw myself. But healing meant dismantling those beliefs, piece by piece.

Therapy was one of the most crucial steps in my healing process. It provided me with the tools and language to understand what had happened to me and to separate my mother's actions from my own identity. For the first time, I was able to see my pain as something that didn't define me but as something that needed to be acknowledged, processed, and ultimately healed. I started to identify the thought patterns and coping mechanisms that had been developed over years of trauma—habits that had been passed down from previous generations—and began to replace them with healthier, more constructive behaviors.

Alongside therapy, I also turned inward. I began to reconnect with the things that brought me joy and peace, the things I had long abandoned because they didn't fit into the role my mother had defined for me. I started drawing, writing, and finding ways to express myself creatively. These small acts of self-care were like small victories, each one reminding me that I had the power to reclaim my life.

Releasing the Burden of the Past

Part of healing from generational curses is releasing the burden of carrying the past. I realized that to move forward, I had to stop living in the shadow of my mother's pain. The legacy of her abuse wasn't mine to bear, and yet I had been carrying it for so long. The weight of it had defined my choices, my relationships, and my perception of myself. But as I began to heal, I understood that carrying her pain didn't make me a better person—it only kept me trapped.

Letting go of the past wasn't easy. There were moments when I felt guilty for wanting to move on, for wanting to let go of the family dysfunction that had been a part of my life for so long. But

I came to understand that releasing the pain wasn't about forgetting or dismissing my history. It was about setting myself free, about permitting myself to live a life that wasn't defined by my mother's abuse.

Forging a New Path for Future Generations

The true power of breaking generational curses is not just in healing your wounds but also in ensuring that the next generation doesn't have to bear the same burdens. As I began to heal, I realized that my journey wasn't just for me; it was for my children, for the future, for the legacy I wanted to create.

I wanted to be the kind of parent I had never had—the kind who listens, nurtures, and provides safety and security. I wanted to break the cycle of emotional neglect and manipulation, to create a home where love was unconditional, where boundaries were respected, and where the next generation could grow up free from the wounds I had inherited.

I knew it wouldn't be easy. The scars of the past don't fade quickly, and old habits are hard to break. But with each step I took toward healing, I saw the possibility of a future that wasn't defined by fear or pain. I saw a future where my children would know their worth and where they would grow up in a home that supported their dreams and their individuality.

And as I began to create this new path, I understood that breaking the cycle wasn't just about my family—it was about making a broader impact on the world. By healing, I was not only healing myself and my family, but I was breaking a cycle that has existed for generations. I was teaching future generations that trauma doesn't have to be inherited—that the past doesn't have to dictate their future.

She Was So Worth It

Looking at my beautiful daughter, I can tell you it was all so worth it. Every tear, every battle, every moment of doubt—it led me to this. I started my healing journey long before I even knew she would exist before I even tried to bring a life into this world. I made healing my top priority because I was determined to be the mother I deserved and, in turn, the mother *she* deserved.

Healing wasn't just therapy. It was a deep, soul-wrenching dive into the darkest parts of me. I confronted the demons of my family, stood face to face with each one, shook their hands, and bid them goodbye. They had no place in the life I was building—not in my heart, not in my home, and certainly not in the space I was creating for her.

When the time felt right, I was ready. I was excited. I was confident. I had done the work. Healing is an ongoing process, but I felt prepared. The grief of my choices—like going completely no contact with both of my parents—will never fully go away. But it doesn't consume me anymore.

Pregnancy was bittersweet. I was mothering myself through it without the mother who, in a perfect world, should have been there. And she could have been—if I had allowed it. But I didn't. I couldn't. I knew that sharing this moment with her would only result in her trying to steal it, to twist it into another weapon against me.

When she found out I was pregnant, she attempted to break through my boundaries, sending messages to my siblings asking if she could send gifts. But I knew better. She wasn't asking to love my child; she was seeking a way back into control, manipulation, and hurt. Loving my child means loving me. You can't hate what you gave birth to and expect access to whom I gave birth to. It doesn't work that way. Her attempts were nothing more than another spit in my face, but I refused to let it linger this time.

Giving birth was everything I could have ever dreamed of. The room was filled with love—pure, radiant, unconditional love. For a brief second, I mourned the absence of my parents, but the angels in my life made sure it was fleeting. This was *my* moment. And I had made it. A day I once thought I'd never see, especially after my mother's curses, claiming I'd never be a mother because I stood up to her.

That day, my little lady came into the world on her terms—24 hours of doing it her way, setting the tone for her life. And let me tell you, she has kept that tempo ever since! As I pushed her out, all smiles and singing Salt-N-Pepa's "Push It," the anesthesiologist earned every cent of his check that day. The nurses couldn't stop smiling, saying they'd never seen such spirit in a delivery room. My daughter was brought into this world surrounded by love and light.

The moment I locked eyes with her, heard her little cry and held her tiny body in my arms, I knew it was all worth it. Every lonely night. Every smear campaign. Every flying monkey was sent to tear me down. Every tear cried in the dark, wishing for the pain to end but always finding the strength to fight another day. It was all for this moment.

Even after her birth, my mother tried to steal the moment. She called my twin, wanting to "congratulate me" and wish she could be there. I told him to hang up. That wasn't her moment—it was mine.

Every day, I look at my precious girl and feel a healing like no other. Loving her heals the little girl inside me. And it reinforces my boundaries. It makes me even more resolved to protect her and myself.

There are days when the pain resurfaces. Milestones in her life remind me of everything I never had. The love I pour into her makes me wonder why my parents couldn't do the same for me. On those days, I cry, and I allow myself to cry. But I keep moving forward.

To those reading this, whether you're a parent, planning to be, or healing for yourself, start your work if you haven't already. And if you have, keep going. You are doing the work of generations. Even if you never have children, your healing is a light for your family, your nieces, your nephews, and every soul touched by your journey.

This is bigger than us. And what a privilege it is to be a part of breaking these cycles. I promise you, it's worth it. And one day, you'll thank yourself for every ounce of strength it took.

A Continuing Journey

Breaking generational curses is an ongoing journey. It's not something that happens in a single moment or with one decision. It's a continuous process of healing, of breaking down old beliefs, and of forging new paths for those who come after us. I may never fully escape the impact of my past, but I now have the tools and strength to rewrite my story to make choices that break the chains of the past.

The road ahead is still long, but with each step, I feel the weight of the past becoming lighter. I no longer live in the shadow of my mother's pain. I live in the light of my healing, knowing that by breaking these curses, I am not only healing myself—I am healing the future.

Living the Life You Deserve

For so much of my life, I was living according to someone else's terms—trying to meet expectations that were never mine to begin with, chasing a version of happiness that was dictated by others. I had spent years measuring my worth by what others thought of me, by how well I could conform to the narratives that were handed to me. But as I began to heal from the wounds of my past, I came to a powerful realization: I was no longer willing to live someone else's life. I was determined to live the life I deserved—one defined by my own standards of love, self-worth, and happiness.

Redefining Love

Growing up, love was something that felt conditional. It was tied to performance, to compliance, to meeting the expectations of someone who couldn't truly give it freely. My mother's love, as much as I wanted it, was always tangled with control, manipulation, and guilt. It was love that demanded I shrink myself, that silenced my voice and kept me under her thumb. I spent so long trying to earn that love, believing it was the only kind I was worthy of.

But as I healed, I began to redefine what love meant to me. I realized that love shouldn't be a transaction, a series of behaviors to be performed to receive validation. Love is not something to be earned; it's something that is freely given without conditions. I started to understand that love isn't about sacrifice at the expense of your well-being, nor is it about trying to change who you are to meet someone else's expectations.

True love, I learned, is about acceptance. It's about being seen and loved for who you are, flaws and all. It's about embracing vulnerability, about letting others into your life without fear of judgment or rejection. The love I was seeking wasn't going to come from my mother or anyone else who sought to control me—it had to come from within.

I began to practice self-love, even when it felt difficult. It started with small steps: learning to speak kindly to myself, giving myself permission to feel and be imperfect, and setting boundaries with others that reflected my worth. As I began to show myself love, I found that the relationships I had with others started to shift. I no longer accepted toxic love or love that came with strings attached. I sought relationships that were built on mutual respect, understanding, and care.

Reclaiming My Self-Worth

For so long, my self-worth had been tied to how others saw me—especially my mother. I believed that if I could just be the person she wanted me to be, I would finally be worthy of love and approval. I internalized her criticisms, her disdain, and her emotional abuse, and I carried them with me, allowing them to dictate how I saw myself.

But as I healed, I began to understand that my worth wasn't tied to anyone else's perception of me. It wasn't about how perfectly I performed, how much I sacrificed, or how well I could please others. My worth was inherent. It was mine by birthright, independent of anyone's approval or disapproval.

Reclaiming my self-worth was a long and sometimes painful process. It meant dismantling years of conditioning, of undoing the belief that I was somehow less than. I had to learn to stop apologizing for being myself and to stop shrinking into the background in an attempt to avoid conflict or rejection. I had to learn to value my own voice, my own thoughts, and my own emotions.

One of the most important steps I took in this process was learning to celebrate my accomplishments, no matter how small they seemed. I stopped waiting for validation from others and began to validate myself. Whether it was completing a project, standing up for myself, or simply getting through a tough day, I began to recognize that I was worthy of celebration just for being me.

Happiness on My Terms

Happiness, for so long, had felt like something I was constantly chasing but could never quite reach. I believed it was something external, something I could only achieve if I lived up to the standards of others, if I finally met my mother's approval, or if I had the perfect relationship. I spent years believing that happiness was something I had to earn or achieve, not something I could simply choose for myself.

But as I began to rebuild my life, I realized that happiness doesn't come from external validation or achievements—it comes from within. Happiness is a state of mind, a choice to embrace joy and contentment, no matter the circumstances. It's not about waiting for the right conditions to appear or for someone else to give you permission to be happy. It's about choosing to live in the present, to appreciate what you have, and to find peace with who you are.

I started small: embracing the quiet moments of joy, the feeling of fresh air on my face, the warmth of a hug from a friend, or the satisfaction of accomplishing something on my own terms. I stopped looking for happiness in the places I thought I needed to find it—approval from others, success, or external circumstances—and began to find it in myself.

I realized that happiness is a journey, not a destination. It's not something that can be forced or manufactured. It's something that comes naturally when you choose to live authentically, to embrace who you are, and to stop waiting for the world to change before you allow yourself to feel joy.

Living Authentically

Living the life I deserve means living authentically—being true to myself, regardless of what others think or expect. It means being unapologetically me, even if that means disappointing others, even if that means stepping away from relationships that no longer serve me. It means embracing my flaws, my imperfections, and all the messy parts of myself that I had once tried to hide.

Living authentically also means honoring my boundaries and standing firm in my beliefs. I've learned to say no when I need to, to walk away from situations that drain me, and to protect my peace at all costs. My life, my time, and my energy are valuable, and I no longer feel the need to give them away to people or situations that don't respect me.

Building the Future I Deserve

As I continue to heal and grow, I realize that I'm not just living for myself—I'm living for the future I want to create for the generations that will come after me. I want to build a life that is rooted in love, respect, and authenticity, and I want to pass that legacy down. I want to teach those around me that they are worthy of love, that their worth is inherent, and that they have the power to create their own happiness.

Living the life, I deserve is not just about personal healing—it's about creating a life that breaks free from the chains of the past, that is not defined by trauma, and that is grounded in the belief that we all deserve peace, love, and happiness on our own terms.

Rediscovering Who I Am

Breaking away after years of being controlled by my mother was a voyage of self-discovery rather than a simple physical act. Years of manipulation, dread, and self-doubt had buried the person I could have been without the abuse, the person I had been before it. As I began to recover, I saw that although separating from her was a win, the true effort was in taking back my identity and creating a completely new self.

Letting Go of a Shaped Identity

For much of my life, my identity had been shaped by my mother's expectations, criticisms, and manipulation. She dictated how I should think, feel, and act, leaving little room for me to develop my own sense of self. My choices weren't truly mine; they were measured against her approval.

Even after I broke free, her voice lingered in my mind, echoing in moments of doubt. When I succeeded, I questioned if it was because of her influence or despite it. When I failed, I felt her judgment, even in her absence. Letting go of this shaped identity was one of the hardest parts of my journey. It meant recognizing that many of the beliefs I held about myself—my insecurities, my fears, even some of my dreams—had been influenced by her control.

To reclaim my identity, I had to unlearn these deeply ingrained patterns. I had to confront the lies she had told me about who I was and replace them with truths I discovered for myself. This process wasn't easy. It felt like tearing down a house that had been built on shaky foundations and starting from scratch, brick by brick.

The Challenge of Remembering Who I Am

The journey of rediscovery was filled with challenges. Who was I outside of the trauma? What did I truly want, believe, or value? For so long, my decisions had been driven by a need to survive, to placate my mother, to avoid conflict. Now, with that pressure removed, I was faced with questions I didn't know how to answer.

Simple things, like choosing hobbies or expressing opinions, became daunting. Did I like this music, or was it what I thought I should like? Was this career path truly mine, or was it something I had chosen to meet someone else's expectations? These questions haunted me, but they also opened the door to a deeper understanding of myself.

One of the most profound realizations I had during this time was that my identity wasn't something I had to "find." It was something I had to create. Who I had been before the trauma wasn't gone; it was still within me, waiting to be nurtured. But I also had the power to redefine myself to build a new identity that reflected the person I wanted to become.

Steps Toward Self-Discovery

Exploration Through Creativity

One of the first ways I began to rediscover myself was through creativity. Writing became my outlet—a way to process my emotions and connect with my thoughts. It allowed me to express parts of myself that had been silenced for so long.

I also experimented with other artistic endeavors, such as photography and painting. The goal of these exercises was to rediscover my delight and curiosity, not to attain perfection. I was able to try new things, make mistakes, and just enjoy the creative process for the first time in years.

Reconnecting with My Values

Another step in my journey was identifying my core values. I had spent so long trying to live up to my mother's expectations that I had lost sight of what truly mattered to me. Through therapy and self-reflection, I began to explore questions like: What do I believe in? What kind of person do I want to be? What brings me fulfillment?

I felt more grounded because of this approach. I came to see that my values—resilience, kindness, and honesty—were wholly mine. They were reflections of who I really was, not influenced by my mother.

Setting Boundaries

A crucial part of rediscovery was learning to set boundaries. Boundaries weren't just about protecting myself from others—they were about defining who I was and what I stood for. By saying no to things that didn't align with my values or well-being, I was able to say yes to the things that truly mattered.

Reflecting on the Importance of Self-Awareness

Through this journey, I came to understand that self-awareness was the foundation of my healing. It was through self-awareness that I began to recognize the patterns of behavior and thought that had been shaped by my trauma. It allowed me to separate what was mine from what had been imposed on me.

Self-awareness also helped me embrace the complexity of my identity. I was not just a survivor of abuse; I was a person with dreams, talents, and passions. I was someone who had endured pain but had also found joy. I was someone who had been broken but had the strength to rebuild.

Regaining my identity wasn't a straight line. On certain days, I felt lost, questioned my abilities, and felt like I couldn't handle the burden of the past. But I learned a little bit more about who I was and could become with every step I took forward.

A Life Reclaimed

Reclaiming my identity has been one of the most challenging and rewarding parts of my journey. It has taught me that healing isn't just about moving on from the past—it's about embracing who you are in the present and creating a future that reflects your truth.

I am no longer defined by my mother's actions or by the trauma I endured. I am defined by the choices I make, the values I hold, and the person I strive to be every day. Reclaiming my identity has given me the freedom to live authentically, embrace my worth, and move forward with hope and resilience.

This journey is far from over, but I am no longer afraid of the road ahead. For the first time in my life, I am living as myself—not as someone else's version of who I should be. And that, I have learned, is the greatest victory of all.

Healing from the Inside Out

Healing isn't just about moving past trauma; it's about addressing the deep scars—both mental and emotional—that linger long after the abuse has ended. For me, the journey of healing required more than time; it required intentional effort and a willingness to confront the pain I had carried for so many years. The wounds left by years of manipulation and control were not visible to the eye, but they shaped every part of who I was. To truly heal, I had to face them head-on, to give myself permission to feel, to process, and to rebuild from the inside out.

Addressing Mental and Emotional Scars

The mental and emotional scars left by my mother's abuse were complex and multifaceted. They manifested as self-doubt, anxiety, and an overwhelming sense of guilt. I often felt like I was walking on eggshells, even in environments where I was safe. My mind had been conditioned to expect criticism, to brace for rejection, and to prepare for the worst in every interaction.

I wasn't even aware that these patterns were signs of trauma at first. They seemed to be a natural part of my identity, a fear-and-survival-shaped identity. However, I discovered that these wounds were temporary when I started to analyze my experiences. They weren't a representation of who I really was; they were the remains of what I had gone through.

Therapy became a safe space for me to explore these scars, name them, and begin the process of healing them. My therapist helped me understand that the self-doubt I carried wasn't my fault; it was a learned response to years of being told I wasn't good enough. The guilt I felt wasn't mine to bear—it was the result of years of emotional manipulation.

Acknowledging these scars was painful, but it was also liberating. It allowed me to see that the things I had internalized as weaknesses were, in fact, the effects of trauma. They were not permanent, and they could be healed.

Finding Self-Empowerment Through Therapy, Self-Care, and Mindfulness

Therapy was one of the most empowering tools in my journey to healing. It gave me the language to describe my experiences, the perspective to understand them, and the tools to begin changing the patterns that had defined my life.

Through therapy, I learned to reframe the narratives I had been living with for so long. Instead of seeing myself as a victim of my mother's actions, I began to see myself as a survivor. Instead of blaming myself for the pain I had endured, I started to recognize my strength in overcoming it.

Self-care also became a cornerstone of my healing process. For so many years, I had neglected my own needs, prioritizing others and suppressing my emotions. But self-care wasn't just about indulgence; it was about learning to honor myself in ways I never had before. It was about setting boundaries, saying no when I needed to, and giving myself permission to rest and recharge.

My ability to remain grounded was greatly aided by my mindfulness. I was able to re-establish a safe connection between my body and mind using techniques like writing, meditation, and deep breathing. I was able to sit with my sadness and let it remain without devouring me during these quiet times, which allowed me to process my feelings without passing judgment.

Rebuilding Trust in Myself

One of the hardest parts of healing was learning to trust myself again. For years, my mother's manipulation had conditioned me to doubt my own feelings, to second-guess my instincts, and to rely on her interpretation of reality. Even after breaking free from her control, that conditioning lingered. I found myself questioning my decisions, my emotions, and my ability to navigate the world on my own.

Rebuilding trust in myself was a slow and deliberate process. It started with small steps—learning to listen to my intuition, to honor my feelings, and to make choices that aligned with my values. I began to challenge the negative self-talk that had become second nature, replacing it with affirmations of my worth and capability.

There were setbacks along the way. There were moments when I doubted myself, when the voices of the past crept back in, whispering that I wasn't enough. But with each step forward, I grew stronger. I learned to trust that my emotions were valid, that my experiences were real, and that I had the power to create a life that reflected my true self.

Establishing New Tools for Coping with Triggers and Stress

Healing from trauma doesn't mean the past disappears—it means learning to live with it in a way that no longer controls you. Triggers and stress were an inevitable part of my journey, but I discovered that with the right tools, I could navigate them without falling back into old patterns.

One of the most important tools I developed was recognizing my triggers. I started to identify the situations, words, or behaviors that brought back feelings of fear or insecurity. Instead of avoiding them, I began to approach them with curiosity, asking myself why they affected me and what I could do to feel safe in those moments.

Breathing techniques became a lifeline during moments of stress. Something as simple as taking a few deep breaths could ground me, bringing me back to the present and reminding me that I was no longer in the environment that had caused me harm.

Boundaries were another crucial tool. I learned to protect my mental and emotional energy by setting limits on what I was willing to tolerate. This included saying no to toxic relationships, limiting my exposure to situations that drained me, and prioritizing my own well-being.

Support systems also played a vital role in coping with stress. I surrounded myself with people who uplifted me, who understood my journey, and who provided a safe space for me to be vulnerable. Whether it was a close friend, a therapist, or a support group, these connections reminded me that I wasn't alone.

A Call to Action for Others Facing Similar Struggles

This journey of healing doesn't end when you recognize your worth—it begins there. It starts when you have the courage to face your past, to look at the pain you've endured, and say, "I will no longer allow this to control me. I will no longer be defined by the abuse, the shame, or the fear that has kept me in chains." Healing requires action. It requires confronting the darkness that's been buried deep within and acknowledging that it is okay to seek help. It is okay to be vulnerable, to ask for support, to stand up and say,

"This happened to me, but it will not determine the rest of my story."

To those who are still living in the silence of abuse, I urge you to take that first step toward speaking your truth. It doesn't matter how small the step is or how many times you have to take it—it only matters that you begin. You have the right to be heard. You have the right to heal. And you have the right to create a life where love, respect, and peace are yours for the taking.

I know how difficult it can feel to break free, to feel that the world is too much, to wonder if anyone will believe you or understand what you've been through. But I want to tell you this: there is hope, even when it feels impossible. There is strength within you that you may not even realize yet. And there are people—therapists, support groups, mentors, and fellow survivors—who can help guide you along the way. You don't have to do this alone.

Healing is a journey, and while it can be painful, it is also powerful. It's not about perfection; it's about progress. Every step, no matter how small, is a victory. You will learn to recognize your own worth, to forgive yourself for the things that were never your fault, and to rebuild a life that is rooted in your own truth.

Affirmation of Hope, Resilience, and the Strength of the Human Spirit

When I look back on the person I was before I began this journey, I see someone who was broken, someone who believed that the scars would never heal. I see someone who felt invisible, as though the weight of her past was too heavy to bear. But now, as I stand on the other side of this journey, I am filled with hope. I am filled with the belief that even the most broken parts of us can heal. Even the darkest stories can transform into ones of resilience and strength.

You have the power to rewrite your story. Your pain does not have to be your legacy. It may shape who you are, but it does not define who you will become. You are capable of more than just surviving—you are capable of thriving. Your strength has carried you this far, and it will continue to carry you as you heal and rebuild.

Healing does not mean forgetting the past—it means learning to live with it, integrate it into your story, and use it as a foundation from which you can grow. It means taking the lessons from your pain and using them to empower yourself, to help others, and to create a future that is free from the shadows of your trauma.

There will be hard days ahead. There will be moments when the past feels like it's closing in when the weight of everything you've been through feels overwhelming. But know this: the human spirit is resilient beyond measure. We have the ability to rise, again and again, from the ashes of our struggles. We can reclaim our lives, our dignity, and our happiness, no matter how much we've lost.

Healing as an Ongoing Journey

Healing from the inside out is not a destination; it's an ongoing journey. There are still days when the scars feel tender when the weight of the past presses down on me. But there are also days of lightness, joy, and peace.

Every action I take, be it engaging in mindfulness exercises, going to treatment, or just deciding to have faith in myself, is evidence of the human spirit's tenacity. I've learned through healing that I am more than my suffering, my trauma, and the person I was expected to be.

This journey has not been easy, but it has been worth it. Through it all, I have learned that healing is not about erasing the past—it's about finding strength in your scars, building a future that reflects your worth, and embracing the person you were always meant to be.

This is a call to action for each survivor reading these words. Your journey is yours alone, but the hope and strength you carry belong to all of us. You are part of a community of survivors, and together, we are rewriting the narrative of our lives—one of resilience, empowerment, and the unwavering truth that we are worthy of a life filled with peace, love, and happiness.

The Impact of Healing on Existing Relationships

Healing has a ripple effect, and one of the first places it became evident was in my existing relationships. I started to notice the ways my trauma had influenced the dynamics of my connections with others. I had often gravitated toward relationships that mirrored my experiences with my mother—relationships where I felt undervalued, unseen, or controlled. These patterns were familiar, but they were also toxic.

As I grew more self-aware, I began to reassess these relationships. I started asking myself hard questions: Did these connections bring me joy? Did they support my growth? Did they align with the boundaries and values I was working so hard to establish? In some cases, the answer was no, and I had to make the difficult decision to step away.

Letting go of old relationships was painful, but it was also necessary. I realized that holding onto connections that didn't serve me was like clinging to weights that kept me anchored to the past. By releasing them, I made space for healthier, more fulfilling relationships to enter my life.

Forging New Bonds

Every action I take, be it engaging in mindfulness exercises, going to treatment, or just deciding to have faith in myself, is evidence of the human spirit's tenacity. I've learned through healing that I am more than my suffering, my trauma, and the person I was expected to be.

Building these bonds required me to show up authentically, which wasn't always easy. Vulnerability had long felt like a risk, a weakness that could be exploited. But as I began to trust myself more, I found the courage to let others see me for who I truly was. I learned that vulnerability wasn't just about exposing your pain— it was about creating space for genuine connection.

I felt safe, something I hadn't felt in years, in these new partnerships. With friends, family, or love partners, I started to surround myself with people who valued me, acknowledged my development, and encouraged me on my path to recovery. These relationships were based on honesty, respect, and love, but they weren't flawless—no relationship is.

The Challenge of Setting Boundaries

One of the most significant lessons I learned in reconstructing relationships was the importance of boundaries. For so long, I had allowed others to dictate the terms of our connections, believing that saying no or asserting my needs would make me unworthy of love. But healing taught me that boundaries weren't just necessary—they were a form of self-respect.

Establishing limits was difficult. I had to unlearn the notion that prioritizing oneself was selfish. It required having tough talks with individuals who were accustomed to the previous me—the one who always agreed, shied away from confrontation, and put up with actions that made me feel bad.

Some people responded with understanding, adapting to the new dynamics of our relationship with grace and support. Others resisted, viewing my boundaries as rejection or betrayal. Navigating these reactions was difficult, but it reinforced an important truth: boundaries are not about controlling others; they're about protecting yourself.

By setting boundaries, I was able to create relationships that were healthier and more balanced. I learned to communicate my needs with clarity and confidence, to address conflict in a way that fostered mutual respect, and to walk away when a connection no longer served me.

Navigating Conflict with Respect and Love

The conflict had always been something I feared. Growing up, it was synonymous with chaos and pain. As a result, I either avoided it entirely or approached it with defensiveness and fear. But healing taught me that conflict, when handled with respect and love, could be an opportunity for growth.

In reconstructing my relationships, I began to see conflict as a chance to deepen understanding and strengthen connection. I learned to approach disagreements with curiosity rather than judgment, to listen with an open heart, and to express my feelings without fear of rejection.

This wasn't always easy. There were moments when old patterns resurfaced when the fear of confrontation threatened to overwhelm me. But with time and practice, I became more comfortable addressing conflict in a way that aligned with my values.

I discovered that the key to navigating conflict was mutual respect—acknowledging the other person's perspective while honoring my own. It was about finding solutions that worked for both parties rather than sacrificing my needs to keep the peace.

The Power of Positive Influences

One of the most transformative aspects of rebuilding my relationships was surrounding myself with positive influences. I sought out people who inspired me, who encouraged my growth, and who reminded me of my worth. These individuals became my support system, helping me navigate the ups and downs of healing with compassion and understanding.

Positive influences didn't just come from personal relationships; they also came from communities and resources that supported my journey. I joined support groups, attended workshops, and connected with others who had experienced similar struggles. These spaces provided validation, encouragement, and a sense of belonging that had been missing for so long.

A New Foundation for Relationships

Healing from trauma doesn't just change you—it changes the way you see and interact with the world around you. For years, my relationships were shaped by survival. I prioritized others' needs over my own, avoided conflict at all costs, and tolerated behaviors that didn't align with my values because I didn't believe I deserved better. As I began to heal, I realized that my relationships—both old and new—needed to be reconstructed to reflect the person I was becoming.

Reconstructing relationships has been one of the most challenging and rewarding parts of my healing journey. It required me to let go of old patterns, to confront my fears, and to embrace vulnerability. But in doing so, I discovered the beauty of connections built on authenticity, respect, and love.

The relationships I have now are a testament to the power of healing. They remind me that I am worthy of being seen, heard, and valued. They reflect the person I have become—someone who no longer settles for less than they deserve, someone who prioritizes their well-being, and someone who believes in the power of connection.

Reclaiming my identity also meant redefining how I interacted with others. I had been conditioned to prioritize other people's needs and suppress my own. Now, I began to build relationships based on mutual respect and understanding. I sought out people who valued me for who I was, not for what I could do for them.

These relationships became a mirror, reflecting the parts of myself that were strong, kind, and worthy of love. They reminded me that I didn't have to perform or prove myself to be valued.

As I continue to grow, I know that these foundations will only strengthen. The journey isn't over, but I am confident in the path I'm on. And for the first time, I can say that my relationships are not a source of pain—they are a source of joy, strength, and hope.

Creating a Life Beyond the Past

For so long, my life had been defined by the shadows of my past—by fear, by obligation, and by the patterns of dysfunction that shaped my early years. Every choice I made, every dream I considered, seemed weighed down by the trauma I had carried. But as I began to heal, I realized that life didn't have to be that way. I had the power to step out of the shadow of my past and into a future that was mine to create, filled with possibilities I never thought I could reach.

Discovering New Passions, Goals, and Dreams

One of the most profound aspects of creating a life beyond the past was rediscovering who I was outside of the trauma. For years, my dreams and passions had been buried beneath layers of fear and obligation. I didn't dare think about what I wanted for myself because I was so focused on surviving the day-to-day struggles of living under my mother's control.

When I finally had the space to breathe, I began to ask myself questions that I had avoided for years: What makes me happy? What excites me? What kind of life do I want to build for myself? At first, these questions felt overwhelming. I wasn't sure where to start or how to begin dreaming again. But little by little, I started to explore.

I reconnected with activities I had once loved but abandoned—like writing, which became a way for me to process my emotions and reclaim my voice. I started trying new things, from painting to hiking, just to see what brought me joy. It wasn't about being perfect or achieving something grand—it was about permitting myself to explore, to fail, and to discover what truly made me feel alive.

Through this process, I uncovered passions I never knew I had. I found that I loved storytelling—not just to process my past but as a way to connect with others and inspire them. I discovered that

I had a knack for helping others navigate their journeys of healing and growth, and I began to see how my experiences could be a source of strength and purpose.

The Liberation of Pursuing Fulfillment

As I began to pursue the things that made me happy, I felt a sense of liberation that I hadn't experienced before. For the first time in my life, I was making choices that were entirely my own—not choices dictated by fear, by someone else's expectations, or by the need to please.

This freedom was exhilarating, but it was also unfamiliar. There were moments when I doubted myself, when the voices from my past crept in, telling me that I didn't deserve happiness or success. But each time I pushed through those doubts and continued pursuing what fulfilled me, I felt a little stronger and a little more confident.

Pursuing fulfillment didn't mean that every day was easy or that I never faced setbacks. There were challenges, moments of uncertainty, and times when the weight of the past still felt heavy. But the difference was that I now had tools to navigate those moments—tools that allowed me to keep moving forward, even when the path was unclear.

Embracing Life Without the Pain of the Past

Letting go of the pain of the past didn't mean forgetting it or pretending it never happened. It meant learning to live alongside it without letting it control me. My past was a part of my story, but it was no longer the defining chapter.

Embracing life beyond the past required me to shift my perspective. Instead of seeing myself as someone who was damaged or defined by what I had endured, I began to see myself as someone resilient, capable, and deserving of joy. I stopped carrying the weight of guilt and shame that had been imposed on me and started embracing the person I was becoming.

This shift wasn't something that happened overnight. It was a process of learning to be present, to find joy in the little moments, and to celebrate my progress, no matter how small. I started to appreciate the beauty of everyday life—the warmth of the sun on my face, the sound of laughter with friends, and the feeling of accomplishment when I achieved a goal.

By focusing on the present and looking toward the future, I began to release the hold the past had on me. I learned that while the pain would always be a part of my story, it didn't have to dictate my future.

Leaving Behind Patterns of Dysfunction

Creating a life beyond the past also meant breaking free from the patterns of dysfunction that had shaped my early years. These patterns weren't just behaviors—I realized they were ways of thinking, reacting, and relating to others that had been deeply ingrained in me.

I started by identifying the patterns that no longer served me. I noticed how I often prioritized others' needs over my own, how

I avoided conflict at all costs, and how I tended to doubt my instincts and decisions. These behaviors had been survival mechanisms, but they were no longer necessary.

Breaking these patterns required intentional effort and self-awareness. I had to learn new ways of relating to myself and others, new ways of thinking and responding that reflected the person I wanted to be. I began to practice setting boundaries, advocating for myself, and trusting my intuition.

As I let go of these old patterns, I felt a sense of empowerment that I had never experienced before. I was no longer bound by the expectations or limitations imposed on me by others. I was free to create my path, define my own values, and live in a way that aligned with who I truly was.

Walking Into a Self-Determined Future

There are a lot of possibilities in the future I see for myself. In this future, my decisions will be made based on my values, interests, and dreams rather than duty or fear. In the future, I will keep developing, discovering, and appreciating all that life has to offer.

Walking into this future doesn't mean that I have all the answers or that the journey will be without challenges. But it does mean that I am no longer afraid to take the next step. I am no longer afraid to dream, to hope, and to build a life that reflects the person I have worked so hard to become.

Developing a life beyond the past is more than simply letting go of things that no longer serve me; it also entails accepting the limitless opportunities that lie ahead and living fully in my identity. It's about living joyfully, intentionally, and with the steadfast conviction that I deserve to be content and happy.

As I continue on this journey, I carry with me the lessons I've learned, the strength I've gained, and the knowledge that I am capable of creating a life that is entirely my own.

A message to my herd

To anyone reading these words who has endured pain, manipulation, and abuse, I want you to know that your story matters. The wounds you carry may seem invisible to the world, but they are real, and they deserve to be seen. I write this memoir not just to share my journey but to extend a hand to you—to let you know that you are not alone, that you are worthy of healing, and that you have the strength to reclaim your life, no matter how broken it may feel right now.

For so long, I believed that I was powerless, that I was doomed to live out the narrative that had been imposed on me since childhood. I carried the weight of my mother's abuse and manipulation, believing that somehow it defined who I was. I lived in fear of the future, haunted by the lies and the cycles of dysfunction that had followed me for years. But as I began to heal, as I found my voice and my strength, I realized that survival is not the same as living. It is possible to break free from the chains of trauma and stop letting your past define your future. And it is possible to create a life that reflects your worth, your dignity, and your capacity for love and joy.

You are enough. You have always been enough. The pain you've endured does not diminish your worth. It does not make you weak. You are stronger than you know, and the fact that you are reading these words right now, that you are still here, is proof of that strength.

You don't have to wait for permission to heal. You don't need anyone's approval to embrace your truth, your story, or your future. You are worthy of love, of peace, of joy, and of everything that makes life worth living. The road may be long, but you are not alone on it. And the best part is that, with every step you take, you will begin to create a life that is entirely yours—one that is filled with hope, with healing, and with the strength that only those who have endured trauma can truly understand.

From One Black Sheep to Another

I pray that my truth has inspired you to live in yours. Let me tell you this: your strength did not come from our abusers or oppressors. I refuse to give credit where it isn't due. What didn't kill you didn't make you stronger—it gave you trauma, self-doubt, shattered boundaries, and struggles with self-love. But hear me when I say this: your strength has been *you* all along.

How else could you have managed to stay in the fight from the very beginning? Sometimes, it's in the darkest times that we discover just how strong we are because the only other option is to give in. And you didn't. Each day you chose to stay in the fight deserves celebration. Don't take that lightly, my herd.

We are Black Sheep, and we are reclaiming a name that was meant to isolate and diminish us. We're giving it a new meaning, one of resilience, purpose, and pride. You were created to stand out. So the next time "Why me?" creeps into your mind, I want you to flip it. Think about how far you've come, the battles you've endured—not just for yourself, but for a healthier lineage, for your children, and for everyone who will come after you. You were chosen to break the cycle so they wouldn't have to instead ask yourself, "Why not me?" Why not be the one to heal, to rise, to transform pain into power? My pain had a purpose, and it brought me here—to my daughter, to my family, and *you*, the person holding this book. My prayer is that you find your purpose, too.

God bless you on your journey to healing and happiness. I am already claiming that it is yours. I love you all, my herd. Keep standing out. Keep shining. Keep fighting.

With all my heart,

Your Fellow Blque Sheep

www.ingramcontent.com/pod-product-compliance
Lightning Source LLC
LaVergne TN
LVHW091708070526
838199LV00050B/2306